OPENING THE DOORS TO
HOLLYWOOD

HOW TO SELL YOUR IDEA
STORY • BOOK • SCREENPLAY

OPENING THE DOORS TO
HOLLYWOOD

HOW TO SELL YOUR IDEA
STORY • BOOK • SCREENPLAY

Carlos de Abreu

and

Howard Jay Smith

Custos Morum Publishers
Beverly Hills

Grateful acknowledgment is made to all sources that provided information and/or
materials that enabled the authors to complete this book.

Library of Congress Catalog Card Number: 94-068044

de Abreu, Carlos, and Smith, Howard Jay
Opening the doors to Hollywood: how to sell your idea, story, book, screenplay
by Carlos de Abreu and Howard Jay Smith

ISBN 1-884025-04-8

Printed in the United States of America

First Edition

Dedication

To my wife, Janice Pennington de Abreu, for her total support and encouragement. Without her, this book would not have been possible.

— Carlos de Abreu

This work is dedicated first to my mentor, the late novelist John Gardner, who taught me to be a writer. Next is Tony Vellani, former director of the Center for Advanced Film Studies at the American Film Institute, who turned me into a filmmaker. Third is Roger Maris, the great Yankee slugger, who inspired me as a young boy never to lose sight of the impossible dream.

And a special thanks to Ruth and Louis Light, Robert and Lillian Smith, and Zachary, Joshua, and Ilissa, without whose support none of this would have been possible.

— Howard Jay Smith

Special Thanks

Our gratitude to the following entertainment industry professionals:

Neil Baggs, Agent, The Agency, **Ann Blanchard,** Agent, William Morris Agency, **Rhonda Bloom,** Producer *(Separated by Murder, Broken Promises: Taking Emily Back)*, **John W. Cones,** Author/Entertainment Attorney *(Film Finance and Distribution, Film Industry Contracts)*, **Christine Foster,** Agent, Shapiro-Lichtman, **Alan Gadney,** Producer *(Moonchild, West Texas)*, **William Greenblatt,** Producer *(Da, Babies Having Babies, Judgment in Berlin)*, **Michael Hanel,** Vice-President, Columbia TV *(Married . . . with Children, Designing Women, Who's the Boss?)*, **Arthur Hiller,** Director *(Love Story, Man of La Mancha, Outrageous Fortune, The Babe, Married to It)*, **Alex Ho,** Producer *(Salvador, Born on the Fourth of July, JFK, Heaven and Earth)*, **Todd Hoffman,** Vice-President, Baumgarten Productions, **Gale Anne Hurd,** Producer *(Aliens, The Terminator, The Abyss)*, **Michael Jaffe,** Producer *(Snowbound, Shattered Trust)*, **Melinda Jason,** Producer *(The First Power, Eve of Destruction, Body of Evidence)*, **George Litto,** Producer *(Dressed to Kill, Obsession, Over the Edge)*, **Mark Litwak,** Author/Entertainment Attorney *(Reel Power, Dealmaking in the Film & Television Industry)*, **Paul Mazursky,** Director *(Bob & Carol & Ted & Alice, Harry and Tonto, Moscow on the Hudson, Down and Out in Beverly Hills)*, **Bob Myer,** Writer/Producer *(Joe's Life, Roseanne, My Two Dads, The Facts of Life)*, **Betsy Newman,** Vice-President, Turner Network Television *(Heart of Darkness)*, **David Permut,** Producer *(Three of Hearts, 29th Street, Blind Date, Dragnet)*, **Mark Rydell,** Director/Producer *(Cinderella Liberty, On Golden Pond, The Rose,*

7

For the Boys, Intersection), **Jorge Saralegui,** Vice-President, Twentieth Century Fox, **John Scheinfeld,** Writer/Producer *(For Ever Knight, The Unknown Marx Bros.)*, **Dr. Linda Seger,** Author/Script Consultant *(Making a Good Script Great, From Script to Screen)*, **Ken Sherman,** Agent, Ken Sherman & Associates, **Tom Towler,** Writer/Producer *(Lonesome Dove: The Series, Gabriel's Fire, Crime Story, The Equalizer, Midnight Caller, Kojak)*, **Greg Victoroff,** Author/Entertainment Attorney, Rohde & Victoroff *(Photography & Law, Visual Artists Business & Legal Guide)*, **Christopher Vogler,** Author/Script Consultant *(The Writer's Journey)*, **Richard Weitz,** Agent, ICM, **Shelly Wile,** Agent, Wile Enterprises, and **Robert Wise,** Director *(Star Trek: The Motion Picture, The Sound of Music, West Side Story, Rooftops, The Sand Pebbles)*.

With many thanks and our appreciation . . .

To Janice Pennington for her creative editing, feedback, and constant encouragement.

To our editor, John Jacobson, Jr., for making this process a lot easier and for all those late nights and weekends spent glued to the computer screen.

To Laurie Horowitz, Gail Kearns, Donie Nelson, and Alice Plato for their assistance.

Acknowledgments

One of the special treats of being in Hollywood is the endless opportunity to work with an enormous range of gifted and talented people, some famous, others not. All of them are important and vital. This is a special town, a world unlike any other, where the ultimate product is magic, movie magic. Collectively we weave the stuff of dreams. We make people laugh, we make them cry. We inspire, we deceive, we commit the perfect crime. The business of Hollywood is tough, demanding, rewarding, and humbling. This book is the product of over a dozen years of work in the entertainment industry. There is no way to thank the hundreds of talented people who have helped and shared their wisdom and experience with us, but we would like to try.

Below is but a partial list of the many friends, acquaintances, and industry professionals who have worked with, assisted, befriended, or simply inspired us through the years.

Steve Adler, Edward Anhalt, Jeff Auerbach, Martin Barab, Carol Baum, Craig Baumgarten, Alex Ben Block, Leonardo Bercovici, Stuart Berton, Lois Bonfiglio, Jeanie Bradley, Joe Byrne, John Cacavas, Fred Calvert, Roy Campanella II, Virginia Carter, Ed Cervantes, Ken Cinnamon, Carl Colpaert, Ken Corday, Sherry Corday, Deborah Curtain, Kerry and Leah Cox, Ann Daniel, John "Danny" Danischewsky, Tony Danza, Elyssa Davalos, Keith Davis, Donald DeLine, Steve De Souza, Mary Agnes Donahue, Doug Draizin, Michael Dugan, Judy Dytman, Ellen Endo-Dizon, Moctesuma Esparza, Bruce Evans, Mark Feldberg, Ed S. Feldman, Owen Ficke, Syd Field, Carrie Fisher,

Richard Fox, Sabrina Fox, Ruth Franklin, Todd Garner, Jo Ann Geffen, Jackie George, Ray Gideon, Marty Gold, Phil Goldfine, Cary Granite, Mindy Green, Robin Green, Peter Greene, Tom Greene, Arthur Gregory, Tom Griffith, Ken Hanes, Ted Harbert, Wes Harris, Michael Hauge, Laurette Hayden, Paul Heller, Kirk Honeycutt, Barbara Hunter, Lew Hunter, Margaret French Isaac, Phil Kamen, Joe Kasperoff, Jeffrey Katzenberg, Jordan Kerner, Brad Kessell, Joe Keyes, Viki King, Sam Kitt, Mitch Klebanoff, Don Kopaloff, Ted Kotcheff, Gene Kraft, Peter Kramer, Rob Lee, Gael Lehrer, Meera and Steve Lester, Jeffrey Levine, Laurie Levit, Al Levitt, Fanny Levy, Hal Lieberman, Kathy Lingg, Helen and Robert Little, Laura Louden, Dara Marks, Paul Maslansky, Fran McConnell, Bill McCutchen, Ian McVey, Ron Meyer, Ann Milder, John Miller, Kevin Misher, Laura Mola, Ray Montalvo, Neal Moritz, Patrick Murray, David Nicksay, Glenn Padnick, Leo Penn, Nancy Peter, Trisha Robinson, Megan Rose, Jeb Rosebrook, Julie Rothenbeck, Leigh Rubin, Esther Rydell, Sol Sacks, Steve Salant, Carl Sautter, Mark Sherman, Jess Siegler, Dov S-S Simens, Joel Simon, Monika Skerbelis, Kathy Sloan-Claster, Matthew Snyder, Peter Soby, Mireille Soria, Luis Soto, Tom Stacy, Geoff Stier, Oliver Stone, Paul Stupin, Joe Sutton, Mary Anne Sweeny, Irwin Tenenbaum, Tony Thomopoulos, Larry Thompson, Barbara Tobolowsky, Andrew Velcoff, Linda Venis, Diane Walsh, Professor Richard Walter, Jim Wedaa, Karen Wengrod, Winifred White, Susan Whittaker, Janet Yang, Dalene Young, and Azita Zendel.

Table of Contents

Preface

It all started in 1991 when two friends of mine, Italian actor Franco Nero and English actress Vanessa Redgrave, were in town. My wife, Janice Pennington, and I invited them for dinner at Locanda Veneta, a small restaurant in the West Hollywood area.

We also invited Ed Feldman, the producer of such films as *Witness*, *Green Card*, and *The Doctor*, and his wife Lorraine; Taylor Hackford, director of *An Officer and a Gentleman*; as well as Lois Bonfiglio, producer of *Old Gringo* and Jane Fonda's partner. It was one of those balmy California nights.

As always, Franco told stories about his worldwide experiences while traveling and making films. After the main course was served, I decided to share my dream with my friends. "I, Carlos de Abreu, am going to get in the movie business. My goal is to discover new writers through my contest, the 'Christopher Columbus Screenplay Discovery Awards.' Then, with my contacts in the industry, I am going to have features made." The table fell silent. It was as if the world had stopped. I didn't know what to do or say. I had no option but to continue with my forceful explanation about how I was going to do it. Vanessa finally came to my rescue and said how great she thought my idea was.

Here I was, sitting with the real pros, from actors to acclaimed directors, and I was telling them how *I* was going to reinvent the wheel . . . to make movies, just like that. Ed Feldman pleaded with me to stay in my business — international marketing. Lois Bonfiglio, with a faint smile, advised me to tighten my belt for at least four years.

15

Taylor Hackford just kept eating and flashed me a courteous smile of approval.

I didn't want to admit it, but my well-meaning friends were trying to save me from agony. It was to no avail. I was more determined than ever to open the doors to Hollywood.

The seed for this book was conceived that same balmy night.

— Carlos de Abreu

A dozen years ago I was in the same position most of you are now, wondering, how do I break into the entertainment industry? Over the desk of my office in Washington, D.C., was a quote from Thoreau: *"If one advances confidently in the direction of his dreams, and endeavors to live the life which he has imagined, he will meet with a success unexpected in common hours."*

For me, the road to my dream ran through film school. I applied to the American Film Institute's Center for Advanced Film Studies and was accepted on the basis of a half dozen award-winning short stories I had written and published. A year later I graduated from the AFI as the top screenwriter in my class. After six more months of intensive networking, job hunting, and writing screenplays on spec, I parlayed my prior management experience and writing skills into a mid-level executive position in the Drama Series Development Department at ABC-TV. That was the year they came out with such shows as *Moonlighting*, *Spenser: For Hire*, and *MacGyver*.

After enduring the rigors of my first network pilot season, Tony Vellani, then the director of the Center for Advanced Film Studies, invited me to stop back at the AFI to give a short talk for the next year's graduating class on what the world of TV was all about. Television was an arena that had pretty much been ignored at the school and few of the students there were interested in what I had to say until I made them aware of one intimidating fact: Out of the seventy-five extraordinarily talented writers, producers, and directors in my class, only five of us had actually found work in the business a year later.

My guest appearance, originally scheduled to last an hour, ran on for three. The questions never stopped. Suddenly everyone wanted to know how to make it, how Hollywood really worked, and how to break through those seemingly impenetrable doors.

I returned to the AFI for the next several years as a guest of the Alumni Association to repeat my lecture. Even as my own career progressed over the years as an executive, writer, producer, consultant, marketing specialist, and teacher in television, radio, film, video, and commercials, I kept hearing the same questions.

The Writers' Program at UCLA Extension finally gave me the forum to answer them properly. Over the past four years I have taught an ongoing series of classes and seminars for aspiring filmmakers in which I've been able to bring in dozens of top actors, writers, producers, agents, and studio and network executives. These guests, such as writer-actress Carrie Fisher, script consultant Linda Seger, and the former executive producer of *Roseanne*, Bob Myer, have been willing and able to share their insights with hundreds of students.

Linda Seger, in fact, introduced me to Carlos de Abreu, who held a similar interest in helping newcomers break in. As Carlos shared his dream with me, we hit upon the notion of collaborating on a book that once and for all would explain how to *Open the Doors to Hollywood*. It was out of that chance encounter that this series became a reality. We hope as you read through it, you too will uncover the knowledge and confidence that allows you to advance in the direction of your dreams and meet *"a success unexpected in common hours."*

— Howard Jay Smith

Your Dream

If you have an idea, a true story, a manuscript, a book, or a screenplay, as well as the burning desire to see your dream project made into a movie, now you can do it.

This book will guide you through the Hollywood maze, from concept to screen. We will share with you stories of successful moviemakers. We will tell you who's who. We will provide you with facts and figures. We will give you tips with the *do's* and *don'ts*.

To be a winner and to sell your idea, story, treatment, manuscript, book, or screenplay successfully, you must learn how the professionals do it: How do you prepare and arrange to pitch your idea, treatment, manuscript, book, or screenplay? How do you package it? How do you write a proposal? To whom do you send it? What should you expect financially? What's the difference between TV projects and feature projects? Between independent contractors and studios?

You must acquire the keys to the secret circles of knowledge. You must learn to understand the minds of the decision makers, their needs and, above all, their modus operandi. These are the inner workings of Hollywood.

Throughout our book, our distinguished entertainment industry friends will give you those keys. Each time a key is given to you, it will be flagged by one of these icons:

You must learn the rules and know who the players are. You must have a strategy so you will know what to do, when, and where.

We will introduce you to industry professionals — treatment experts, writers for hire, screenplay consultants, packaging experts, entertainment attorneys, agents, etc. — who can help you make it happen.

By revealing the mysteries of breaking into Hollywood and providing the keys to unlock the doors of opportunity, this book will give you the knowledge to achieve your dreams.

Let's do it.

— Carlos de Abreu
Howard Jay Smith

PART I

FROM CONCEPT TO SCREEN

Introduction

Fairy Tales Can Come True,
It Can Happen to You

By Christopher Vogler

The title *Opening the Doors to Hollywood* suggests that Hollywood is some kind of vast building or walled city-state, closed off to outsiders by well-defined walls and accessible only by well-guarded doors or gateways. There's a lot of truth in that metaphor, and exploring it can help you to open your own doors to Hollywood.

Metaphorically Speaking

In approaching a career in Hollywood, metaphors may be useful tools of comparison for understanding the film community and how it works.

There are many ways of looking at "the business," and people have crafted all sorts of metaphors to describe what goes on in the entertainment industry, including that it is a kind of army, a rat race, or a great madhouse. We speak of "getting that project off the ground" or "making it fly" as if movies and TV series were jumbo jets. The process of getting a film or TV show produced has been compared to a war, thievery, baseball, football, and sexual intercourse. However, since we're trying to open the doors of Hollywood, it's appropriate to explore the metaphor of architecture.

In many ways, writing a film story, getting a project to the screen, or making a career is like finding your way around a vast building. Hollywood can be viewed as an enormous labyrinthine edifice, whose twisty corridors lead to countless doors of possibility.

Hooray for Hollywood

Hollywood itself is a metaphor for the worldwide entertainment community. What is this place or state of mind called Hollywood that everyone is so eager to get into? What are the boundaries of this walled city, and where are the doors in this metaphor?

Hollywood, California, is a real physical location on the globe, an unincorporated district of Los Angeles where movie studios were first planted in 1911. The movies that flowed out of this factory town became the world's standard for entertainment, and Hollywood gave its name to the whole film business, whether films are produced in Culver City, Glendale, Burbank, or Bombay. A few production facilities such as Paramount, the Gower Studios, the Raleigh Studios, and others are still located in the physical Hollywood, but it's the metaphorical doors of Hollywood that we're knocking on.

"Hollywood" is the world's metaphor for the entirety of the film business. Whether films are shot today in North Carolina, Vancouver, Iceland, Africa, New Zealand, Hong Kong, or France, the filmmakers think of themselves as part of the Hollywood community. No matter where you live in the world, if you start fooling around with a camera, people will say you've "gone Hollywood," even if you never visit the physical place.

Metaphoric Hollywood's borders are porous and constantly shifting with new developments in technology. As Renaissance painting changed with new methods of mixing paint and creating perspective, so Hollywood changes as new ways of delivering stories and entertainment experiences are being generated.

24

The concept of Hollywood has expanded radically in the last ten years from the business that provided about two hundred feature films and five hundred TV shows a year for seven or eight studios and three national networks.

The New Global Hollywood

Now the concept of Hollywood is much larger. It encompasses the vast new world of cable TV, global satellite networks, and computers. Video games must be written and produced just like movies, and can make as much money or more — witness *Sonic the Hedgehog*, a video game which has made over four hundred million dollars worldwide, compared to two or three hundred million for a blockbuster picture.

Top movie executives are quitting their studio jobs to run interactive video companies and home shopping networks. The lines between movies, videos, publishing, computer games, TV shows, and interactive entertainments are blurring, and Hollywood is the only metaphor big enough to enfold it all.

There is still some truth to the notion of Hollywood as a place located in Southern California. The district of Hollywood is still more or less the geographic center of a cluster of production facilities, soundstages, office buildings, and studio ranches, stretching from Culver City, Venice, and Santa Monica in the south, to Glendale, Burbank, North Hollywood, and even the Simi Valley in the north. The dozen or so companies that control more than half of the world's entertainment have headquarters in Los Angeles, within a thirty-mile radius of Hollywood. The executives, agents, producers, actors, and directors are there. The meetings to decide what movies will be made are held there. At some point, every major figure in world entertainment has to come to Hollywood, if only to accept an Academy Award.

The Corridor of Doors

But whether we're speaking of the physical Hollywood, or the great metaphoric Hollywood of global entertainment, it can be visualized as

25

a long corridor of doors, that familiar infinite hallway we have all encountered in our dreams. The corridor goes on forever, and behind its doors are infinite possibilities.

As you walk along the hall, you see that some doors are open to you, some are closed. Some are bolted and barred, chained and guarded. Some are just faces of wood with no hardware, no doorknob to grasp, no keyhole to try your keys in. While some work perfectly well to admit other people, they seem impassable to you alone. Some are crowded with people screaming to get out, others are jammed with people trying to get in. Some are bricked up completely, with only an outline to show where there was once a doorway.

Each door leads into a different room or space, into a different experience or set of possibilities. In some rooms there is an entire lifetime. Other rooms are full of monsters, or love, or money, or sex, or creative satisfaction. And still others open into an abyss of blackness.

In some rooms it seems wonderful parties are going on, with people milling around, talking, and making deals enthusiastically. You notice in some rooms as you walk by that certain people in the crowded parties are elbowing their way purposefully across the room, making for another door on the opposite side, that leads perhaps to more exclusive parties, or to another corridor of doors and possibilities.

Many Mansions, Many Doors

Someone said, "There are as many doors into Hollywood as there are people." The roads into the business are highly individual, and there is something to be learned from each person's story. I always like to ask successful people, "How did you get to your current position?" I always learn something from the particulars of luck, timing, and skill that people reveal in telling their stories. The movies of the 1930s, '40s, and '50s give a distorted, glorified, but somewhat accurate picture of the Hollywood system.

The studio gates are important symbols in these pictures. The most memorable is perhaps the elaborate Paramount gate, which still stands. In countless movies, stars were depicted as cruising confidently through these wrought-iron gates, while wanna-bes — the Hollywood outsiders — were shown trying to crash the gates, outwit the gate guards, get over or under the walls. The gates still stand, the walls and guards still bar uninvited intruders, but more than that, the invisible doors and parapets still defend the invisible fortress of Hollywood.

The Doors of Film School

If you want to knock on the doors of Hollywood, one method is to go to a good film school — such as the University of Southern California (USC), the University of California, Los Angeles (UCLA), or New York University (NYU). Get a solid background, good formal training to support whatever practical experience you already have. In school, give yourself time to find out what you're good at, what you really want to do.

The film school as a method of getting into commercial movie-making was a breach in the Hollywood wall that had been blasted by George Lucas and his contemporaries, John Milius, Francis Ford Coppola, Martin Scorsese, and others, who had found mentors at USC, UCLA, or NYU to show them through the Hollywood doors.

Before their time, most people got into Hollywood through other doors. They were born into the industry, as sons and daughters of Hollywood pioneers, or they were brought in from the worlds of Chicago and New York newspapers and playwriting, or they found some other way into the maze.

Lucas and his fellows made film school a clear door to Hollywood. There are still only a handful of first-class film schools, and the competition to get in is savage because so many young people are drawn to that door.

Thousands want in, but there's only room for a few hundred at a time.

Patience

Patience is essential. You'll need it at many stages, waiting a semester to direct a film, waiting to find a job, to get into a union, to get

27

your script read, to get an agent, to get a part, to make a deal. It can be frustrating.

Hollywood is very hard on the impatient. It would be easy to conclude that you don't have the talent or drive when you repeatedly hit the wall of frustration, but that would be a premature judgment.

A Matter of Timing

Frustration goes with the territory. Things don't always happen when you want them to, and if you meet resistance, it may not be because you are unsuited for the work. It may be simply that the timing is not right, yet. Hollywood runs in cycles, and you may have to wait for another turn of the wheel, for another season, before the key and the lock line up and the door opens for you.

The doors of Hollywood are like valves, opening and closing at different times to regulate the flow of talent into show business. A patient seeker may have to camp near a door that seems likely and wait until the time is right, when the door is open (a little like hovering in a parking garage, waiting for someone to leave so you can take their spot).

When the stakes are high, you may have to play the waiting game for years. It took ten years of trying to sell *One Flew Over the Cuckoo's Nest* as a movie, and seven years to develop the script for *Beverly Hills Cop*.

If you want to play the Hollywood game, you should make the adjustment to its being a long game: a career, a lifetime, not a hobby or a brief fling. One of the secrets is simple perseverance — consistent commitment to a goal over a long period of time. This can open doors that all other methods have left locked.

Success by Association

It's been observed that successful people often get to the top by associating with people who are already successful in the field they are trying to master.

28

Going to a film school is one way of associating with like-minded people who are all trying to succeed, and with teachers who have proven themselves in the field. But you can open a similar door by other means. There are film societies and networking groups for aspiring screenwriters and producers.

There are writers' conferences and seminars where you can meet experts and people who have already succeeded at selling their ideas and realizing their dreams. If you have relatives or connections in the film business, by all means make use of them. If you don't, then your job is to create associations — business friendships — that will connect you to Hollywood or whatever world you are trying to enter.

Local writing groups across the country and around the world bring in Hollywood speakers to share information and new ideas. The Independent Feature Project, an organization whose members are independent producers, brings in speakers for panel discussions, as do the Writers Guild and many others.

You can also study aspects of Hollywood or hear speakers by taking classes at UCLA Extension's Writers' Program and Film Studies division. Individual teachers and authors of screenwriting books, such as Dona Cooper, Syd Field, Michael Hauge, Viki King, Robert McKee, Tom Schlesinger, Dr. Linda Seger, John Truby, myself, and others, give seminars for the public.

In film school and in all of these other venues, there is a benefit which may actually outweigh the formal training, confidence, and mentorship you get there, and that's the connection with the other people in the classes and seminars.

Writing Groups

If you feel screenwriting is an appropriate door for you to knock on, then you might consider joining a writers' support group, critique group, or writers' club in your area. These range from small, informal groups that just get together to read each other's material, up to huge organizations with newsletters, annual conferences, and hundreds of members. Some writers' groups sponsor seminars and workshops where you can learn more about your chosen craft. Such groups can be good places to meet writing partners and keep up with the latest developments in the field.

Conferences

Writers' conferences, often sponsored by local writers' groups or by colleges, can be great places to learn about the business and make connections. Such events bring together film teachers, successful writers, agents, and studio executives who can open doors to Hollywood.

Writers get a chance to pitch ideas to potential buyers, and many agents come to these gatherings looking for clients and properties to sell. You get a chance to socialize with people who are already doing what you want to do. It can help banish illusions about the business, and bring the gods of Hollywood down to human size. *Writer's Digest* publishes an annual listing of such conferences around the country.

Contests

In the past few years, screenwriting contests have become an increasingly important door to Hollywood. Film students compete fiercely for the Nicholl, the Goldwyn, the Diane Thomas, or the Christopher Columbus Screenplay Discovery Awards screenwriting prizes, because the winners reap more than just a financial reward. They get recognition.

Winning one of these contests or getting honorable mention is not a rock-solid guarantee of a Hollywood writing career, but it does mean that your work will be read. You are automatically ushered through a door into a smaller, more exclusive room, and your chances of getting to the right people are greatly increased.

Dreams Made Real

When you are lucky enough to know what you want, you can apply your full energy to making your dreams real. This sounds easier than it is sometimes. It would be easy if we were simple, monolithic beings who entertained only one idea or attitude at a time. But in fact, we are complex, multilayered beings who usually maintain different attitudes at the same time, often quite contradictory ones.

Sabotage

Even when the upper levels of our awareness are pulling for positive change, the sneakier lower levels may be gleefully sabotaging our progress. Deep down we are often resistant to change because the dark stuff within us feels its "life" threatened. Efforts to build a new structure or knock on new doors may be undermined by the neurotic shadow-selves who dwell within us. Like Dracula, they fear the light of change.

Centering

The only way to overcome this self-sabotage is by getting centered. Try to move the center of your attention away from the doubts so that it's in exact alignment with your deepest needs and highest goals. This is the meaning of the word "concentration" — a state of being totally with your center. When we concentrate on a goal, we are lining up all the levels of our being with our deepest, truest selves.

"I Will"

To make things happen, you need to make a firm act of will. This consists of a statement that rings out in two directions: outward to the universe around you, and inward, to the many levels of your own self.

This statement must be phrased precisely. It's no good saying, "I'm going to try to be a director, a producer, a writer, or an executive." That imposes too many steps and conditions, and sets the goal vaguely in the future. As much as possible, try to bring your dreams into the present or make your future goals definite. A stronger statement is "I AM a producer," or "I AM a writer," or "I WILL achieve my goal within the next six months."

Clear Intention

When you've made your choice and phrased it strongly, stand up and say it out loud to the world. Tell friends and colleagues what your intentions are. Make an announcement to your bosses and potential employers of what you want. Broadcast the statement of your choice as far as your imagination can carry you, out to the angels and gods, out to the stars: "This is what I need and want."

Make the same statement of intent inwardly. Lean over the lip of the well of your being, and shout down to all the levels, "This is what I need and want." Ask all those levels to get into alignment with your new direction. Only then can energy flow cleanly through your whole system, with no binding or friction, with no doubts dragging at you, blocking you, or holding you back. Only then can you be in focus about making your dreams real.

Once you know what you want and have focused your intent on getting it, make a simple, clear plan with a series of small, realistic, achievable steps. Great ambitions are sometimes thwarted by the impossibility of achieving so much all at once. Of course you can't achieve all your goals at once. They have to be broken down into manageable steps that can be done in a logical order. Each of these steps is another door that can be negotiated.

It seems you never run out of doors. New corridors and crossroads appear every day. That's the ever-changing architecture of Hollywood, where few people settle into comfortable, unchanging jobs. Every new idea, treatment, manuscript, book, script, every new show is another door of opportunity.

If you've hesitated about approaching the doors of Hollywood, or if you're well inside the labyrinth but are stuck in a corridor hammering on a particular unyielding door, take heart. Your dreams can come true, if you're willing to put in the effort and time to open those doors or figure out a way around them. Hollywood is built on dreams, but the successful people are the dreamers who set their intention on making the dreams come true.

Dreams draw us into the labyrinth and keep us going in the dark times, but ultimately they only have value if they are realized. If you focus and persist, you can make your dreams real. That's what Hollywood is all about.

"If you work at that which is before you," the wise Roman Emperor Marcus Aurelius wrote nineteen centuries ago, "following right reason seriously, vigorously, calmly, without allowing anything else to distract you . . . if you hold to this, expecting nothing, fearing nothing, but satisfied with your present activities according to nature, and with heroic truth in every word and sound which you utter, you will live happy. And there is no one who is able to prevent this."

Christopher Vogler is an award-winning author (The Writer's Journey) *and script consultant. He has evaluated more than six thousand screenplays for major motion picture studios including Walt Disney, Warner Bros., United Artists, Touchstone Pictures, and Hollywood Pictures. A specialist in fairy tales and folklore, Vogler consulted on Walt Disney's feature film hits* The Lion King, Aladdin, The Little Mermaid, *and* Beauty and the Beast. *For information on how to contact Christopher Vogler and Storytech, his literary consulting firm, see Chapter 24.*

Chapter 1.

The Keys to Unlocking
the Secrets to Hollywood

"If you believe in yourself, just hang in there because you will get your chance."

— Mark Rydell,
Director-Producer
(Cinderella Liberty, The Rose,
On Golden Pond, For the Boys, Intersection)

Hollywood is the storytelling capital of the world. It's a place where you can easily hear many tales of how people were able to sell their projects: from bedroom tales to hard work to mere luck. The great news is that anyone who really wants to can find a way to enter the "closed kingdom" of the movie business.

The first step is to understand what we call the "Geography of Opportunity." The selling of one's project is a business. Ultimately, no matter how brilliant or wonderful your project might be, the bottom line is still, "Will it sell?" and when it's sold, "Can it be produced?" and if it's produced, "Will it draw an audience sufficient to earn a profit?"

All too often producers and writers, even experienced, talented veterans, work in a vacuum, isolating themselves from the realities of the marketplace. And each year thousands of projects are created and scripts are written by sincere, hardworking, and determined artists which never sell, are never read, and never even see the light of day.

By understanding the marketplace, you can gain entry into it. And the marketplace called Hollywood can be richly rewarding to those who create the products that achieve some measure of success.

Breaking through and staying successful are obviously difficult achievements that do not come easily or without work. How do you increase your chances of making it? By understanding the rules that affect the market and outsmarting those players who don't grasp them. Many veterans fail to grasp or apply these rules. But you can, and if you do, you increase the chances of opening the doors to Hollywood immeasurably.

Understanding the rules, though, is not enough. Once you comprehend how the system works, you can learn strategies to penetrate it. The single purpose of this book is to teach you the rules of the game and how to break them on the road to success.

Make no mistake about it. To win in Hollywood, you've got to be determined. It can be done, it's done every day, and we will teach you how to do just that.

The path to success is different and unique for everyone in Hollywood. Gale Anne Hurd, a successful producer, has produced some of the most memorable movies of the last two decades: *Aliens, The Terminator*, and *The Abyss*. Here is the story of how she opened the doors to Hollywood:

> I studied communications (both film and broadcasting) and economics at Stanford University, graduating in 1977. My former film professor, Steven Kovacs, had been hired by Roger Corman, the famous producer-director, to head up production. When an opening as Roger's assistant became available, I was recommended for the position. I received a letter (which I have framed in my office) inquiring as to whether I was interested in the job. I was living in Northern

California at the time, but I nonetheless flew down to Los Angeles (at my own expense), interviewed for the position, and the rest, as they say, is history.

My advice to aspiring producers is to start at the bottom and work up. I had two degrees from one of the top universities in the country, yet I was eager to learn. I applied myself to every task presented to me, whether it was photocopying screenplays as Roger Corman's assistant or making coffee on the set as a production assistant. I did not refuse a request, even if it meant canceling my personal plans and working nonstop for seventy-two hours. The industry is full of aspiring filmmakers; if you don't make the commitment to your job your top priority, someone else will, and you'll never succeed. I am proud of my humble beginnings in Hollywood, and I've never stopped learning.

In selecting a project, I try to find something new in each endeavor, whether it is a combination of genres (e.g., *Tremors* was a humorous horror film) or a new twist on an old standard (*Aliens* is essentially a war film set in outer space). I like character-driven pieces (like *The Waterdance*), and settings where my imagination can run wild (such as the Insider's Camp in *No Escape*). I never select a film project merely because I think it will be a huge hit at the box office.

If you want to guarantee a green light, package your project. Find the most appropriate director, the right cast, and then approach financiers or studios. This was the formula which enabled *The Terminator*, my first independent feature, to make it to the big screen.

I hope we'll see more independent films — and independent financing entities — emerge from the end of the recession. With successes like *The Crying Game* and *Four Weddings and a Funeral*, money will become available for less mainstream films, made for a price, and distributed by mini-majors.

— Gale Anne Hurd

UNLOCKING THE SECRETS

Over and over again, studio executives, producers, and directors ask us if we know of any good projects. There are never enough to satisfy the creative machinery of the film industry. Over 500 films are made for theatrical release yearly by the studios and another 125 or more for television broadcast. Plus, another 400 to 500 movies are made by small independent film producers, so the need is always there. The competition to find the next great story or concept never stops.

It doesn't matter who you are, how old you are, or what sex you are, as long as you have a story that a buyer (studio, producer, director, writer) values. They will buy it from you. Our book will tell you where you can find such projects. Also, we will give you access to industry professionals who can assist you at all levels of packaging.

❧ **Every year Hollywood spends over half a billion dollars on developing projects. Hollywood needs what you have, if what you have is what they want.**

The following is a crucial question, and, according to your answer, you'll be able to evaluate whether you have what it takes.

Question:

What is the most important thing you need to have to sell your idea, story, manuscript, book, or screenplay to Hollywood?

Our distinguished friends, director-producer Arthur Hiller (*Man of La Mancha, Love Story, Outrageous Fortune*), producer Alex Ho (*Salvador, Born on the Fourth of July, JFK*), writer-director Paul Mazursky (*An Unmarried Woman, Moscow on the Hudson, Faithful*), director-producer Mark Rydell (*Cinderella Liberty, The Rose, On Golden Pond, For the Boys, Intersection*), and legendary director-producer Robert Wise (*The Sound of Music, West Side Story, Star Trek: The Motion Picture*) will share with us their answers to the same question.

38

⚷   **Answers:**

"You must feel passionately about your project."
                    — Arthur Hiller

"You must love your project and be passionate."
                    — Alex Ho

"You must be obsessed with your project."
                    — Paul Mazursky

"You must have passion and love your project. You must be moved by it."
                    — Mark Rydell

"You must have passion for your project."
                    — Robert Wise

⚷ **As you see, the consensus is unanimous. You must have passion and believe in your project**. This key is crucial because if you don't, who will? If it is just a so-so idea or mediocre manuscript or screenplay, it is not enough.

You must be wondering why so many bad movies are made. Well, the answer is that . . .

⚷ **Whoever sold them had passion and was obsessed with their projects.** Even though the projects were bad, their creators were able to infuse the buyers with their enthusiasm. Quality was overlooked.

Don't let that happen to you. Director-producer Mark Rydell strongly recommends that ⚷ **"the emphasis on your search for projects should be placed on the quality of the stories. Be a creative producer, a person of taste."**

Chapter 2.

Opening the Doors

THE DAVID PERMUT STORY

"Dear Mr. Permut: Congratulations on your decision to enter the motion picture industry. I can think of nothing that would offer you as much future security, with the possible exception of going over Niagara Falls in a leaky raft. But if you are really interested in pursuing this reckless endeavor, please call me."

— Sidney Sheldon,
Writer

Before we begin our step-by-step process to assist you in selling your dream project, we are going to introduce you to another Hollywood insider, David Permut, the producer of *Three of Hearts*, *Consenting Adults*, *Dragnet*, *29th Street*, and *Blind Date*, among other films. His story will give you insights into the business, while encouraging you on your Hollywood journey.

There are no definitive rules in the picture business. This makes it somewhat difficult for somebody struggling to get into the business. This is also what makes it terribly exciting at times because anything is possible. That's been proven many times.

Getting into the business was always a dream of mine. I had tunnel vision. When I was in school, in the seventh grade, I used to subscribe to *Variety* and *The Hollywood Reporter*. My teachers would always confiscate my trade papers because I didn't do terribly well in Spanish class. Still, I knew who was running every studio in Hollywood. I've always been very driven. I always knew that I wanted to be in the industry, though I wasn't certain what aspect of the business I wanted to get into. At first I thought directing was it, from having made films on 8 millimeter.

Actually, my first job officially in the business was selling maps on Sunset Boulevard to the stars' homes. Believe it or not, it was a rather profitable business at the tender age of sixteen. I also met a lot of people. Katharine Hepburn used to come by and sign the maps, and Fred Astaire came by, too. Randolph Scott's wife gave me an umbrella; she thought I was getting too much sun during the days. Also, there was a prominent attorney named Sam Zagon who lived across the street. He represented Stanley Kramer and numerous prominent directors in the business. He used to come over and chat with me.

The long and short of it is that even by selling maps to the stars' homes, I was able to establish relationships very early on in my career, with people like Sam Zagon. Interestingly enough, Sam was one of my first attorneys in the business — representing me on the acquisition of rights to a book which I got involved with years later.

Aside from the maps, I got my real start in the agency business. I went to work for a small talent agency. I was interested in the literary side, and began by representing a few writers. I even had my own agency for a short while at the very early age of nineteen. I had gone to UCLA for a year but quit when somebody offered me a job as a gofer on a picture. I

41

worked on a couple of films and then got involved in the agency business shortly after that.

I was very lucky. A lot of what we do is about luck and timing. The first produced film that I made was a fluke. We made the movie in one night on videotape in 1975. The quality was horrendous; the tape to film transfer was primitive. It looked terrible and it was grainy. We made the movie for $230,000. Every studio passed. They didn't want to have anything to do with this little video transfer to film.

A guy in the lumber business, who was one of the largest shareholders of Georgia-Pacific, fell in love with this project. He wrote a check for $230,000. We taped the movie in the theater and we transferred the tape to film. We released the film ourselves. We booked the theaters. We called Salah Hassanein at United Artists and Sumner Redstone and Hank Plitt (from the Plitt theater chain). We really didn't know too much about what we were doing; we just kind of did it. We booked about 750 theaters to play this movie.

The film was released three weeks after it was shot. The actor in the movie was nominated for Best Actor in 1975 for an Academy Award. His name is James Whitmore and he did a one-man show of *Give 'Em Hell, Harry*, portraying Harry Truman. We had six videotape cameras watch him being brilliant on stage in front of a live audience. People had no idea we were going to be filming. They came to the theater in Seattle and found cameras in some of their seats. We had to pay them to go out and have a steak dinner on us because they couldn't see the show from their seats. It was literally one take with the entire show covered by six cameras. The picture did about $11 million on a $230,000 budget, which is a damn good ratio and, as they say down South, we were "shittin' in high cotton."

The whole concept of filming live events was very appealing to me. I wanted to do Lily Tomlin's show at one time. I've been approached to do every one-man show, every one-woman show, since then. The next film I put together was even a greater success than the 1975 film. It was shot in two consecutive nights. It wasn't on video — it was on film. We released the film ourselves the same way we released *Give 'Em Hell, Harry.* We booked the theaters ourselves because every studio passed on the movie. It cost $750,000 and it grossed about $32 million domestically. It was *Richard Pryor, Live in Concert.* Richard was brilliant at the Long Beach Terrace Theater.

That was the most successful film in concert history. And it was really my greatest monetary success, thus far. You know if a $750,000 film does $32 million, it's pretty good. So, I got started in a rather unconventional way, making both *Give 'Em Hell, Harry* and then later *Richard Pryor, Live in Concert.* Ray Stark saw the movie one night, and he called me up and said, "You should be in a studio." I had never met Ray before, so we met and spent some time together. Before I knew it, I had a first-look deal with Columbia Pictures in 1979. That's when I started making more conventional films.

The first feature that I executive produced was a film called *Fighting Back*, which was based on a *60 Minutes* episode. It was a story about a vigilante from New Jersey named Anthony Imperiale. I saw him on *60 Minutes* one Sunday night like everybody else watching the show. I called the gentleman in New York and then flew there. He had been approached by other producers but fortunately I stayed with it and wound up with the rights to his story. I developed it originally at Columbia. Then I left Columbia after a year or so and went with Lorimar. I took this project with me. After Lorimar the project was still in active development. I finally made the film. It took three years to get it made with Dino DeLaurentiis. Paramount released it. The problem with the picture was that it was a vigilante movie which had lost its timeliness over the three-year period of development. *Fighting Back* could have been a more topical picture had it been released earlier, but *Death Wish*

43

and a number of other vigilante-themed movies had preceded it. That took some of the wind out of its sails.

At the same time, in 1987, I also produced *Dragnet*. *Dragnet* came about late one night. I was watching TV and "channel surfing," going from one channel to the next as I often do. I saw an old rerun of *Dragnet*. Three channels away there was Dan Aykroyd in a rerun of *Saturday Night Live*. I started thinking about the idea of doing a send-up of *Dragnet* for the big screen.

The next morning my first call was to Bernie Brillstein, Dan Aykroyd's manager. My next call was to Frank Price, who was running Universal at the time. Then I went in with one of the shortest pitches in movie history, which was "Dum, da, dum, dum." Frank Price said, "Let's make the movie." It was that simple. Of course we went through the process of getting a script and getting a picture agreement. These didn't take too long. It was about a year from the moment when I uttered "Dum, da, dum, dum" until we actually had a camera rolling. It moved pretty quickly. The picture did close to sixty million dollars domestically and was a big hit for the studio, one of the top-ten movies of the year.

Dragnet was also one of the first movies to translate a TV show to the big screen. There are so many out there now, when you walk down the aisle of a movie theater, it's like looking at *TV Guide*. You're channel surfing at a movie theater complex. Since the success of *The Addams Family* and *The Fugitive*, TV's been fertile ground. I think now the mines have been excavated. I'm responsible for some of that because after *Dragnet*, I was approached by just about every franchise imaginable: *Sky King*, *F Troop*, *Fury*. I went aggressively after the rights to several of them. One was *The Little Rascals*, which was produced by Steven Spielberg's company, Amblin Entertainment. While I'm involved monetarily, I'm not involved creatively. There are a lot of cooks in the kitchen. We spent several years developing the script. Fortunately, Spielberg's company became involved with King World Productions. I bowed out of producing the film. *The Beverly Hillbillies*, which I also set up and brought to Twentieth Century Fox, was also a successful film. It did over forty million dollars and a sequel is in development. I recently sold *Green Acres* to Fox. We're in development on *Green Acres*, which Rita Rudner and her husband, Marty Bergman, are writing. *F Troop* is in development over at New Line Cinema.

One of the biggest pictures we have on our slates for this year is kind of funny and it brings a smile to people's faces when I mention it. I went to Aaron Spelling and proposed doing a film with him. Fortunately, he responded very enthusiastically. It's *National Lampoon's Love Boat*.

We're going to take this innocent and pristine show and really put it on its end. Obviously, marrying *Love Boat*'s name to *National Lampoon* couldn't be a stronger icon, not only in this country but around the world. *Love Boat* was the number one syndicated show in more countries than I can even remember.

This picture could be huge. We're talking about casting Ice T, whom I just finished a film with, as Isaac, the bartender, giving advice to everybody. Being highlighted with *National Lampoon*'s name married to it, I think it has instant recognition and identification around the world. People know the kind of ride they're in for. When you say *National Lampoon's Love Boat*, people generally laugh.

Targeting the Audience

Our goal is to get a crossover audience. That's the key to success with a lot of pictures. With *Dragnet*, many people went because they remembered the show fondly. They also went because it was a comedy with Tom Hanks and Dan Aykroyd. You also draw a whole new generation of audience, whether it's *The Addams Family* or *The Flintstones*.

45

Finding the Idea

Good stories come in many fashions. ❦ Some of my projects evolve from ideas that I'm **sparked to by the newspaper**. As an example, ten years ago there was an oil freighter off the coast of Florida. It was lost hopelessly in a big storm. The oil freighter literally crashed into the backyard of a Palm Beach socialite, who lived next to the Kennedys. She became a fifteen-minute celebrity. She was in *People* magazine. She was a very gracious hostess who served beluga caviar and paté to the freighter's twelve swarthy Venezuelans. They hardly spoke English, but she still played hostess to them in Palm Beach.

That's not necessarily a story; it's an incident. What I saw in that was the idea of doing a cultural clash comedy, and a movie which was like *The Russians Are Coming* meets *Down and Out in Beverly Hills* set in the world of Palm Beach. It's a very insular world unto itself. I acquired the rights from Mollie Wilmot, who in turn became a technical consultant on the project. I'm currently in active development on the film at Hollywood Pictures.

This story caught a lot of people's imaginations. I went after the rights and was able to get a writer and to get Disney (Hollywood Pictures) interested in proceeding. But really, the incident was not the story of the movie. It just initiated the idea. You pick up the newspaper and every day there's a story that is interesting. Whether it makes a feature film or not, or a TV movie perhaps, who knows? ❦ **It's about enthusiasm and getting excited and believing in what you're selling, regardless of what medium it's for.** A lot of the ideas I have are generated by things like *Love Boat*. The idea of transforming *Love Boat* to a big-screen movie and skewing it the way we are is something that I thought would make sense. It would be a terrific idea.

❦ **The other source of ideas is writers**. The power of this business is material. If you have a 120-page script that the studios want, they will do anything they have to do to get it. I cultivated relationships with Dale Launer when he was selling stereos in the San Fernando Valley, California, before he wrote *Blind Date* for me, and before he wrote *Ruthless People* or *My Cousin Vinnie*; and with Adam Greenman, who was a bartender in Echo Park, California, before he wrote *Three of Hearts* and a two-hour CBS movie for me called *Breaking the Silence*. The real challenge of what I do is finding new talent, whether it's actors or cinematographers or other creative elements. One of the areas where I've had a lot of good fortune is working with established writers. I've worked with Neil Simon and George Gallo. George and I go back ten years, so he wasn't at the point in his career that he is today. Neither was Dale Launer.

Many of the projects also come from ideas that writers have. Writers will come to me and if they have a great idea, it's terrific to know that they potentially can go the distance and deliver a script. Somebody may have a great idea, but they may not have the capacity to go the distance with the script. Fortunately, I have a lot of confidence in most of the writers that I'm currently in business with. They can do it.

Magazine shows are a great source of material and so are your own instincts. If I come up with an idea that I think is exceptional, I'll kick it around with some writers to see if they share my enthusiasm for it. Those are some of the avenues that one can explore.

Breaking In

There are a number of things to do to break in. First of all, it depends on what aspect of the business one wants to break into. If you are looking to produce films, that's probably what you should do. Figure out a way to raise enough capital to make a film and then produce it.

47

As I said, ✿ **the power in the business is material. If you have a piece of material and the studios want it, they'll do anything they can do to get it, including making you a producer,** whether you're waiting on tables or selling stereos in the San Fernando Valley. It doesn't really matter, if you've got the goods. Obviously, it's getting the material seen by the right people and that takes somebody with connections.

As a producer you are always a storyteller. I don't think there's a definition of a shy producer, because no such thing exists in the business. You have to be tenacious and aggressive and inventive and clever. When I started, I didn't know anybody in the business, even though I sold the maps to the stars' homes. I wrote letters, and my letters basically were: "Dear Mr. So-and-So: Before you make a drop shot to the wastepaper basket, please allow me to introduce myself." I told them I made my own movies on Super 8 and I was attending UCLA, etc., etc., and my closing in the letters went something to the effect of "I'd appreciate any advice you might have that might further my career." I sent hundreds of these letters out and I got hundreds of form letters back. However, I also received some very nice letters back and I met a lot of interesting people through the letters. Sidney Sheldon wrote back to me (I was eighteen when I wrote to him): "Dear Mr. Permut: Congratulations on your decision to enter the motion picture industry. I can think of nothing that would offer you as much future security, with the possible exception of going over Niagara Falls in a leaky raft. But if you are really interested in pursuing this reckless endeavor, please call me." I did. He invited me up to his house — I've never worked with Sidney Sheldon but it was certainly a nice opportunity to be able to spend an hour talking to him. I can go through a number of other very prominent people in the business whom I met through writing letters. If anybody says to me that writing letters is a waste of time, I say "bullshit," because it seemed to work for me. Not only did it work for me, but I was offered a few jobs through that approach, including the job in the agency business I mentioned earlier.

When you're asking somebody for advice, you're also dealing with established people in the industry. Most of the people I know in the business have a little bit of an ego, maybe some more than most. I know I do. When somebody calls you up or writes you a letter that's impressive and from somebody looking for advice, it's hard for most of us to turn them down. As a result ♪ **I met a lot of people through writing letters**.

Also, it's ♪ **being at the right place at the right time.** I know that's difficult because if you're starting in the business, you're not invited to the black-tie dinners. Any way you can get someone's attention is important. Being tenacious and aggressive certainly counts for a whole lot.

♪ **So write letters and just be inventive and clever**. People do meet people and it is a people business. If I were out there and didn't have the access that I currently have, I would do what I did initially. Aside from writing the letters, I would also try to be at whatever party I could finagle my way into. If you want to meet somebody, you meet somebody, and if you really want, truly want something, I believe you get it. You just have to have the tenacity to hang in there, and **that's what this business is really about — just hanging in there long enough.**

But in terms of material, let's get back to the goods, because the goods are about material. Establish relationships with writers because the key to the door is material, unless you have major relationships with stars and with star directors. It doesn't matter if you don't have any produced credits. If you have the 120-page script, that's sometimes all it takes.

♪ **School, colleges, and film courses are also important**. Make friends with the professors at these schools. ♪ **Find out who the big shiny stars are in literary classes.**

Get out there as much as possible. Every time I used to see

a film truck on location, I stopped. I met a lot of people that way. I met directors that way, directors who invited me up to their houses. I got to be social with some of the people I met at a young age because I was very compelled by the business. I used to hang out at Universal, uninvited. Later I got invited by one of the producers on a series there, who asked me if I wanted to run some errands on the show. I did that for a short while. This was when Steven Spielberg was doing his first *Night Gallery* at Universal.

Access to Buyers

Let's go back to *Dragnet*. If I had gone in and said, "Dum, da, dum, dum" without Bernie Brillstein's support and Dan Aykroyd's enthusiasm about starring in the movie, they would have said, "The door's over there." The reaction could have been quite different even though they respected what I thought was an inventive idea. I had that support in 1987.

If somebody is starting off, I think it's important to have support, whether it's from a producer, or an agent, or a manager. 🎬 **It really doesn't matter what the person's title is, but it must be somebody who has the connections, who will lend credibility to a given project. He also must be able to pick up the phone and get people on the phone**.

It's important to have an agent who loves the material. Sometimes having the material come through a third party is better. It's a lot easier for a studio executive or a buyer to hear that it's a great script from somebody who hasn't written it or somebody who isn't hungry to produce it, such as an agent who has a more objective opinion about it.

Forecasting

Regarding the future of the film business, there are no answers even with respect to interactive film and the information superhighway. There's still a lot of mystery to all of this. Even the guys who are at the forefront of that business can't put their fingers on it exactly until it's here. What makes the business exciting is the constant rolling of the dice. Nobody knows the trends in the industry. Nobody can project them, even though everybody desperately tries. I think the future of the business is exciting, especially when you talk about fiber optics compared with the archaic way in which we make films and lug film canisters around to movie theaters. The whole technical aspect of the film business will be revolutionized. There will always be films. People like to experience certain things with other people. Films are one of those things. There are certain movies that one can see in the privacy of a living room and not lose a lot. But there are other films with the scope, dimension, and wide-screen projection that are exciting to watch in theaters.

New Technologies

The only way technology will impact on the creative aspects of movies is that the audience will be able to become more of a participant. This is not just with interactive shows but with "popcorn movies," as I refer to them, such as *Jurassic Park*. I can picture that movie in high definition, and I can picture it as an interactive film. It's terribly exciting. It's the theme ride, it's the E ticket at Disneyland.

In *Three of Hearts* we wound up shooting two endings to the picture. If interactive films were available now, maybe that's the way we would release it. Of course, years ago Paramount did a movie called *Clue* and released one version on the West Coast and another version on the East Coast. A movie that's more intimate and about people in relationships probably isn't going to have that much play in interactive as opposed to the more "popcorn-style" film.

It's exciting. It's a great time for somebody to want to enter

51

the business, because the business is going to go through dramatic changes in the foreseeable future.

In terms of my own future, as I try to project what kinds of ideas I'm looking for, my only barometer in looking for projects is something that ◦ **I would want to line up to pay seven dollars for**. My taste tends to be very eclectic. The area I lean toward more than most is probably comedy, as is the case with my next picture. I think there's something for everybody and I think that's what movies offer you, especially today. There's so much product on the market, it's overwhelming. Every weekend there are five or six major releases that hit the screen. It's staggering.

Chapter 3.

Project Sources

"If you want to get into the business, acquire the rights to a story, a book, or a screenplay."

— **Paul Mazursky,**
Director
(An Unmarried Woman,
Moscow on the Hudson, Willie & Phil,
Down and Out in Beverly Hills, Faithful)

DEFINING YOUR ROLE

I t is important to establish what your role is in the industry. Because your goal is to be able to sell your project, we suggest that you position yourself as a "Producer." According to director-producer Mark Rydell, a producer should be a creative artist and not just a hustler. A producer at his best is a person who should have the ability to judge material — magazine and newspaper articles, novels, short stories, pieces of literature, and screenplays.

For our purposes, there are five main producer titles — Executive Producer, Producer, Co-Producer, Associate Producer, and Line Producer/Production Manager — which we define on the next page.

As in any endeavor, you should try to get the most you can for yourself. However, if you are just starting out in the entertainment business, you may have to be flexible and accept whatever is offered to you.

— Executive Producer
The person who provides the finances or a major element to make the project happen. You must have power to secure this title. He/she is the boss.

— Producer
The person who generally finds and develops the project, from concept to screen.

— Co-Producer
The person who brings some element to the project. Normally this title is given to the person who finds or owns the project. A partner with the Producer.

— Associate Producer
Credit given to an executive assistant, a line producer, or the person who found the project. **If you can't get the title of Producer or Co-Producer, this is your title.**

— Line Producer/Production Manager
The supervisor of the film. An employee of the production company. The nuts-and-bolts person.

Now you know where your place is in the moviemaking hierarchy.

As long as you have a project to sell, and you are actively pursuing it, you are a producer.

Don't worry about anything else but finding that great project. The executive producer or studio will hire the people who have the expertise to actually make the movie.

54

WHAT IS A GOOD STORY?

Judging a story is a very subjective task. Every producer and executive has his/her own taste. What one person may love, another may hate. During our interview with Mark Rydell, when asked what a good story was, he smiled and said, "Directors and producers spend most of their time reading, evaluating material. I am always looking for a piece of material that makes me shake, makes me tremble, where I can feel the art in it, or I can feel somebody's passions have been engaged, the writer's passions have been engaged to the extent that mine are going to be engaged. I'm a voracious person, and when I go to work on material, it's an experience of deepest examination and testing of the material all the time, looking to make sure that I have the strength to last the two to four years that it takes to make a picture happen. I throw material away all the time because it does not contain the deep investment of the artist, who is the originator of the material. Sometimes I start to read and all of a sudden the hair stands up on the back of my neck. That's when I know I have responded to that material in a way that is going to give me the fuel to go forward in a world that is trying to stop me all the time. It's a world where we have to climb over rejection after rejection, but you get to the point where rejection doesn't affect you because you are so determined to make your picture that anybody saying 'no' is just going to be wrong, so you go to the next person to make it. You know you can't be deterred."

As Mark pointed out, the story must touch you deeply. If it's a comedy, you must laugh; if it's a drama, you must cry. In addition to the emotional appeal, there are certain basic elements you should look for when evaluating a story.

❧ Those basic elements are:

- **How relatable is your concept** (could it happen to you)?

- **How unique is your story?**

- **How castable is your story** (what stars are perfect to act in it)**?**

- **How much entertainment value is there?**

❧ **Relatability** (means it could happen to you). This situation is something that you could imagine. How would you respond to this situation if you were to find yourself in it? For example, take the story of Jennifer and Jim, a couple who were driving from one place to another, got caught in a snowstorm with their baby and had to survive. That's a very relatable story. Another is the story of the couple whose little girl fell into a well. Stories about people who are victims of crime are good examples.

People overcoming obstacles; that's another relatable situation. For example, a woman has a child, the child dies, and she's accused of killing the child. She's imprisoned and while she's in prison her husband and her attorneys fight to prove her innocence. They discover that the child had a rare disease which manifested itself as poisoning but was, in fact, a sickness.

Again, a very relatable story, one where an ordinary person endures a nightmarish, extraordinary experience and is exonerated. **Relatability is very important.**

❧ **Uniqueness**. If it's a crime story, is there an aspect that we haven't seen before?

Look for relatability, look for uniqueness, and look for twists and turns — if it's fiction, there should be lots of clever twists and turns.

❧ **Castability**. Buyers always look for projects they can take to their favorite stars. Having a great project to introduce to those same stars becomes vital for producers. Furthermore, the international market provides nearly 60 percent of the revenue source for most movies, so it is crucial to have a project that's attractive to stars with box office clout. (See our list "How the Stars Rate Worldwide" on page 287.)

🐎 **Entertainment value.** This, of course, is a very important criterion. Is this entertaining? Is it a good story in the old-fashioned sense? Are these characters that we care about? Are we frightened if it's a thriller, do we laugh if it's a comedy, do we cry if it's bittersweet?

Heart is important. Your story needs characters that we care about.

🐎 For **network television,** your movie idea has to have **an appeal to women,** because these films are primarily targeted at a female audience. That's ABC, CBS, and NBC.

🐎 TV movies at Fox are skewed less toward women. They have an interest in appealing to a slightly younger, more male audience. They are beginning to move closer to the middle, that is, closer to their competitors. They still tend to be less interested in true stories and more interested in a broader range of genres. They'll do comedies whereas the other three networks do very few.

🐎 Generally speaking, for TV movies the three major networks, ABC, CBS, and NBC, want contemporary dramas, true stories, and thrillers, particularly about women in jeopardy, that is, women in situations where they are threatened either emotionally or physically and have to extricate themselves.

Now that you know what buyers look for in a story, let's go out there and find the next *Die Hard, On Golden Pond,* or another *Bobbitt* story.

Here is how you do it.

STORY SOURCES

There are many sources for stories, manuscripts, books, or screenplays. In the industry, be it motion pictures or television, from studios to independent production companies, everybody is on the lookout for the next great story or next great book or next great screenplay.

We have a name for those people who dedicate their full time to it.

57

They are called "golden retrievers." In fact, to track down and bring in a story faster than the competition is so important that Michael Eisner, chairman of the board of the Walt Disney Company, noted in the *Los Angeles Times* that Jeffrey Katzenberg, his former chairman at Walt Disney Studios, is "still the best golden retriever I ever met."

This shows you that it doesn't matter who you are in the movie business; the key still is ✎ **to be able to find the next great story.**

WHERE AND HOW TO FIND PROJECTS

According to Dr. Linda Seger, international script consultant and author of *Making a Good Script Great, Creating Unforgettable Characters, The Art of Adaptation*, and *From Script to Screen,* to find stories, you should first look in your own backyard:

✎ **Look in your local newspaper** because if you are outside of L.A. you have access to stories before the people in L.A. become aware of them.

Study what has been done as a movie of the week. For example, Lorena Bobbitt is not from Los Angeles or New York. Her story broke in a small newspaper before it broke in a big one. So you say, "Well, if I had been the person who noticed that story in my local newspaper, I could have done something."

Linda comes from a town with 2,500 people. They had a bank robbery when she was ten. The guy who did it lived six miles from her home. Lieutenant Calley, who gave the orders to kill villagers in the My Lai massacre during the Vietnam War, lives in a neighboring town.

Very few people live in towns smaller than Linda's, yet she had two big stories in her own backyard. If she had wanted to go after those rights, she might have been quick enough to get them.

Don't even try to compete with the big Hollywood stories where producers can offer loads of money. Look for the stories in your own backyard, in your neighboring towns, and in your local newspaper. Think about whether there is a story in your family.

After you find what you believe to be a good story, have a professional help you evaluate it. Sometimes people don't understand what's good and what's not. If you're outside the business, there's no way you can really know.

If you can't find any great stories in your backyard, as Linda suggests, broaden your base. Here we introduce you to multiple strategies to acquire projects.

True Stories

True stories are normally made for television. However, more and more, feature producers are attracted to them. Producer Rhonda Bloom (*Separated by Murder, Broken Promises*) from the Larry Thompson Organization, shared with us how she normally finds her true stories:

☙ Stories come from many sources. One is **newspapers and magazines,** which range from *Rolling Stone*, *People*, the *Los Angeles Times*, the *New York Times*, the *Washington Post*, and *The New Yorker* to more obscure magazines and local newspapers.

☙ The **library** is a great place. Go there and look up older publications, and don't forget to look for old, obscure, public domain projects. For example, look at old true crime books. They may have come out some time ago and may not have been of interest then. However, the stories may be as timely today as they were when they occurred. Keep in mind that the marketplace changes over the course of time. Old materials may have a new life.

☙ Use **computer information systems** like Nexis. They will give you access to true stories, legal cases, and crime stories.

☙ Watch **television magazine and news programs**, such as *Hard Copy*, *A Current Affair*, *Inside Edition*, *20/20*, and so forth. Other kinds of programs which also feature true stories are another source. How-

59

ever, these are primary sources, so you will be competing with everybody in the business.

Magazines and Newspapers

If it's a magazine article, you can do two things. Call the magazine and ask for the name of the article's author. That person may in some instances have access to the rights. Or you can be a detective. If the article is about a person, a man or a woman who lives in, say, Kansas City, Missouri, you could call Kansas City information and ask directly for that person.

To gain access to people you want to contact regarding whatever you read in the papers, call the newspapers. Ask for the journalist or reporter of the story. If not available, look in the telephone book for those same names. If again, no success, go to city hall and look through vital records, such as birth, marriage, and death certificates, etc., if permissible and available.

If the story is an extremely well known one, the chances are that that person may already have some sort of representation, either a local lawyer, or a lawyer or agent in Los Angeles. That person would tell you if you were to call, "Yes, I already have somebody handling the film and television rights."

Books

If it's a book, call the publisher. The publisher will tell you who controls the film and television rights. It will be controlled by one of three entities: an agency, an author, or by the publishing house itself. Look in the front cover and see who the publisher is. Most major publishing companies are based in New York City.

🔑 Call the publishing company and ask for the subsidiary rights department. They will tell you who controls the rights. If it is an agency, they'll most likely give you the agency phone number.

Also ask for the expiration date of the option. Sometimes you can find out the option will be expiring soon. Keep your eye on it. You may be able to jump in when a window of opportunity occurs.

Other Sources for Manuscripts and Books

There are two principal publications for the book industry. One is *Kirkus Reviews* and the other is *Publishers Weekly.*

Each of these magazines reviews books a month to two months prior to publication.

They are good sources. However, the best way to get information about upcoming books is to go directly to the publishing companies themselves, all of which **publish two advance forms of information about new books.**

➤ They publish advance **lists,** which are rough in format. They are released months or even years in advance of publication dates. They subsequently publish **catalogues,** which are slick and colorful and are closer to the publication date of the books themselves.

➤ Publishers can make this information available to you. **The lists and the catalogues both describe upcoming publications,** which *Publishers Weekly* and *Kirkus Reviews* will eventually review.

Anybody can subscribe to *Publishers Weekly* or *Kirkus Reviews.* Your local public library may subscribe to these publications and have copies available.

➤ To acquire the lists or catalogues, contact the subsidiary rights department and describe yourself as an independent producer.

They may or may not be cooperative with their lists. It's probably easier to get the catalogues because they are less confidential than the lists. If you describe yourself as an independent writer/producer, it may be possible to get copies of these lists and even to get on their mailing list.

✎ You want to get on their mailing lists so that the catalogues and/ or advance lists will automatically be sent to you. The catalogues and lists are published three or four times a year: fall, winter, spring, and summer.

There may be costs, depending on whether or not they feel you're a small organization versus a larger organization. Assume that they are free, unless the publisher indicates otherwise.

Television Magazine/News Shows

If it's a story you see on a magazine show, call and ask which transcript services they use. For a few dollars, transcripts are available through those agencies. Each magazine show has its own transcription service. Journal Graphics is one, for example. To obtain transcripts, call the show, such as *Hard Copy*, *Inside Edition*, or *A Current Affair*, and they will tell you what company they use.

✎ The best thing to do is to get the written transcript of the segment that you saw. Transcripts will give you the names you need to contact, whether it's the name of a reporter or the name of the people in the story. Then you follow the same process you would use to track down a true story from a magazine.

✎ Techniques to Acquire the Rights

In order to secure the rights, you have to convince the person whose true story you are trying to acquire that you are the person with whom they should be in business. **There are two ways to do that:**

✎ **One is to throw a lot of money at them. The other is to demonstrate that you have something different to offer.**
Let's analyze the first method: money. A typical option purchase structure might be two thousand dollars or less for a year. The two primary elements of the option are money and time. Both are nego-

tiable. Your goal is to acquire the rights for the maximum amount of time for the least amount of money.

So let's say you offer two thousand dollars for a twelve-month option that would be applied against a purchase price of twenty thousand dollars. The typical ratio of option to purchase price for many years was 10 percent. If you offered two thousand dollars, it would be against twenty thousand dollars. If you offered ten thousand, it would be against a hundred thousand.

These days those ratios have changed. Often, the option money can be as much as half the eventual purchase price so that there's more incentive to get the project made. If you're spending 50 percent (a hundred thousand dollars against two hundred thousand or ten thousand against twenty thousand), there is more incentive to work harder to move the project forward.

It's all relative. As an independent writer or producer, if you can convince a rights holder, author, agent, or a person whose true story you are trying to acquire, **that ❧ you have the passion, that you have the right vision for the story**, and that you believe you can sell it or develop a great script, then you'll have a shot at getting the opportunity to prove yourself.

❧ The other way to obtain the rights to a project is to demonstrate that **you offer something different from other people.** If so, you might be able to acquire that story or that book for very little money. If you are new in the business, or if you can demonstrate that your skills and your vision are what's important in developing the story, you may win out over a major Hollywood production company.

The big players may throw a lot of money around, but they may have fifty other projects that they're working on. In contrast, this may be the one thing that you want to do, that you believe in, that you can, hopefully, bring to the attention of a studio or network.

❧ So the selling point for you as an independent is that **you can bring focus,** energy, and concentration to that particular story. You care about it. We are encouraging you to be enthusiastic and to have passion for your projects, but we don't want you to run amok.

✎ **"Be up-front and honest about things. Be straight."**
—Alex Ho,
Producer
(Salvador, Born on the Fourth of July, JFK)

✎ **Don't misrepresent who you are or what you are able to do. Be enthusiastic but don't lie.** It's a small business. If you say, "You know, my brother is best friends with Steven Spielberg," eventually a hole will be punched in that story, so be truthful. Represent yourself fairly and enthusiastically. Don't tell stories and don't make up credits that you don't have. The best approach is just to be honest, tenacious, and passionate.

ACTION PLAN

✎ Family and Friends

Your relatives may have great stories about some of your family members. Your friends may also have great stories about some members of their families. Ask them. Let them know that you are in the market for a great story. Tell them that you have access to Hollywood buyers.

✎ **Advertise in your local newspaper or in your office newsletter, if any exists.**

With a few dollars you can place an advertisement in the classified section of your paper asking for true stories for television and/or motion pictures. For example:

> Film Producer looking for dramatic true stories to buy.
> Please send two-page information to Mr. So-and-So at:
> [your address] or call [your phone number]

Note: When speaking with potential sources of stories, let them know that you will be considering it and you will give them a response within a few weeks. Don't promise anything or try to speculate how much it is worth.

As a serious professional, you must take every step, one at a time. Also the less you say, the fewer the chances you have of creating potential misunderstandings.

Tell everybody you meet that you are a producer looking to buy interesting and unique stories.

☙ Your Local Courthouse

Go and look through their files. You may run across fascinating true stories. They should be accessible and open to the public. Ask the court clerks if they remember any special cases.

☙ Police Officers, Firefighters, and Attorneys

These three professions have hundreds of stories to tell. They are a wonderful source of true stories.

☙ Newspapers and Magazines

Stories are found in feature articles or in local, regional, or national newspapers.

If you see a story you believe in, go after it. You will be surprised how you may find a story that nobody picked up or was interested in.

☙ *Kirkus Reviews*

It is expensive to subscribe to this service ($355 yearly) and you will be competing with everybody else in the industry. Still, if you can afford it, we recommend that you subscribe. (It may be available at your local library.)

The Kirkus Service, Inc.
200 Park Avenue South, Suite 1118, New York, NY 10003
(212) 777-4554
Fax (212) 979-1352

☙ *Publishers Weekly*

Again you will be competing with the industry, but if you can afford it ($139 yearly), it's worth it. (It is normally available at the local library.)

Publishers Weekly
P. O. Box 1979, Marion, OH 43306
(800) 278-2991

☙ *Writer's Digest*

This is a monthly publication that can provide you with all types of information related to the publishing world, from writers for hire and book reviews to book fairs.

Writer's Digest
1507 Dana Avenue, Cincinnati, OH 45207
(513) 531-2222

☙ Libraries

If you make friends with librarians, they can tell you what books are special, what is coming out, or what is happening with the book trade.

You can also gain access to a lot of publications that may provide you with information regarding potential true stories. (Look into old newspapers. Research the sections on crime, scandal, gossip, etc.)

If you are not familiar with how to work with the different research tools in the library, ask for assistance; it's free. Librarians love to help readers.

❧ Bookstores

Use the same technique. Make friends with the manager or the salespersons. Ask them what's new and what's selling. Also ask them if they know of any old title that they believe is a good read.

Collect as much information as you can. Tell them that you are a producer and that you are always looking for good stories to buy.

❧ It doesn't matter how much money you have. If you find the right story, money will be available. Remember, every year Hollywood spends over half a billion dollars developing stories.

All you need to do is find the stories and be able to secure the rights to them.

❧ Book Fairs

Through *Publishers Weekly* and other publishing-related journals you can find out when and where these book fairs take place.

They are great events to network with potential sources of material. They also provide access to publishers, distributors, wholesalers, sales reps, and, above all, writers.

❧ *Writer's Market*

In this annual reference book you can find information on most of the publishing houses and magazines in the United States.

Writer's Market
F&W Publications
1507 Dana Avenue, Cincinnati, OH 45207
(513) 531-2222

Writing Groups

Writing groups are potential sources for books, plays, or screenplays. But be careful. The quality of work generated by new writers in their manuscripts or screenplays is often not up to the standards expected by the film industry. You have to know what to look for.

Also, tap into local playwrights' groups as a source of material. In New York City, there are Broadway, Off Broadway, and Off Off Broadway theaters and writers. Smaller cities and rural areas have their own theater writing groups, as well.

Writing groups are a good resource for finding potential writing partners for a spec screenplay based on your idea, story, manuscript or book.

Note: For samples of query letters, releases, and option agreements, see Chapter 25.

Chapter 4.

Story Rights Acquisition

By now you know what a good story should be, and you know where to get it. What do you do next? You protect it. We recommend that you CONSULT AN ATTORNEY when you engage in any transactions relating to the acquisition of rights. Whatever we and/or our contributors explain or suggest is not to be construed as being "the law" and/or the only way to protect your interests.

☙ How to Protect Your Idea

How does someone protect an idea or a story? A good starting point is to explain the difference between an idea and the expression of the idea.

Copyright in the United States is very helpful to creators of all kinds. It gives them exclusive rights to their creation, but in order to be entitled to copyright protection under the law, the creation has to be fixed.

What we mean by fixed is that the idea must be written down or recorded somehow. An idea that is not fixed is just in your mind, and is not protected by copyright law. So, the first step is to write it down.

☙ If a person with an idea for a movie or a book writes that idea down, or makes a one-page treatment or a pitch or a letter, copyright protection only attaches to the *expression* of the idea, that is, the selection and arrangement of the words comprising the treatment or letter. No registration is necessary and no copyright notice is necessary to acquire these rights.

The individual who created the idea has a copyright at the moment that they write down their idea — they have a copyright in the expression, the words. They do not have a copyright in the idea itself.

We'll take an example from history. The presidents of Burundi and Rwanda are shot down in a plane. We say, "Gee, this would make a great spy novel." That's an idea.

When we write down the plot, list the main characters, and document that Denzel Washington should star and we should get Spike Lee to direct, what we've written is copyrighted. We have a copyright in those actual words. No one can take our actual words.

But the *idea* is not protected by copyright. Anyone reading our script or our one-page treatment with whom we don't have a contract is free to take the idea and write their own spy novel set in Africa in the 1990s.

They cannot take the actual words, the expression of the idea that we've written. If we write a script on spec, they cannot take our dialogue, the words, the lines the actors are supposed to speak, or the descriptions of the scenes that we've written.

❧ They *can* take the idea unless there's a contractual relationship to prevent it.

Now to the discussion of protecting ideas.

❧ Ideas are protected only by contract law.

When a person with an idea goes in to sell it, a relationship exists between the person who has the idea and the person that they're pitching it to, and that's a contract, that relationship.

❧ It can be an **oral contract**, where the people agree in advance: "I'm about to disclose an idea to you; you agree if you use it, you'll pay me the reasonable value for it." It can be a **written contract**: "I'm about to disclose an idea to you. You hereby agree if you use it or any part of it, you'll pay me the reasonable value," or it can be an **implied contract**: You go into a producer's office and you sit across the desk from him or her. He's not there to chat; he is a movie producer — he's there to buy ideas, so if you just have a meeting with him and explain to him what your idea is, a court will find an implied contract exists. So under certain circumstances, if a producer hears your idea, steals it, and uses it for a movie, you have legal recourse: breach of implied contract.

↘ The "Barstool Rule"

↘ Be careful of what we call the **"barstool rule."** If you go into a bar and sit down on a stool, and a guy sits down next to you, and you say, "I have this great idea for a movie, you know, *Die Hard at the Eiffel Tower*," the guy in the bar has no contractual obligation to you.

The guy sitting next to you in the bar or the one you talk to at a cocktail party can take your idea and use it any way they want without owing you anything.

To protect ideas you must have a contract with the person you are disclosing the idea to. It's best to have that contract in writing and to have it understood in advance how much you're going to get paid if they use your idea.

This also protects the person who is listening to the idea. The studios get pitches for ideas all the time and on any given day a studio already has several projects with the exact same idea or similar ideas in development.

Studios and producers don't want to be stuck having to pay you for an idea if they already are in development on that exact same idea. Studios are very careful about accepting pitches.

Agents play an important part in this process. An agent adds a professional level. They keep careful records of meetings that are held, who is in attendance, and what idea is pitched. The agent gets paid if the idea is sold. They function as a sort of check and balance against the producer.

If you have a private meeting with a producer, it's very hard to prove what took place.

If you have a meeting set up by an agent who has a secretary, a receptionist, and an assistant, you can be assured that they have a thorough paper trail of all documents and communications that have been exchanged.

❧ How to Protect True Life Stories

There are potential problem areas for writers, people who are writing about true life events, and people who want the rights to true life stories. Let's start with an example.

A few years ago, a baby fell down a well. For a week the whole country focused on a little town in Texas and this baby. It was a very heartrending, true life, human interest story.

If we are moved by this and think, "Gee, we would love to dramatize this story. What permission do we need? Whose rights do we need to get? Can we do it without permission?"

The law to be aware of here is called **"the right of privacy"** for those involved in the story.

People have a right not to be portrayed falsely, and not to have false things said about them — **those are two different rights.** Third is the right of private persons (not public figures) to keep their lives private.

However, when a private person is thrust into the public eye because a crime occurs in his neighborhood or his baby falls down a well, he may be totally innocent, but he's just been catapulted to public figure status, thus losing some of his right of privacy.

If you or a relative of yours is involved in a terrible crime, and you're seen on television at the funeral, you lose some of your right of privacy.

You lose the right to stop someone from writing about you, writing true things about you, or writing public facts about you.

If you run for public office, you lose more of your rights because *you* become news because you have chosen to place yourself in the public eye. We balance a person's right of privacy in this country against a tradition of free speech.

The First Amendment of the Constitution is very powerful. Society benefits from a free flow of information and ideas. If someone is genuinely a public figure and the circumstances of his/her life are of interest to the public, he/she can't stop somebody from writing the truth.

There's a spectrum of free speech protection, depending on the type of writing. The most protected writing is the news writing in newspapers.

You'll have a very hard time suing a newspaper, such as the *Los Angeles Times*, for writing about you if your baby falls down the well.

At the other end of the spectrum you have *commercialization*. If we wanted to sell ashtrays with "Baby Falls Down a Well" on them, that kind of commercial speech isn't given the same kind of protection that newspaper speech is.

Somewhere in the middle of that spectrum, between commercial merchandising and news reporting, is screenwriting and television.

Television is an outlet for information as well as entertainment. It's a product. Millions of dollars go back and forth in connection with movies and TV.

You can write a story without anyone's permission if you write it based on "public domain facts."

Public domain is really a misnomer since it refers to a copyright that has expired or has been abandoned; something that is out in the public and is no longer protected by copyright. But for shorthand purposes, we talk about "public domain facts."

When information is published in the newspaper, or is made a public record within a court transcript, those facts become public. No one has the right to stop you from publishing those public facts in a screenplay. So if a baby falls down a well in your neighborhood, and it's a much publicized event, you can use facts that are in the public record. You can write a screenplay and dramatize it without permission from the baby, the baby's mother, or the baby's relatives.

☜ However, you can write a better story if you have a private interview with the mother of that baby, if you have access to facts that are not public. That's why you want to get a **life story option agree-**

ment to have access to those private facts.

If you have interviews with the actual subjects, you'll be able to do a more in-depth, insightful story than you could using only a news story as your source.

A news story is very factual, very dry. On the other hand, if you sit down with someone, such as Charles Manson, for an afternoon, or a week or a month, you're going to get insight into their character.

Also, when people are interviewed by the press as an event is happening, they're not being paid for the interviews. They may be traumatized, and may not be very articulate or very helpful. But people tend to be calmer a month or a year later, particularly when they stand to profit from the project. They've had a chance to reflect on the events and their reactions to them. They may have some special twist or take or angle on the story that didn't come out in the newspaper — their own personal view. If they bond with the writer, they may add something special to the story, making it more than just the dry facts.

🔑 Major Legal Dangers

The major legal dangers lie in writing a story without contractual permission with the subject. It's called **"false light invasion of privacy," "defamation," "libel" (written lies), or "slander" (verbal lies), and "public disclosure of private facts."**

These are the types of privacy invasions that create the biggest problem for people who don't have the cooperation of the subjects they are writing about.

As an example, let's take the case of a famous, terrible crime involving the kidnapping of dozens of children. One of the networks made a movie about it. One of the criminals convicted of the crime has now sued the network and the producers because that criminal claims to have been falsely portrayed in the movie.

It's true that the criminal perpetrated the crime, but the writers are accused of taking artistic license with the facts. Even though the person they portrayed was really involved with the crime, the criminal is claiming that he was falsely portrayed, that he didn't really hit, beat, or shoot the children and that the crime really wasn't his idea.

✎ Even criminals have legal rights to be portrayed truthfully. An important rule to follow: **Fact check anything that you put in a book or screenplay.**

Be careful. Get court transcripts. Find out what that person actually did say under oath in court and then be absolutely faithful to the exact words that were spoken. Use newspaper reports and multiple sources to double and triple check the reliability of your facts.

✎ As a footnote, regarding stories about criminals, **the "Son of Sam" laws, which prevent criminals from benefiting from their crimes by making contracts with writers, are unconstitutional and have been struck down in a number of states**, even though they are still on the books in some states.

✎ **You can make contracts with criminals to have their exclusive story and write with them.**

Remember that not only does the subject have privacy rights, but the witnesses, relatives, and anyone else involved also have rights. If there was a policeman who was the hero, you can't show that policeman as a heroin addict. If there was a nurse who successfully resuscitated the baby when it was born, you can't show the nurse as incompetent. If there was a relative who was prominent in the facts, he/she can't be falsely portrayed. Remember to go beyond just the individuals involved in the incident. Discuss the people surrounding them.

✎ Take your facts from public record. You need to have **at least two or, better, three sources for any fact** that you portray in your screenplay. If you're saying "This is what really happened," have two or three sources to support your facts, and create what is called an **"annotated script."**

❧ Once a script is produced, television networks and motion picture distributors require producers to obtain an "errors and omissions" insurance policy before the film is broadcast or exhibited, covering both the producer and the network or distributor. Often, before an insurance company will issue a policy covering a non-fiction film, the company will request **an annotated script** — a script that has citations or annotations to verifiable, reliable sources for all of the dialogue and scenes in the film.

What newspapers reported this? What witness told you that this happened? Do you have a signed permission form from this person to portray them in the movie?

An annotated script covers you and gives you the greatest amount of protection when your movie gets made. ❧ **Writers should keep careful records of the sources for each fact that they portray in a true life or non-fiction story.**

During pre-production, the completed shooting script can be sent to a research company where all the characters' names are checked out to make sure there are no living persons who may be mistaken for characters portrayed in the film with the same or similar names. Other applicable references in the script are also verified and confirmed to the producer of the project.

True Stories about Deceased Individuals

Normally, dead people have few, if any, legal rights. However, in certain states they do have certain rights that may be violated by unfair or unauthorized portrayals in motion pictures.

❧ If the likeness of a person or their name has been registered with the Secretary of State in California, even after the person's death, the deceased party's estate has the right to stop commercial exploitation of the deceased's name, signature, or likeness.

For example, in California, Laurel and Hardy, W.C. Fields, John Wayne, James Dean, and Elvis Presley are all dead, but are registered celebrities with the Secretary of State. You cannot market James Dean

T-shirts, John Wayne ashtrays, or Elvis Presley cocktail napkins without permission from their estates. But you can write a true story about James Dean even though he's dead, because that falls more on the information side and less on the commercial side of the spectrum.

➣ Spouses or estates can register the names and likenesses of dead people with the California Secretary of State. However, if a deceased person is not registered, you can't invade the privacy of a dead person. However, watch out: You *can* defame the dead person's relatives, and you can invade the privacy of people close to a deceased individual.

➣ It is best to have a written contract with everyone involved with a story in which they give permission and release their rights.

There are rules that insurance companies follow when they do clearances on scripts to see what releases they need to get. Releases, which are permissions from living people, generally should be obtained from anyone who is portrayed in the property.

You want to avoid potential litigation expenses whenever possible. A disclaimer, a statement at the beginning or end of a movie saying that it isn't a true life story, and that it is purely fictional, doesn't always work. If people can recognize themselves in the story, they have a right to sue you if they are falsely portrayed. ➣ **The disclaimer is not a license to libel people. A disclaimer isn't going to be enough in every case to legally cover you.**

➣ The best scenario is to get a life story option contract with one of the principals that gives you permission and the cooperation of that individual for interviews, to look at their diaries, their scrapbooks, etc. They may give you access to other people, such as their third grade teacher or previous victims or other persons who will improve the story. All this may provide you special insight into the thesis of the story, maybe an angle that other people or the newspapers don't have.

➣ **It's always best to have permission.**

🔑 Also, for creative reasons you may want to fictionalize some aspects of your story. You definitely want permission to do so.

🔑 When you make an option agreement with an individual, get the right to embellish, to enhance, to fictionalize, so that it doesn't have to be verbatim. **If you can get the rights to a life story, you're going to have a better chance to write a better book or screenplay than if you don't, but if you can't get those rights, it shouldn't prevent you from writing a good story.**

Works Made for Hire

Because of the complexities regarding copyright law, we feel compelled to explain briefly what works made for hire consist of. If you are a producer or you want to hire the services of a writer, you should know that, under copyright law, there's something called **"works made for hire."** Works made for hire are copyrighted works in which the *employer* automatically owns the copyright in a work from the instant the work is created. Works made for hire fall into two main categories.

🔑 The first category includes **works which are created or written in the ordinary course or scope of employment by an employee.** No written employment contract is required.

We are talking about a formal employee — someone who works regular hours for a salary, in an office or quarters that the employer provides, has federal tax withholdings from his/her paycheck, and receives employee benefits.

🔑 The second type of work-for-hire situation covers works which are **"specially ordered or commissioned,"** which applies to about nine special categories.

One of those special categories of "specially commissioned works" is a contribution to an audiovisual work, including a motion picture.

🔑 If you write a screenplay that falls into one of the categories of specially ordered or commissioned works and are not a salaried employee, your employer will not own the copyright unless there is a written agreement. You must **have a signed written contract that says you're going to write a screenplay, and that it will be a "work made for hire." It has to have those words, and recent federal copyright cases suggest that the agreement must be signed by both you and the producer** *before* **the script is written.**

✏ **If the script is already written, it can't be turned into a work made for hire. The only thing you can do then is to sell the copyright to the producer.**

Note: We want to thank Greg Victoroff, a lawyer handling contracts and lawsuits involving entertainment and copyright law, for his invaluable contribution to this chapter.

For information about Greg Victoroff's services, see Chapter 24.

ACTION PLAN

Copyright Registration

To protect your material, you should register it with the Copyright Office in Washington, D.C.

Copyright Office
Library of Congress
Washington, D.C. 20559
(703) 557-INFO, (202) 707-3000

Writers Guild Registration

To protect your **screenplay or treatment** you should register it with the Writers Guild of America (WGA). They have two offices, one in New York and one in Los Angeles. They are dedicated to the television and motion picture business.

Writers Guild of America East
555 West 57th Street
New York, NY 10019
(212) 767-7800

Writers Guild of America West
8955 Beverly Boulevard
West Hollywood, CA 90048
(310) 550-1000

The WGA registration service assists members and non-members in establishing the completion dates of their literary properties.

Registration provides a record of the writer's claim to authorship of the material.

When the registration office receives the material, a numbered receipt is given to the registrant as official documentation of the registration. Notice of registration can be placed on the screenplay's title page.

Outlines, treatments, synopses, screenplays, stage plays, novels and other books, short stories, poems, commercials, lyrics, and drawings are accepted for registration.

The registration lasts for a term of five years and can be renewed for another five years.

Note: Registration with the WGA does not take the place of copyright, protect titles, help a writer to become a member of WGA, or help to determine writing credits.

For further information, contact:

Writers Guild of America West
Registration Services
9009 Beverly Boulevard
West Hollywood, CA 90048
(310) 205-2540

To protect yourself when acquiring the rights to a story from a third party or parties, ask the person(s) with those rights to **sign a release form** and also make sure that you have **a written contract that gives you the right** to acquire those rights.

Samples of different agreements are provided in Chapter 25.

Chapter 5.

The Art of Storytelling

Y ou may be wondering how you are going to write your own idea or story, or how you can put on paper the story that you just secured the rights to.

We can't teach you in a few pages how to become a great storyteller, or for that matter, an accomplished writer. But we can guide you through our simplified approach on how to write a story, step by step. It is very important for you, as a newcomer, to have the best written story possible. The more you read and learn about storytelling, the better off you'll be. After all, your passport to Hollywood will be based on the strength of your story's concept or the quality of the writing.

THE BASIC ELEMENTS OF STORYTELLING

Storytelling is nothing more than the art of one person being able to tell others the beginning, middle, and end of a story.

There are certain elements of a story that we must know in order to understand it.

In this chapter we present the simple basics of story structure. However, in Chapter 8, to illustrate what we believe to be a good example of storytelling, we have provided the story breakdown of the Academy Award–winning film *Ghost*.

EXAMPLE OF SIMPLIFIED STORYTELLING:
BEGINNING–MIDDLE–END

"A Love Story"

- **Beginning of the story**

  1) Where does it take place? Middle America somewhere, at the high school prom.
  2) How does it start? Good Boy and Pretty Girl fall in love.
  3) What happens? Bully takes Pretty Girl away from Good Boy.

- **Middle of the story** (the more the conflict the better the story is)

  1) What does the Good Boy want? To get Pretty Girl back.
  2) What does the Bully do? Beats up the Good Boy and doesn't let Pretty Girl go back to him.
  3) Every time Good Boy tries to get Pretty Girl back, what happens? Bully beats him up.

- **End of the story** (against all odds the good guy wins)

  1) Against all odds Good Boy beats Bully and gets Pretty Girl back.
  2) Good Boy and Pretty Girl live happily ever after. Their ordeal is over.

This is a very simplified way of telling this story, but at least we can give you an idea of how easily the basic elements of a love story can be put on paper.

Further along in this chapter we will give you a breakdown of the basic elements of other story genres, so you will know how to formulate your stories.

Of course, only trained and talented writers are able to tell or write a story that will keep a listener transfixed, or the reader glued to the pages. What makes a story interesting is creativity, what makes it believable is form. We can teach you form, but you have to be born with creativity or develop it through study and practice.

🦒 **A believable story is one that the reader or audience can understand and relate to**. It is a story that communicates. Another key to storytelling is character.

🦒 **It is human nature for people to compare themselves to one another, and as a result, they relate to the characters on paper or screen. If a story is viewed as a model of human behavior, then the most effective story will contain familiar characters.**

In the oldest stories, familiar character types combine with familiar story structures. Fairy-tale romances, tragic epics, heroic adventures — these are the stories that audiences recognize. The challenge lies in using the familiar structures to create an inventive story.

MAJOR TURNING POINTS OF STORYTELLING

Like any other business, Hollywood has its own lingo. And even among ourselves we use different words when referring to the same events. For our purposes, we will be using the same terms throughout the book and, where applicable, we will familiarize you with their meanings.

Once again using the simplified love story example:

Beginning

Hook:

(Visual event/information that secures one's attention and curiosity.)

–Pretty Girl fights with Bully outside prom's dance hall, rejecting him.

Inciting Incident:
(Event that impels the character into pursuing a specific goal.)

–Good Boy invites Pretty Girl to dance; she accepts. They are in love.

Plot Point A:
(Initial problem. What is at stake?)

–Good Boy loses the Pretty Girl to Bully.

Middle

Chain of Conflict:
(Protagonist/Antagonist plans. Plotting is what the characters do, feel, think, or say that makes a difference to what comes afterwards.)

–Good Boy at the end of prom loses Pretty Girl to Bully. Every time Good Boy tries to get the Pretty Girl back, and Bully finds out, Good Boy gets beaten up.

Story (Plot) Points:
(Major events that create a change of direction in the story. They are turning (plot) points.)

(Plot Point A, Plot Point B, Plot Point C, Climax)

Plot Point B:
(Compounding problem. What/who is forcing the protagonist to fight harder?)

–Good Boy can't get the Pretty Girl back because Bully won't allow it to happen.
–Bully is forcing Good Boy to fight harder.

Plot Point C:

(Ultimate complication.)

–Good Boy tries to fight back but Bully once again beats him up badly and warns him that next time it will be even worse. There is no hope. Even the Pretty Girl is starting to think that maybe it wasn't meant to happen with the Good Boy.

Clock:

(Protagonist is faced with limitations to reach final goal. Urgency to solve problem.)

–After last major beating, Pretty Girl tells Good Boy that she is contemplating going to college and leaving town soon.

End

Climax:

(The highest point of crisis after which the conflict or confrontation is over.)

–Against all odds, Good Boy faces Bully and beats him.

Resolution:

(Should be a payoff of the initial problem.)

–Good Boy and Pretty Girl become engaged and go to same college to finish their education and eventually get married.

Now that you have learned our terminology, we are going to introduce you to our **"genre breakdown."** We believe that this is a very important part of learning how to properly tell a story.

As in anything, exceptions will always apply. In the case of true stories, you will be limited as to how much you can manipulate the events in order to create a better story.

CATEGORIES OF GENRE

GENRE: Term used in Hollywood to define the theme of a film — western, comedy, drama, thriller, etc.

Classic Categories of Genre

	Comedy	**Drama**	**Tragedy**
Basic Elements	A sane human being in a crazy world. A crazy human being in a sane world.	Human being in a human world.	Human being in a super-human world (gods/royalty).
Conflict	Is expressed humorously. Conflict between protagonist and antagonist.	Is expressed seriously. Conflict between protago-nist and antagonist.	Is expressed catastrophically. Conflict between protagonist and a superior force.
Resolution	UNION of the protagonist and antagonist.	SEPARATION of the protagonist and antagonist.	DEATH of the protagonist.

Today, most movies are a mixture of different genres; therefore, the writer must be alert to the different common requirements, chain of conflicts, and resolutions required for each one.

Table of Genre Examples

Action	Espionage	Relationship
Adolescence	Family	Religion
Adventure	Fantasy	Renaissance
Americana	Friends	Revolution
Biography	Future	Saga
Business	Horror	Satire
Character Study	Journalism	Science Fiction
Civil War	Law	Sexual Obsession
Comedy	Love Story	Show Business
Comedy - Adult	Medical	Slapstick
Comedy - Black	Military	Sports
Comedy - Romantic	Murder Mystery	Supernatural
Comedy - Teenage	Music/Dance	Suspense/Thriller
Courtroom Drama	Nature/Animal	Vietnam War
Crime/Gangster	Non-Fiction	Vigilante
Detective	Period Piece	War Story
Docudrama	Political	Western
Dramedy	Prehistoric	World War I
Education	Prison	World War II
Ensemble	Psychodrama	World War III

THE BASIC ELEMENTS OF EACH PRIMARY GENRE

Every film is different, yet the elements of the primary genres in Hollywood share basic themes and components. Following, in brief, graphic form, are descriptions of those storytelling elements. (The singular has been used for expediency in the genre descriptions, i.e., we refer to the "protagonist," the "opponent," the "ally," and so forth. In all cases, the plural is equally applicable; there can be one protagonist or there can be many.)

THE BASIC ELEMENTS OF GENRES

ACTION/ADVENTURE

Basic Elements

An action/adventure film requires a protagonist and his opponent. Usually, the protagonist has an ally. Lots of special effects are normally used in their confrontations, and the protagonist is often outnumbered and betrayed.

Inciting Incident: Protagonist's life is in danger.
(Event that impels the character into pursuing a specific goal.)

STORY STRUCTURE

BEGINNING	MIDDLE	END	
	Chain of Conflict	**Climax**	**Resolution**
Fleeing	Battle(s) with antagonist(s) Nonstop action	Protagonist wins final battle	Antagonist loses/dies

COMEDY

Basic Elements

Comedies often take an outsider (the protagonist) to an unfamiliar "world." Plot points are created by protagonist's weaknesses and problems created by the antagonist.

Inciting Incident: There is a different/unusual problem.
(Event that impels the character into pursuing a specific goal.)

STORY STRUCTURE

BEGINNING	MIDDLE	END	
	Chain of Conflict	Climax	Resolution
Complications	Fights between protagonist and antagonist	Major fight	They get together "Wedding"

COURTROOM DRAMA

Basic Elements

It requires a victim, an attorney, and a lawyer defending the antagonist. Police and expert witnesses.

Inciting Incident: An injustice takes place.

STORY STRUCTURE

BEGINNING	MIDDLE	END	
	Chain of Conflict	Climax	Resolution
Attorney gets involved	Evidence gathering–Twists Revelations–Specialists	Trial Verdict	Justice prevails

DRAMEDY

Basic Elements

An emotionally unstable protagonist with weaknesses. Emotional confrontations, yet they incorporate humorous elements along the way.

Inciting Incident: An unstable relationship among family members or others.

STORY STRUCTURE

BEGINNING	MIDDLE		END	
	Chain of Conflict		**Climax**	**Resolution**
Protagonist is not accepted	Emotional confrontations		Death of antagonist	Acceptance

HORROR

Basic Elements

Horror films require a monster and victims. An opponent to the monster, who often is the protagonist/victim or a friend. Killings/murders.

Inciting Incident: A killing is committed.

STORY STRUCTURE

BEGINNING	MIDDLE		END	
	Chain of Conflict		**Climax**	**Resolution**
First kill/fight	Monster kills victims		Protagonist fights/kills monster	Monster killed

MYSTERY – DETECTIVE

Basic Elements

A detective, victim(s), red herrings and/or false trails. Secrets. Killings and revelations of the secret(s) drive the film forward.

Inciting Incident: A murder is committed.

STORY STRUCTURE

BEGINNING	MIDDLE		END	
	Chain of Conflict		**Climax**	**Resolution**
Detective is "hired"	Clues–Criminal is winning Red herrings–False trails		Detective catches murderer	Mystery/ crime(s) solved

ROMANTIC COMEDY

Basic Elements

A man and a woman, an antagonist to their marriage, and a rocky relationship.

Inciting Incident: Couple meets. They usually dislike each other at first meeting.

STORY STRUCTURE

BEGINNING	MIDDLE		END	
	Chain of Conflict		**Climax**	**Resolution**
Forced together	Love/hate relationship		Breakup	Marriage

SUPERNATURAL

Basic Elements

A protagonist, a superhuman "evil force," protagonist and antagonist allies, and supernatural events.

Inciting Incident: A supernatural occurrence takes place.

STORY STRUCTURE

BEGINNING	MIDDLE		END	
	Chain of Conflict		Climax	Resolution
Protagonist slowly begins believing	Fooled by supernatural force(s)		Protagonist fights "force"	Evil force is destroyed

THRILLER

Basic Elements

A protagonist, a victim, and a "friend" who is a betrayer. Lies and betrayals.

Inciting Incident: A crime and/or a betrayal takes place.

STORY STRUCTURE

BEGINNING	MIDDLE		END	
	Chain of Conflict		Climax	Resolution
Protagonist accepts fact that he has to fight	Deception–Lies–Fights		Against all odds, protagonist wins final fight	Protagonist gains wisdom

Our genre charts are meant to guide you. However, every story is unique, and some of the suggested basic elements may not apply to the structure of your story.

Now you should be more comfortable putting your story/idea/concept on paper or revising the existing structure of your treatment, manuscript, or screenplay.

❦ If your writing skills are not very strong, **contact your local college or high school and ask for their English and/or communications departments. They may be able to help you by giving you the names of some talented students, tutors, or writing classes.** Very inexpensively, you can find someone qualified to help you with your project.

❦ **Do not be embarrassed**. Students love to be part of projects, especially if they relate to Hollywood. Or, you can ask a relative or a spouse to assist you. Do not let a good story go unnoticed.

Hollywood needs you, whether it's for stories, buying tickets to their movies, or watching their television programs.

Chapter 6.

How to Write Your Dream Story: A Step-By-Step Guide

HOW TO PUT YOUR IDEA/STORY ON PAPER

We are going to give you a checklist of questions that will help you focus on your story. If you don't have the answers to some of the questions, don't worry, just keep going and eventually ideas will come to mind.

Let's start:

Genre

(Go back to the genre categories and see which one fits best. You may choose more than one.)

1) What is the genre, and is it the best genre to support your story?

Log Line

2) Tell us in two to three clear sentences the description of what your story is about (i.e., Boy and Girl fall in love, Bully breaks up their romance. Against all odds, Boy gets Girl back, they marry and live happily ever after.).

Idea/Concept/Story

3) Is your story rich enough and innovative enough for a movie?

4) Are the characters the right characters to support the story?

5) Is the story big enough for a full screenplay/script?

6) Why will an audience respond to this story?

A. STORY STRUCTURE

BEGINNING

(Please refer to the chart on page 163.)

Back Story
(Tells us a bit about the setting, where it takes place, who the players are, etc.)

7) What is the background of your characters and the situation leading up to the beginning of your story?

Hook
(Visual event/information that secures one's attention and curiosity.)

8) Does the opening scene(s) capture your attention and propel interest in the story to follow?
Tell us all about your opening scene.

9) What is the scene that you are going to use as a hook in your story?

96

Inciting Incident
(An event that compels the character to pursue a specific goal.)

   10)   Is the inciting incident big enough to force the protagonist to stop, or fight to maintain his or her usual life?

   11)   What is the scene that you are going to use as the inciting incident?

Plot Point A
(A major event that creates a change of direction in the story/initial problem.)

   12) What is at stake?

   13) What is the scene in your story that you are going to use for your first major plot point?

MIDDLE

Protagonist's Plan

   14)   Does the protagonist's course of action/plan require several steps which can encounter obstacles? What is at stake? Is it important enough?

   15)   Does the protagonist have a friend? Tell us about him/her.

   16)   Does he/she complement or contrast the protagonist in a character-revealing fashion?

Antagonist's Plan

   17) Does the antagonist's plan present some of those obstacles?

18) Does the antagonist have a friend? Tell us about him/her.

19) Do they add tension because of their rivalry with the antagonist, and thereby make a potential ally for the protagonist?

Mid-Plot Point B
(Compounding problem.)

20) What happens so that the protagonist's problem requires a higher level of commitment due to higher stakes?

Clock
(You can place a clock whenever you want in your story.)

21) Is the story structured in such a way that we have a race against time for the protagonist to achieve his/her goal?

Plot Point C
(Ultimate complication.)

22) What does the protagonist (and the possible antagonist) do to advance to an even higher level to accomplish his goal?

END

Climax
(Self-Understanding — moral/psychological. Your story can have more than one climax to accommodate the conclusion of subplots that you may have.)

23) What takes place? Is this the highest point of crisis and confrontation?

Resolution/Balance

24) Is the resolution visual/non-dialogue and a payoff to the opening of your story — inciting incident? Tell us what happens.

B. CHARACTER

Now that you have established what your story is about, we are going to guide you through the character development phase.

Protagonist's Goal
(Final objective.)

25) Is the protagonist's final objective defined?

26) Is there only one from beginning to end?

27) Is the protagonist's external desire a committed, obsessive drive?

Protagonist's External Conflict
(Affects others.)

28) Is the protagonist's external problem interesting and complex, and will it allow the inner conflict to surface?

Protagonist's Internal Conflict
(Affects oneself.)

29) Is the protagonist's inner conflict illustrated through action?

Protagonist's Friend – *if any*

30) Is he/she similar to the main character without having the same moral need, or does he/she contrast with the main character yet have a similar moral need?

Antagonist's Goal

31) Is the goal in conflict with the protagonist's goal?

Antagonist's Desire

32) Is it clear and does it directly oppose that of the protagonist?

Antagonist's Friend – *if any*

33) Is he or she motivated to remain with the antagonist for personal gain?

C. CHARACTER ARC

(Please refer to the charts on pages 167, 168, 169.)

Character Change A *(Caused by Plot Point A)*

34) Does the character see the problem, and does he/she take a step forward to change it?
Is it an unconscious or conscious choice?

Character Change B *(Caused by Plot Point B)*

35) Does the character start to see the effects of his/her problem and the value of change?

Character Change C *(Caused by Plot Point C)*

36) Does the character decide it is not worth it to continue to change, and revert to old behavior instead?

Character Change – Climax *(Caused by Climax Scene)*

37) Does the character decide to change to achieve goal? Is it a conscious choice?

D. SUBPLOTS

Now that you know how to break down a story, both for story structure and character development and change, you should be able to apply the same steps to your subplots.

Aside from the main story, it's beneficial to have one or two subplots to enrich the story.

Chapter 7.

How to Write Outlines, Treatments, Manuscripts, and Screenplays

One of the first problems people face when trying to put together a project is how to express their ideas on paper. In Hollywood there are numerous formats, but the most commonly used are the outline pitch, outline, treatment, and, of course, screenplay.

In the publishing world, we have the treatment, manuscript, galley, and published book.

Although we provide definitions below, people in Hollywood use these terms interchangeably at times, which only adds to an outsider's confusion. In order to sort through the maze, let's take a look at each of these and see what they are and how they are used.

Outline: A preliminary treatment (a rough sketch) of an idea/story as you intend to pitch it. Should be five thousand words or less.

Treatment: An essay-style description of the story and characters. There is no specific length, ❧ but it should run between four and eight pages if it is a short treatment or twenty-five to fifty pages for longer ones. Typically, treatments run between eight and twelve pages.

Manuscript: An essay-style description of the story. Normally double-spaced and using a 12-point font size. There are no limitations on the page length. This is the basic format for writing a book.

Screenplay: The working format for a film. Includes scene descriptions and dialogue. Special formatting applies.

OUTLINES

There are two types of outlines: the Pitch Outline and the Step Outline.

Pitch Outline

Even at their most complicated, pitch outlines are really rather simple documents. Rarely are they formal; formality is a sure sign of a novice. They are not very detailed, and rarely are they actually given to anyone.

Pitch outlines are meant to sell projects, but the selling is most often done verbally, in person, at a pitch meeting. In a pitch session, you are expected to articulate the high points and the hook of your story idea. What is it that makes your idea different from the thousands of others presented in the course of a year?

When pitching, story is key. One should not be concerned about the film budget, the stars you think should be in it, or the director you think is perfect for your project. After all, you're pitching an idea, and your primary objective is selling that idea.

Because so many ideas flood into Hollywood daily, the only way buyers (producers, executives, studios, and networks) can deal with the onslaught is by saying "no" to 99 percent of what comes their way. If they find anything in your project that gives them an excuse to say "no," such as the wrong star being attached, they will say "no."

The best way to sell is to avoid complications. Stick to the narrow, hard-core essence of your idea. Have a one-liner in mind that hooks everyone who hears it, such as, "This is the story of the President's body double who's forced to take over when the President suffers a stroke." (*Dave.*) Or, "This is *Die Hard* on a ship." (*Under Siege.*) Then add in a few lines about each phase of the story. How does it begin? What is the crisis that kicks off the action? What are the complications? What is the crisis? And how does it conclude?

Don't try to sell it by pointing out audience demographics, or tying it to holidays. A smart buyer will already be looking for these things and as the saying goes, a good executive will "know it when they see or hear it."

Now, as we've indicated, pitches are verbal and done in person. Frequently, however, the person you pitch to is not the one who has the power to buy your project. You may not get to see the actual buyer. Therefore, what you sometimes will want to do is to carry with you a neat, concise printed version of your basic ideas written in simple paragraph form. It should carry your name and contact phone number, the name of the project, and a few lines recapping the highlights you've just pitched verbally. This is a synopsis/pitch outline. The shorter the better.

The best pitches, however, are those that are so tight and compelling that the buyer needs no further explanation. Remember, every extra word you write only gives your enemy, in this case the buyer, one more target in his or her search for a reason to say "no."

On the other hand, don't be so Spartan that they have no clue what you're talking about. The shortest pitch for a TV movie on record was two words: "California Girls." But if you walked in and said "New York Dolls," you'd be tossed out. Relationships and reputations have as much to do with selling projects as do raw ideas. Your goal is to use the exact amount of words needed to sell your project — no more, no less. There are no exact rules, no precise guidelines except this: When you pitch an idea and see you've got a buyer hooked, shut your mouth and stop talking. Don't un-sell them. Let the buyer's own enthusiasm take over. Let them fill in the blanks.

Practice your pitch. Pitch to friends and see what holds their interest and notice when their eyes start to wander. If they're fading, you're dead. Rework it until you can capture someone's attention and hold them, and when they are looking for more, stop. Your synopsis/pitch outline should be the same. Let it hook them, but not fill them up. Leave them wanting more.

Step Outline

Outlines are a writer's tool used to develop and work out the kinks in your story. It is really a work in progress and rarely will you ever show it to anyone. It is the earliest draft of a script that contains the sequence of all the basic scenes and actions. It doesn't include dialogue or narration, the two components of an actual script draft. It's merely your road map to follow when you write the full draft.

Outlines are necessary tools to use because scripts are difficult and complicated animals to bring to life. It is much easier to correct a story or character flaw in the outline stage than it is to write fifty or sixty pages before you realize you don't know where you're going, or what the story is really about. Solve these problems early on in outline form. The moment you're asked to show someone else your "outline," it becomes, by informal definition, a "treatment." So now you may ask: how does a treatment differ from an outline, and when do you need one?

Treatments

If outlines are the writer's tool to work out story kinks, then a treatment is your executive's tool to determine if you've done so, and if you're still on track with the story that they bought from you, or you want to sell to them.

How do they differ? Externally, they don't. They may look the same, and act the same, but they are different. They are different because a treatment is what you show to someone else AFTER you've worked out all the problems, nuances, and dramatic arcs involved in plotting and character development. An outline is what you hold in your hands for your eyes only before you risk showing it to anyone else.

There are a lot of doors in Hollywood, but the same door will rarely open twice. It is a mistake ever to give anyone anything that is not the absolute best you can make it. An outline is for you; a treatment is for them.

Normally, a producer or executive will ask you or your writer to prepare a treatment after you agree to move along in the development phase of your script. There may or may not be money involved. Most times there isn't. Most deals with newcomers fall outside the contractual protection of the Writers Guild of America.

Nonetheless, the creation of a treatment is almost always a required step in selling your script.

To summarize, what is a treatment? It is a polished document, ranging from four to twelve pages in length, that clearly spells out all the major scenes or sequences in your script. If it's for a half-hour sitcom, it will, of course, run just a few pages. A treatment for an hour episode of a TV drama might be five to eight pages, and for a feature or TV movie, eight to twelve pages. There are no exact rules, save this one: Tell only as much as is necessary to convey what the producer wants to see, no more, no less.

In good treatments, each paragraph covers a scene or sequence of the script. Feature treatments are sometimes broken up into first, second, and third acts. The first act is roughly the first quarter of the treatment, the second act corresponds to the next two quarters, and the third act is the final quarter.

For a TV movie, the treatment is broken up into the seven acts typically used by most MOWs (movies of the week). These seven acts correspond to the seven commercial breaks inserted in a two-hour block.

For miniseries, the act breaks are roughly similar to an MOW, with seven acts for each two hours of airtime.

Sitcoms are broken into two acts with an occasional introductory short tease or a laugh-producing tag segment at the conclusion. The use of a tag or tease depends entirely on the conventions of the show one is pitching. *Murphy Brown* doesn't use either; *Roseanne* occasionally uses both. *Murphy Brown* is also an exception to the two-act sitcom rule. Its stories are broken up into three roughly equal acts.

Hour shows are broken up into four acts but these, too, may also have a tease or tag.

The bottom line in TV is to know the format of the show you're developing for. Samples of some of these forms are included.

106

SAMPLE OF PITCH OUTLINE FOR TELEVISION
(A rough sketch of the story, as you intend to tell it.)

This is a sample of excerpts of a pitch outline that we used before we introduced this story to a network.

HUSBAND, LOVER, SPY

A True Story

(Excerpts)

1974 I MEET FRITZ - - AN EXTRAORDINARY MAN

I MAKE FRITZ'S LIFE MY OWN. I feel that I've found

"home" with him. My life will never be the same

again.

- - We meet in July, he proposes in September.

WE MARRY THE FOLLOWING MAY.

I live a whirlwind life in L.A. and Aspen.

- - He is a printer, publisher, lecturer, writer

and mountain climber.

- - I try to fit in with Aspen crowd.

- - I buy an antique store.

- - We spend romantic days on picnics in the country. Fritz teaches me how to climb.

There are times when he travels alone and when he returns he is distant and moody.

A MYSTERIOUS side of Fritz emerges.
- - I remember STRANGE MEETINGS he had while we were on our honeymoon. I begin to think, "I DON'T KNOW THIS MAN."

We talk about the importance of trust in a relationship.
- - "Don't believe what you may someday hear about me."
- - "MAYBE I'M A RUSSIAN SPY."
- - "You may have to go away one day to an island where there is no one else."

1975 We plan to go to Pakistan together, but my work schedule is changed at the last minute. He tells me, "I'll only be gone three months at the most."

- - Instead of the usual excitement about the
trip, Fritz is remote and quiet. Undercur-
rent of tension. He asks for the book,
DEAR AMERICA, to read at base camp. He
makes a point of it.

GOOD-BYE NIGHT: we don't make love. SILENCE.
He falls asleep with his head on my stom-
ach. I feel torn between staying with him or
leaving and returning to work. I decide my
fears are in my imagination - - I leave for
L.A.

I receive SEVEN LETTERS from him en route to
base camp. Then there is only silence.

WEEKS PASS. I think maybe he's been arrested for
climbing without a permit. I begin to panic. It
is 5 weeks now and FRITZ IS MISSING.

END OF ACT I

* *

I START MY OWN INVESTIGATION.

- - I am afraid that I might find something I

don't want to know.

 - - A MIKE HILLMAN comes to see me

saying he's received an urgent message to

meet with me - - HE PROBES ME ABOUT

FRITZ and leaves a PHONE # with me.

1977 That night I have a dream that - - FRITZ IS

ALIVE IN A MONASTERY.

I contact BOB PELOQUIN a private investigator

 - - He agrees to take the case.

 - - MEET IN ASPEN. We get F's dental

records and fingerprints on an international

FBI bulletin. Intertel discovers that the #

Mike Hillman gave me was for an agent's

"SAFE HOUSE."

 - - Bob Peloquin tells me: "THERE'S MUCH

MORE TO THIS THAN MEETS THE EYE.

Your husband was involved in something

that you were not aware of."

END OF ACT III

* *

- - "FRITZ IS ALIVE, he'll be HOME FOR CHRISTMAS."

END OF ACT V

* *

WEDDING plans are to go ON HOLD.

> - - Carlos tells me that I am putting my life on hold, in someone else's hands. I WILL NEVER LOVE ANYONE THE WAY I LOVED FRITZ.

I am struggling with the ghost of the past versus a future with Carlos. TOGETHER WE DECIDE TO SEARCH FOR FRITZ. One last time.

END OF ACT VI

* *

Our next sample, on the following page, is the national best-seller, *Husband, Lover, Spy*, written in a feature treatment format. This is the treatment used as a sales device to entice a potential buyer.

SAMPLE OF TREATMENT FOR MOTION PICTURE
(Short treatments can be from four to eight pages, and long
treatments up to fifty pages plus.)

HUSBAND, LOVER, SPY
(Excerpts)

A True Story

Life for JANICE PENNINGTON couldn't be better. She's beautiful, successful, and passionately in love with FRITZ STAMMBERGER, a tall, muscular, handsome, intelligent man and world-renowned mountain climber who challenges the most formidable peaks around the world and finds no fear to climb alone.

They meet in the tony opulence of Aspen and wed three months later... until the call of the next mountain, TIRICH MIR, lures Fritz to the remote outreaches of Pakistan. Fritz has such inner strength, a sense of destiny, that Janice quickly centers her life around Fritz. Even a short absence leaves her rudderless...

SUBJECT: W/W Fritz Stammberger was 10 days overdue returning to the U.S., reported to be mountain climbing in Kashmir...Department of State...Embassy has no record of subject...

Fritz is gone and Janice must live with the fear he will never return. Fueled by encouragement from Fritz's network of powerful friends throughout the world — princes, presidents, and celebrities have all been touched by the charismatic mountain climber — Janice embarks upon her long and tortuous journey to reconcile the mystery of Fritz's disappearance.

She vividly remembers their days and nights together, but she savors each moment, a votive to a love that still burns deeply within her, that drives her to continue to hope. Memories...everything Janice touches or sees reminds her vividly of Fritz...their honeymoon in Yugoslavia, romantic picnics, weekend retreats, the park in Germany where he jogged, the shops they visited...she could feel what it would be like to be with him, to be him.

She submerges her existence in the memories of the past and hopes for the future.

Finally a call comes from the CIA. Her persistent letters petitioning them to release any information on Fritz have been denied but they still want to meet with her...why would they spend such time if there was nothing to the story? The man from the CIA visits ... *the security of our government is at stake here,* they say. ***"Your husband is dead,"*** he says.

The CIA man leaves, requesting her to stop the petitions under the Freedom of Information Act, insisting she will not get any information from them.

Copyright © 1991 by Carlos de Abreu & Janice Pennington

Our next sample, on the following page, is the same story in manuscript format, used in publishing.

SAMPLE OF A BOOK MANUSCRIPT
(You can have as many chapters as you want.)

Husband, Lover, Spy

Chapter 3.

(Excerpt)

Aspen

November 1975

The snow thundered down on the men trapped
inside their sleeping bags. Chunks of ice and
rock mingled with the powder as the avalanche
rumbled through the valley, echoing off the
mountain walls, the Himalayas. The three men
yelled, and wailed, intoning a death knell.
Then, as suddenly as it had begun, the noise
died out, until it was replaced with an ominous
silence. Their breath rasped in and out as they
greedily took in oxygen. A small pocket of air
had been trapped under the snow. It would keep

them alive for maybe an hour. Long enough to suffer. Long enough to think about the end that awaited.

Fritz's climb the previous August had ended under that avalanche. In spite of the odds, he managed to dig his way out, saving himself, and then his companions. Back at home he told me how he clawed through the weight of the snow, not knowing if he would survive. It made him rethink his whole life, he said.

He was gone again. And although he had been two weeks late from climbs before . . . this time was different.

I thought about our life together. Moments from his courtship, our wedding, the honeymoon surfaced like a rapid montage. We'd been seeing each other for three months when he proposed: "Will you share your life with me?" We spent our honeymoon in Europe, living on coffee, croissants, and each other.

116

I desperately tried to recreate his image. I remembered how he looked in the first light of dawn, his hazel eyes, aquiline nose, full lips. I captured each feature for a moment, then it faded: the way one arm would be raised above his head, its well-defined muscles leading to his broad shoulders, his chest, his taut belly. His sensuality was powerful. Pictures of our intimacy flooded through me. I could almost feel the warmth of his mouth as he bathed me with his kisses, the smell of his hair and his body, the feel of his skin.

I touched my body as if he were touching me— gently, tenderly, passionately. The illusion faded. Tears streamed down my face and neck. No matter how I fought to bring him back, I couldn't. I was alone in our bed.

SAMPLE OF TREATMENT FORMAT
FOR TELEVISION MOVIE
(Several sections from a two-hour movie sample treatment.)

FORGET-ME-NOT

PAULA MEYER's desperate and deadly search for her husband, ROBERT, starts when he disappears while purportedly on a business trip. Little does she know that he's been in a car accident while in Mexico breaking off an affair with a co-worker, LIANNE SMITH. ROBERT's leg has been shattered and he suffers from a case of amnesia. LIANNE takes advantage of the situation and kidnaps him so she can rebuild his memory, substituting herself as ROBERT's wife.

THE STORY:
ACT I
In a slow-motion dream punctuated by the sound of running water, PAULA MEYER stands on a diving board and waves to her husband. From the

other end of the backyard pool, ROBERT smiles and waves back. Paula runs and jumps into a swan dive. As she gracefully arcs high up into the air she sees Robert, in silhouette, locked in the arms of another woman. Terrified, Paula looks down and finds the distance between her and the pool has grown to over thirty feet and all the water is gone.

She plummets helplessly toward the hard concrete. In desperation she screams Robert's name for help, but he's too engrossed with his lover to respond. At the moment of impact...

Robert shakes the screaming Paula from her nightmare. He's still wet from his morning shower. Outside the window a jackhammer rattles the earth. A construction crew begins work for the day on excavating the hole for their new swimming pool. Robert holds Paula close and comforts her as another day dawns at the Meyer household.

ACT IV

At home, the tension on Lianne is constant. As she tries to continually recreate the past, she keeps making small errors. She worries about Robert remembering too much. Little things come back to him that he can't understand. Where's his favorite blue shirt? Why isn't Tommy coming to breakfast? Who's Tommy?

Paula's personal life has also become more and more complicated. She's even started smoking again. Not only must she try to make ends meet, she must also explain Daddy's absence to her son. She's forced to cut her expenses to a minimum and even halts construction on the pool, leaving a wide open pit in the backyard.

ACT VII

As soon as Lianne steps out, Robert calls a cab.

Paula puts Tommy to bed and tells him she's got to change and then go out for a little while. Paula heads to the bathroom and starts to undress for the shower.

Using Robert's key, Lianne slips into the kitchen. Lianne flips the circuit breaker on the powerbox.

Paula's in the shower when the lights go off. She throws on a robe and starts to look through the cabinets until she finds a flashlight and a can of mace.

Outside, Robert pulls up in a cab and sees Lianne's car in front of the darkened house. He's jealous with rage.

The normal steps in writing a screenplay are: ➹ **idea, step outline, treatment, and screenplay.** Script formats vary from features to television and within the television realm there are some variations as well. Here we try to give you some examples of the different major formats.

MOTION PICTURE SCREENPLAY FORMAT

These are suggested formats. They are not the only way. Others may apply. There are a number of helpful script writing, formatting, and story development computer programs on the market. They include Movie Master, Final Draft, ScriptWare, Scriptor, Warren Script Applications (with Microsoft Word), SuperScript Pro, and Script Perfection (with WordPerfect) for script writing and formatting, and Collaborator, Storyline, Plots Unlimited, and IdeaFisher for story development. Also, the Writers Guild of America has a booklet on formats.

Properly formatting a screenplay is critical. There are essentially six format elements in a screenplay. They are **Slugline, Action, Character Cue, Dialogue, Parenthetical,** and **Transition**.

The **Slugline** is written in full caps and has either one or two blank lines before it.

Action is typed single-spaced, upper and lowercase in short paragraphs. There should be one blank line before each paragraph.

Character Name (**Character Cue**) is typed in full caps, appearing more or less centered on the page.

The **Dialogue** is typed in standard upper and lowercase and is placed directly beneath the character cue, beginning at space 28 from the left-hand side of the page and ending at about space 56, also appearing centered on the page but wider than the character's name above it.

A **Parenthetical** is written lowercase, and typed beneath the character cue in parentheses on a separate line from the dialogue.

Transitions are such things as CUT TO:, MATCH CUT TO:, FADE TO:, DISSOLVE TO:, and the like. These are justified with the right margin, typed in full caps. However, FADE IN is aligned on the left and always placed at the beginning of the screenplay.

Overall Notes on Format

Screenplays are typed in 10-pitch (i.e., 10 characters per inch) typewriter type on 8 $^1/_2$ X 11-inch paper. On some computers, the equivalent font and typesize would be Courier and 12-point. The margin should be an inch to an inch-and-a-half at the top and bottom of each page. It's best to avoid large blocks of text or dialogue as much as possible, and the narrative should be broken into short paragraphs. Do not include camera directions unless it is absolutely critical to do so. The script should not have scene numbers.

Cover

No fancy covers. A professional script's cover should be either a solid color or none at all.

Title Page

The title is centered in full caps; below it, centered, is the word "by," and below that, centered, the name of the writer. The name of the writer and/or agent and address and phone number are typed at the bottom of the page, one inch in from the left and two inches from the bottom. Also, if the script has been registered with the Writers Guild, "Registered WGAW" (Writers Guild of America West) or "Registered WGAE" (Writers Guild of America East) may be typed on the right-hand side of the page on the same line as the name and address or it may be typed below the address.

Settings (the number of typewriter characters, counting from the left-hand side of the page)

17	Left margin
28	Dialogue
35	Parenthetical
43	Character Cue (name)

66   Transitions
72   Page number (in the top right-hand corner of the page)
75   Right margin

Spacing

Use single spacing: **Use double spacing:**

For character actions   Between scene locale and narrative
For camera directions   From FADE IN to first scene
In dialogue   locale designation
For scene descriptions   Between narrative and character
For sound cues   cue
Between character cue   Between speeches of characters
   and dialogue

Use triple spacing:

Before scene locale designation (scene heading)

Length

❧ **A feature film script should be approximately 100 to 120 pages in length.** It's best not to go more than a few pages over or under these numbers. As a general rule of thumb, one page of a script is roughly equivalent to one minute of screen time.

Capitalization

The following should be capitalized in the script: CAMERA MOVES, CAMERA SHOTS, CHARACTER CUE, CHARACTER'S NAME (the first time the character is introduced in the script's narrative), DAY or NIGHT, EXT. or INT., FADE IN, SCENE LOCALE, and SOUNDS.

124

**SAMPLE OF MOTION PICTURE SCREENPLAY
COVER PAGE FORMAT**

HUSBAND, LOVER, SPY

by

Carlos de Abreu

Carlos de Abreu

433 N. Camden Dr., Suite 600
Beverly Hills, CA 90210
(310) 288-1881

Registered WGAW No. 058324

SAMPLE OF FEATURE SCREENPLAY FORMAT

{Top margin is approximately 1.0".}

FADE IN
{The slugline is typed in FULL CAPS.}
EXT.   GILGIT - HIMALAYAS, 1975 - DAY
{Double space, i.e., blank line here.}
A rock-lined polo field in a small village of
Northern Pakistan. A polo chukker being
played. We can feel the rush of energy.
Horses galloping, snorting, sweating.

NERU, a bearded Pakistani, charges against
an AMERICAN RIDER.

The AMERICAN takes the challenge.

At full gallop they try to dismount one
another.

AMERICAN RIDER
{Margins of descriptions are approximately 1.7"-7.5".}
pulls his horse out for a brief second and
with a twist of his hip comes back with
added spin throwing his weight against Neru,
riding him off.

NERU

nearly slips... but at the last moment
rights himself.

C.U. OF THE HORSES' HOOVES

126

2.

[Page number, at approximately 7.4"-7.5". Always use page numbers.]
The ground shakes. Hooves cutting the
dirt field create clouds of dust and flying
gravel. *[Descriptions are single-spaced.]*

C.U. ON RIDERS' BOOTS

Spurs digging into the horses sides, blood
dripping from the wounds.

Villagers and armed soldiers watch the game.
Military trucks surround the field.

Suddenly...

WE HEAR ONE SHARP POP SOUND

The American Rider slumps on his mount, he
has been shot...he falls off crashing to the
ground.

                    AMERICAN RIDER
                  (mumbling)
            "Blowback"

INT. HIGH RISE/LOBBY, D.C. - NIGHT

JAMES WHITELAW

a wiry know-it-all, rushes in the lobby. The
doorman greets him. As he waits for the

3.

elevator, a PRETTY BLOND joins him. The
elevator arrives, people come out.

INT. ELEVATOR - NIGHT

James lets the woman go in first. She faces
the door, he faces her. She is uncomfortable. He gives her the once over.

INT. TENTH FLOOR HALLWAY - NIGHT
{Watch paragraph length and break long sections into shorter paragraphs.}
Elevator reaches tenth floor, James gets
out. He walks to his apartment and opens
door.

INT. JAMES' APARTMENT - NIGHT

A typical bachelor pad. Pictures of <u>horses
and polo scenes</u> cover the unmirrored walls.

He goes to the kitchen and pours a drink--
Coca-Cola mixed with Courvoisier. He takes a
sip, squinting his eyes.

INT. JAMES' LIVING ROOM - NIGHT

Walking into the living room, he takes off
his shoes and settles into his armchair. The

red light of his answering machine is blink-
ing. He presses the playback button and
listens to his messages.
{Character name begins approximately at 4.3".}
                    FEMALE VOICE
               (low husky voice)
          James, James, where are you?
          Here I am ready for you ... you
          better call soon.

                    SAME FEMALE VOICE
{Margins of parentheticals are approximately 3.7" to 5.5".}
               (different tone)
{Dialogue margins are approximately 3.0" to 6.2".}
          Idiot, where have you been?
          Had tickets for a concert,
          Maurice Ravel...right, the
          "BOLERO" guy! Suzanne, Bye.
               {Single space dialogue.}
                    MALE VOICE
          James call MATT SHAW at the
          <u>Agency</u>. It's urgent!

He shakes his head. And we read his lips.

                    JAMES
               (mouths the word)
          F...

TELEVISION SCREENPLAY FORMATS

Currently in prime-time network television there are five types of scripts that air. They are the half-hour situation comedy (sitcom); the one-hour drama series; the two-hour MOW or movie of the week; miniseries, which can range anywhere from four to twenty hours; and the two-hour drama series pilot episode.

Whenever a writer attempts to produce a sample or spec script, it's essential to know and understand the format and structure of the type of script he or she has set out to emulate. Each type has its own set of rules, parameters, guidelines, and conventions.

Further, when a writer attempts to write a spec script for a specific show, such as a *Roseanne*, or a *Northern Exposure*, it's critical to follow the precise style used by that show.

The single best way to know what the format is for a given show is to **call up the production office and ask one of the assistants or secretaries for a sample script**.

Most shows will be glad to send you one. If that route fails, try libraries and bookstores or ask anyone else you know who may have contacts in the entertainment industry.

Don't waste time or money going to agencies or dealers that sell scripts. There's not much mystery in Hollywood about obtaining scripts from shows.

Dozens of copies of each draft are distributed to everyone in the cast, crew, studio, talent agency and network offices. After a new draft is produced or a show airs, most copies end up in the trash. Shows are often only too happy to give old copies away for free.

In this section we're going to look at the basic formats used in each of the five types of writing. The goal is not to teach you how to write the scripts, but rather to make you aware of some of the main principles involved in creating each of the formats.

130

Sitcoms

The first breakdown in sitcoms is the split between those shows that are filmed and those that are taped, usually in front of a live audience. Film shows such as the classic *M.A.S.H.* are shot on location and on sets built inside studio soundstages.

Tape shows, such as *Roseanne* or *Home Improvement*, are shot on videotape, usually by three or four cameras, exclusively on soundstages.

The distinction between film and tape has blurred over the years, but the essential distinction as it applies to scripting is this: Film shows shot on location have the potential of going anywhere, indoors or out. Tape shows by contrast are most frequently bound to a basic set of interiors.

When watching your favorite show or rerun you can easily see the differences. *M.A.S.H.* had the look and feel of a real outdoor medical encampment in the mountains of Korea. However, when Tony and Samantha went skiing on an episode of *Who's the Boss?*, the ski scenes were all shot on a soundstage doubling for a downhill slope. The viewers know they're really not outdoors, but they're willing to momentarily suspend their disbelief for the sake of the story.

Show runners (writers who are producers as well), such as Bob Myer, who was the executive producer of *Roseanne* for several years, would easily agree that tape shows try to avoid faking exteriors whenever possible because they never do look quite real and the cost of creating them can all too easily inflate their budgets.

When creating sample scripts for film or tape shows, it's essential to recognize and be aware of how the show handles moves beyond the basic set. Most shows, such as *Murphy Brown,* almost never use exteriors. Ninety percent of the action takes place on basic sets, such as the office pool area, Murphy's living room, and Phil's bar. Only as the story dictates are there moves to other sets.

When a writer creates a sample, the script should mirror the general tendencies of the show being emulated. Adding in unusual sets and moves will immediately mark the writer as an amateur and hinder acceptance of the script.

⚐ **Most half-hour sitcoms run for twenty-two to twenty-four minutes. Unlike feature film scripts, pages of sitcom scripts are double-spaced, with the result being that most sitcom drafts run forty-four to forty-eight pages.**

Until recently most comedies were split into two acts of eighteen to twenty-four pages each. Within each act there would be anywhere from two to six scenes. Preceding the first act there would usually be what is known as a "tease."

In the case of a program like *Cheers*, the tease might be a one to two-minute run centered around an extended joke. Once the punchline is hit, the script will cut away for commercials and opening credits. The tease will not necessarily be connected to the story at hand that night. Its purpose is to capture the audience immediately after the close of the preceding show and discourage them from switching channels.

Now, as channel zapping or surfing has become far more commonplace, shows have moved more to what is called a "cold opening." Much like a teaser, it kicks in immediately after the previous show, but unlike a tease, the cold opening is usually an integral part of the full story. Cold openings may run anywhere from two to five minutes.

The longer opening tends to hook the viewer for a long enough period of time to discourage channel zapping. After all, who wants to switch stations when you're already five minutes into a show and that movie you were considering watching has already jump started?

Once the cold opening has run its course, we then hit the commercial break and pick up with opening credits.

John Scheinfeld, a writer, producer, TV executive, and lecturer at UCLA, has been involved in the creation of numerous sitcoms. John advises that the first act of any sitcom must first introduce the basic story line and give the audience a dramatic hook within the first few minutes. What little crisis in the lives of our regular characters is going to arise? What seems to be the logical outcome, and what can our character do to resolve it?

Soon after finding out what the crisis and potential solution is, we're then thrown a new set of curves or obstacles the protagonist must overcome.

132

The midpoint of the script, that is the break between the first and second acts, is in essence a cliffhanger. There's an identified problem, possible solutions, and a roadblock that serves to complicate the story. Just when the viewer is concerned about the outcome, the act ends and the commercials pop in.

Because we want to know the outcome of the story, we hang in through the commercials and pick up again in the second half.

Act Two will generally complicate the original situation even further before bringing us to a resolution at the last minute.

A good many shows now also use a "tag" at the end of the show. A tag could be thought of as the opposite of a tease or cold opening.

Tags usually run for a minute or two at the end of a show. They come after the last commercial break. Dramatically they add a final joke to punch up the conclusion of a show and give it a sense of finality.

From a network point of view, tags allow them to place the final block of commercials before the story ends. Audiences are held through this last block of advertising by the prospect of hearing that final punchline. Once the last note has been sounded, the network can then segue right into the next show and its tease or cold opening.

Never forget that shows are merely the filler that enables commercial sponsors to present their products to you. To achieve this goal, the basic laws of dramatic structure are of necessity altered and modified to fit the sitcom format.

As the art of storytelling has grown and improved over the years there have been a number of attempts to alter the basic sitcom format. Generally these changes have been designed either to give a freshness to the genre or to bring it more in line with traditional three-act dramatic structure.

Seinfeld, for example, has taken on occasion the teaser and tag and turned them into stand-up bits. Jerry will appear onstage as if he were engaged in a nightclub act and run off with a short monologue. The theme of the comic bit will usually reflect upon the story being told that night, without actually being a part of the dramatic story line.

And although Jerry's bits come across as a modern-day innovation on the standard tease and tag, its origins go back to the beginning of TV.

The *Burns and Allen* comedy shows, which were among the first sitcoms ever produced, also did similar variations on this concept. Every show concluded with George and Gracie doing a schtick for the audience in front of the curtains. "Say 'Goodnight,' Gracie" became a signature closing for Burns that most fans remember to this day.

Traditionally, dramatic structure for all forms of storytelling has been expressed in three acts: Beginning, Middle, and End. To fit the conventions of television, this structure has been forced into two acts. Act One of a sitcom includes the standard beginning of play as well as the first half of the middle act. Then, a somewhat artificial cliffhanger is inserted into the center of what should be the middle act. The remainder of the middle act kicks off Act Two, which then concludes with the end segment.

A number of shows in recent years have attempted to get away from the cookie-cutter formula for sitcoms and return to the more natural three-act structure. Most prominent among them is *Murphy Brown*.

From its inception, *Murphy Brown* has eschewed the two-act structure and dispensed with tags and teases. The show is split into three distinct acts, which conform to our notions of a beginning, middle, and close.

A typical episode will begin in the office pool area. A situation or problem will arise which must be dealt with. After a commercial break, the action traditionally shifts to Phil's bar. The original dilemma is then complicated with additional twists and turns. After a second commercial break, Murphy ends up in her living room where the original problem is resolved.

Of course, there are a multitude of variations on action and the use of sets, but it is this basic pattern that maintains a sense of consistency and fulfills viewers' expectations.

❧ **When writing sample and spec sitcom scripts it's essential, as noted earlier, to understand and use the basic conventions of that show. The style of *Murphy Brown* is vastly different from that of *Seinfeld*, which is also miles away from *M.A.S.H.***

Michael Hanel is the vice-president of comedy series development at Columbia TV. He's been with the company for nearly a decade, during which time he's been involved in the production of literally thousands of episodes. A major function of his job is to read scripts in a never-ending search for new and talented writers. Michael knows that using the wrong format, or being ignorant of a show's format, is the single biggest mistake that inexperienced writers make. Before you write, study the show. Tape as many episodes as you can. Understand and internalize its rhythms, act breaks, and tone.

Once you understand the structure, the next area to analyze before you write is characterization. First, does the show have a single main character as *Murphy Brown* does, or is it an ensemble cast as seen in the original *Taxi*?

In *Murphy Brown* all of the action revolves around Murphy. Even if the problem to be resolved belongs to a supporting character such as Miles or Jim, Murphy is always intimately involved in the ultimate solution or resolution. Any spec script that fails to keep a focus on Murphy would be tossed as being atypical of the show.

On the other hand, *Taxi* and *Cheers* tended to revolve less around the stars, Alex and Sam respectively. Although the leads were always in focus and involved in the action, the secondary players were allowed to have a much more prominent role.

Contrast both of these models to that of *Seinfeld*, which frequently uses three distinct story lines in each episode. Although Jerry is featured prominently, there is nearly equal time devoted to the bits revolving around Kramer, George, and Elaine.

In all sitcoms the regular characters have distinct personalities. Staff writers try to make each character as unique and distinctive and full of quirks as is humanly possible. There's no mistaking *Seinfeld*'s Kramer for *Murphy Brown*'s Miles.

When creating spec episodes it's vital to know the characters on the show. Watch and record as many episodes as possible. Listen to the language the characters use. Pick up on regular tics and mannerisms. Watch how they react under different circumstances.

What, for example, makes Roseanne distinct from Murphy? How

would they react in the same situation such as meeting the President at a town hall session? Both might be argumentative, but their approaches would be modified significantly by their personal histories and backgrounds.

To write existing characters, you must know everything you possibly can about them. You must get inside their skins to know that Kramer might say one thing, but George another. Their voices are distinct, and only when you can replicate those distinctions should you attempt to write them.

🐸 **Another flaw in scripts that new writers create is introducing new characters and giving them a major role in the story, a role that frequently dominates those of the regulars.**

When you analyze scripts, pay attention to how frequently outside characters are used. And when they're used, just how big is their role? Usually it's small, and at best they function as pivotal characters that force the regulars to react one way or the other.

🐸 **It's a network axiom that viewers watch the same shows week in and week out because they want to welcome those characters into their homes.** Stories are secondary; it's Jerry or Murphy or Roseanne or Tim Allen they want to see.

When you introduce outside characters or for that matter vastly change the nature of the show in a spec script, you deprive the audience of seeing what they expect. And if you fail to fulfill expectations, you'll lose your audience.

🐸 **Another common error of spec sitcom scripts is that they're not funny, or the humor used is the wrong kind.**

Before you ever send a sample sitcom off to a professional in the industry, be it an agent, writer, producer, or network executive, try it out on friends you trust. Do they laugh? Is the material funny? Does it fit the show you're emulating? Do the characters ring true?

If the answer to any of these questions is no, then don't send it out.

136

Rewrite it, and keep rewriting until it's a masterpiece. And when you're done, immediately write a second one.

Producers and agents figure that given enough time, anybody, even a monkey, can produce one good sitcom script. But show runners need writers who can work quickly and on demand. By producing two or more high quality scripts to show around town, you've already lifted yourself out of that first category. In other words, if you want to sell yourself, create the marketing tools that will allow you to accomplish that task.

Look at your spec scripts as if they were a prime-time advertisement to sell a product. You are the product, the scripts are the commercials. If the commercial is flawed, no one will buy the product, and that's you. If the scripts are brilliant, then you're opening the door.

Now that you know how to flawlessly structure a wonderful sitcom script with totally realistic characters that are hysterically funny, you've got to decide what show to write.

First rule: don't waste your time writing an original sitcom. No one in Hollywood could care about your original characters. It's not going to get turned into a pilot, nor is it going to catch the attention of a producer, agent, or executive.

There's an odd Catch-22 about sitcom scripts. Many times the best aren't really funny on paper, unless the reader knows who the characters are. A *Roseanne* script will read funny because we know how Dan and Rosie relate to each other and their kids. We understand their humor, their put-downs, their good-natured knocks at each other.

But who knows that the "Aunt Louise" you create is so eccentric she doesn't mean anything she says? Who can visualize your physical schtick if they don't know how your characters move?

Even experienced writers have a tough time getting the networks to understand their pilot scripts until AFTER they're filmed as pilots or put through a staged reading.

Second rule: don't write a spec script for a show that is no longer on the air.

137

Write what you know best, which is a show you genuinely love. First, your affection for all the characters and their quirks will come through in your work. Second, you'll have an innate understanding of the style of humor used. After all, you like the show because it makes you laugh. It strikes a chord with your own sense of humor. Make use of that. Don't fight the river currents, go with them.

The bottom line is to present nothing but the best you can possibly do to represent your talents. Anything less and you sell yourself short.

One-Hour Drama Series Shows

The rules for selling yourself through a one-hour drama series script are not much different from those involved in creating a top-notch sitcom script. All you need to do is to take a show that's on the air and create an episode that's better than anything anyone has ever seen.

Unlike sitcoms, drama shows are never filmed before a live audience. Basic sets on soundstages and on location are used. What this means for writers is that they are freed from the confines of the stage and allowed to move anywhere that's called for by the story they're telling. The only constraints on location will be the budget for a given show and the general style and philosophy of the show.

By philosophy we mean the basic tendencies. For example, *L.A. Law* took place primarily in the office and the courtroom. Ventures farther afield were rare. It's not likely we'd have seen a car chase, speed boats running drugs, or our heroes jetting off to Europe, events that were more than typical of *Hart to Hart*.

Every show has a style and look all its own. At a moment's glance it's easy to tell whether you're watching *Murder, She Wrote* or *Northern Exposure*. The pace, tempo, and conventions vary enormously. But what all one-hour shows share in common is a three-act dramatic structure spread out over four segments.

When writing hour scripts it's critical to be aware of the basic conventions of the show you're writing for. As with sitcoms, the sample script should mirror the general tendencies of the show being

138

emulated. Straying from the basic style will again mark the writer as a beginner not worthy of being taken seriously.

Most one-hour dramas run for about forty-eight minutes. Just as with features, scripts should be single-spaced. Time is measured at an average of one page per minute. Consequently scripts are approximately forty-eight pages. That's a general rule and there are, of course, variations.

Tom Towler, a writer-producer for such shows as *Lonesome Dove: The Series*, *Gabriel's Fire*, and *Crime Story*, advises that each show has conventions that may be unique to its own method of storytelling. *Moonlighting* was a notable example. The style of storytelling was very loose. Narrations tended toward a breezy shorthand. The usual rules of cutting from one scene to another were often dropped, and instead we just tracked along with a character. White space was used to tell a story and give a sense of urgency. And ellipses . . . (dot, dot, dot) were everywhere.

This loose method fit with the zip and zing of the dialogue. The story seemed to rip along. And the end results were forty-eight-minute scripts that ran upwards of ninety pages.

If a sample *Moonlighting* came in at under fifty pages, it was tossed. No way could the writer have caught the essence of the show.

On the other hand, if an *L.A. Law* came in at ninety pages, it too would have been tossed.

The lesson again remains to know your target and mimic its nuances to the very best of your ability.

The forty-eight minutes of a one-hour drama are split into four fairly equal units. The number of scenes per segment varies enormously from show to show and even episode to episode of the same show.

Many one-hour shows use the same tag and tease devices that half-hour shows do. Some ensemble shows, such as *L.A. Law*, that tend to have ongoing story lines, begin their tease with a quick recap of the previous week's highlights before launching into new material that opens the current episode.

Unlike sitcoms, teases almost exclusively belong to the stories being told that night. When used, tags are again designed to add a sense of finality to the story.

Although all one-hour dramas share the same basic three-act dramatic structure, there are three basic variations on how they accomplish this.

First there is the single story-line script with a distinct beginning, middle, and end, such as *Murder, She Wrote*.

Then there is the multiple story-line type of show, popular in such ensemble shows as *Hill Street Blues* or *St. Elsewhere*. These scripts have two, three, or even four main story lines. One may have started in a prior episode, one might start and finish in this episode, and another may overlap into the next episode.

And lastly, there are the prime-time soaps that became so in vogue during the early 1980s, and again in the mid-1990s. *Melrose Place*, *Dynasty*, *Dallas*, and *Knots Landing* are prime examples of this. There are always several story arcs in play at any one time which are conceived of, and designed, to last over any number of episodes. Each story arc has its beginning, middle, and end, but these elements can be played out over weeks, months, or even years.

The soap opera structure has fallen out of vogue for this very reason. Shows such as *Dallas* with extended story lines fared very poorly in the syndication market. Viewers need to see them sequentially or risk being confused. This is a far cry from the self-contained episodes of a show like *The Cosby Show* that broke all syndication sales records.

Ensemble shows by contrast have fared reasonably well in the syndication markets even though some of their story lines overlap from one episode to another. The reason for their success is simple: There is always at least one main story line that begins and ends each week.

When Jordan Kerner, producer of such feature films as *The Mighty Ducks*, *D2*, and *When a Man Loves a Woman*, was the vice-president of drama series development at ABC, he would remind the staff that viewers need and expect a sense of closure in drama. Open-endedness makes people uncomfortable and dissatisfied with what they've seen. The ensemble shows found a way to have their cake and eat it too by using multiple story lines and insuring that at least some of them end when the show's over.

The first act of any drama corresponds to the first act of the three-act dramatic structure. In those first ten to fifteen minutes, the first act must introduce the story and hook us with a conflict in need of resolution.

The first act break or commercial break most commonly ends on a note of suspense. We've been introduced to some dilemma, and when that first break comes, we're left with a strong cliffhanger. The nature of the cliffhanger will correspond to the nature and style of the show.

On *Murder, She Wrote*, this is usually the point where somebody turns up dead. In *L.A. Law* we were usually in the courtroom and the opposition had presented some sort of damning evidence against one of our heroes' clients.

The second and third acts of a TV drama correspond to the second act of basic dramatic structure. These two segments serve to complicate the situations our protagonists must face.

Our protagonists struggle to overcome the new crises as they arise. The half-hour commercial break comes in the middle of this section. The split between the two segments is usually slightly off the half hour, occurring a few minutes before or after that point. The purpose here again is to discourage viewers from switching channels.

There's usually an attempt to break between these two segments on another note of suspense, but it's not considered as crucial as is the first quarter-hour mark.

The most significant cliffhanger occurs at the forty-five minute mark. This moment corresponds to the basic story crisis which kicks the final act into gear. Again, because we want to know the outcome of the story, we hang in through the commercials.

Hour dramas that occur at either 8:00 p.m. or 9:00 p.m. are more likely to have a tag than those at 10:00 p.m. The earlier shows are designed by the network to keep you watching into the next hour. The ten o'clock shows are the leads into the local affiliates' 11:00 p.m. news shows. The locals will generally pop in a promo for their news broadcast between the final segment of the ten o'clock show and its credits. The news promo serves as its own tease for the next half hour.

Just as with sitcoms, the biggest mistake an inexperienced writer can make is to be ignorant of a show's format and style. We can't stress enough the importance of studying the show you want to emulate. Again, tape as many episodes as you can. Learn and internalize its rhythms, act breaks, and tone.

After learning the structure, a writer must next analyze the characterizations. Does the show have a single lead character such as *Magnum, P.I.*, an ensemble cast such as *Northern Exposure*, or does it have co-leads such as *Moonlighting*?

In *Murder, She Wrote*, everything revolves around Angela Lansbury's character, Jessica Fletcher. She is the one who undertakes the investigation in which almost all of the other characters are possible suspects. Deviations from this pattern are rare, except in cases where a "guest detective" takes over the lead. Any spec script that fails to keep a focus on Angela's character would be considered inappropriate.

By contrast, shows such as *L.A. Law* and *Hill Street Blues* give fairly equal time to all of the members of the cast. Granted, a specific episode may give more weight to several of the characters than others, but this imbalance is usually corrected over a span of several nights.

You must know all of the characters you're going to write about. The more complex the show, the greater the degree of studying you must apply. Ensemble shows obviously have more characters than a single- or dual-lead show.

You must know the quirks of each of these characters and be aware of how they relate to each other. Read and watch as many shows as you can. Tape the episodes so that you can listen to the language the characters use over and over again. You want to get to a point where you hear their rhythms in your head. See how they react under different circumstances.

What for example makes the characters in *Picket Fences* different from those in *In the Heat of the Night*? How would each police chief react to a murder in town? How would they conduct an investigation?

As with sitcoms, you must study the manner in which guest characters are used. Are they given a dominant role or are they just bit players? It's easy to figure out the answer to this question. The show will provide you with it every week.

When you watch shows, see how often outside characters are used. And when they appear, how big is their role? The range in drama shows is considerable, far greater than in sitcoms. But . . . this all depends on the show itself.

Unlike sitcoms, the longer length of a drama show enables the writers to give greater depth to the relationships between regular and guest characters. However, it is always the regular characters or star that predominate. If your guest character becomes the protagonist of your story, then you're writing the wrong script.

There have been a few exceptions to this rule. *Hotel*, *Love Boat*, and *Fantasy Island*, all products of Aaron Spelling's company, gave the prominent role each week to the guest stars. These shows were specifically designed to meld two opposing concepts: that of a regular drama series with a consistent cast of characters and an anthology where the cast changed completely each week.

Anthologies have rarely worked on network television. If the audience doesn't know what to expect and what characters they'll be seeing each week, they won't tune in unless the show is heavily promoted. That costs money, which becomes an additional burden. Networks would rather invest the time and effort it takes to promote a new story each week with a concept that's easier and more profitable to sell, such as a two-hour TV movie.

Even some of the more famous anthologies, such as *The Twilight Zone* and *Alfred Hitchcock Presents*, were never big ratings winners. Most of their fame comes from long-term success in the less competitive syndication and rerun marketplace.

The Spelling shows, on the other hand, were all very successful during their heyday of the late '70s and early '80s. They in part achieved this success by giving the viewer both a consistent cast of regulars and locale, and also by bringing in guest stories that could be as unique and varied as any of TV's great anthology shows.

Whether or not you're a fan of the style of these shows is less important than the fact that they successfully filled a niche in the marketplace.

If a common error of comedy scripts is that they're not funny, then the parallel mistake for drama scripts is that the dramatic conflicts are either not strong enough or they're ill-suited for the show you're trying to write for.

After observing a show often enough and seeing how the characters relate to each other, it's critical to study the patterns used to add conflict to the show.

On *L.A. Law* we almost always learned about what the night's cases were going to be in the daily partner meeting in the boardroom. You also saw that the cases the firm was engaged in that evening had a tendency to reflect different aspects of a similar question. The arena may have been how parents relate to children or how lovers come into conflicts with each other or how friends betray each other, etc. Regardless of what the situations were, there was an overriding manner in which the cases came into being.

In a typical *Murder, She Wrote*, Angela Lansbury's character usually goes on a trip, someone turns up dead, she investigates the case and solves it at the last minute.

Rarely are the conventions violated. And when they are, it's done deliberately and with a specific purpose in mind. As a spec script writer though, you're trying to prove you can observe a show, understand its guidelines and write a script that is true to form.

To venture far from the rules, no matter how wonderful your story may be, does not prove you can write for a specific show. At its most base level, TV is a commodity like toothpaste or soap. If someone needs and asks you to buy them Crest and you give them Tom's of Maine natural toothpaste because you feel it's a superior product, you've failed the test.

Similarly, don't put car chases in a program like *L.A. Law*, or a courtroom scene in a medical show like the old *St. Elsewhere*. Stick to the core of the show, and to that core, add something genuinely brilliant and original.

Also, don't make the mistake of thinking that action and fighting represent drama in a story. Drama must come out of the conflicting needs of the characters involved, such as when you throw a single slab of meat into a pen with two starving junkyard dogs.

❧ It's worth mentioning here, too, that as good as you make your spec script, probably the last place you want to send it is the show you wrote it for. Why? Because rarely will they ever like it or think it represents their show.

No matter how hard you try, you can never be inside the head of the team of writers and producers who create the episodes of a show. If you do something very original, they may reject it as not being something they think their characters would do. If they thought their characters would do it, they'd have already written it themselves.

And if you stick to something very conventional but well written, you'll get poor marks for failing to be original.

❧ You'll have better success with your work if it's seen by the staff of a different show that has a somewhat similar style. The staff of the second show is not locked into a preconceived notion about the first show. Just like you, they're viewers and hopefully fans of the other show. They'll appreciate your work far more and may even hire you for their show.

As a precaution though, we'll again repeat the same advice we gave before.

❧ Never send out a spec script unless you're absolutely convinced it's the best you can do, and you've tried it out on people whose opinion you trust. This rule applies to both features and TV.

❧ Never give your script to anyone who you know is going to tell you they love it. Give it to someone who's not afraid to tell you the truth. The last thing you want to happen is to have no one tell you what's wrong with your script. Otherwise, you'll be like the emperor who stood naked thinking he was wearing new clothes because all of his subjects were afraid to tell him the truth.

The rules about what one-hour dramatic show to write are the same as those for sitcoms:

Don't try to push an original story; don't write for a smash hit; don't write for a show that's already off the air; and don't write for a show that will probably go off the air.
Do write what you know and love most.

Movies of the Week (MOWs)

In the television realm, as a newcomer, the movie of the week is the area where you may have the best chance to sell your story or manuscript, book or screenplay.

If you have the rights to a wonderful original story that fits the current conventions employed by the networks, you may be able to catapult your career into hyperspace.

Primary among the reasons why seasoned writers shun MOWs is that TV movies lack the cachet of a feature film while requiring nearly as much work. To a great extent this is true.

Those of us who grew up loving film equate those feelings with the great movies we've seen in theaters. If asked to name a favorite, some might say *Gone With the Wind*, *Chinatown*, *Star Wars*, or even a low-budget wonder such as *Repo Man*. It's all a matter of taste.

MOWs suffer by comparison in our collective memories. Yet they fill a critical niche in the TV marketplace and have proven to be enormously popular. And interestingly enough, if on a good night an MOW attracts thirty million viewers to the tube, that's twice as many as most successful features draw in a year of domestic release. It's this ability to pull in viewers that gives them their clout.

Another reason writers shy away from MOWs is financial. While the average budget of studio-released features may be around thirty

146

million dollars, the typical TV movie is made for one-tenth that amount. Wages paid to writers also tend to be significantly less, though WGA minimums on both are not appreciably different.

Most agents would concur that, as we noted earlier, there is a firm belief that TV viewing is controlled by the women of a household. True or not, programmers work off this belief and consequently the great majority of TV movies are geared for women.

☙ Family stories, tales of women in jeopardy, and accounts of women overcoming long odds to success are common topics. Romantic themes, whether they revolve around a love triangle, love lost, or love found are also frequent themes.

The most common source of stories is the true life saga ripped from the headlines, whether it be the Amy Fisher tale or a trip inside the lives of the royal family of England.

☙ As we'll explain shortly, the broadcast networks break their MOWs into seven acts over a two-hour period with commercials inserted in between. Actual running time is only 96 minutes out of 120. The remaining minutes are devoted to commercials and station promotions.

Since cable stations HBO and Showtime are supported by viewer membership instead of advertisers, there is no need to break up a movie into segments or to restrict its length to ninety-six minutes. They have a greater flexibility than commercial stations in both length and act structure with their original programming.

When writing MOWs you must be aware of the general conventions that the networks depend on. Nine times out of ten the protagonist is going to be a woman. It is women who are the predominant viewers of MOWs. If you are unable, unwilling, or too unaware to write a strong female lead, then this format is not for you. Try another venue.

The biggest exceptions to this rule are shows like *Columbo* and *Perry Mason* and other franchise TV movies. These are targeted toward a male audience and are best used to counter-program against a female-oriented MOW run on another network. Because they are based on a franchised character, there is a built-in recognition factor that draws an audience to them.

❦ **If you want to write a spec script for a franchise, you severely limit the possibilities of a sale. Further, you face the same complications as one who undertakes to emulate an existing drama series.**

❦ **Most female leads tend to be portrayed by actresses between the ages of thirty-five and forty-five. There is a dearth of roles for leading women in feature projects, yet stars in this category often have a large following. These fans readily tune in to watch them in MOWs.**

❦ **As mentioned, most MOWs run for about ninety-six minutes. Just as with features, scripts should be single-spaced. Time is measured at an average of one page per minute.**

The ninety-six minutes of an MOW are split into seven units or acts. The number of scenes per segment varies, but there are several conventions that remain constant.

Unlike sitcoms and hour drama shows, teasers are almost never used. Tags occasionally appear, and when they do, they usually add closure to a story.

All MOWs use the basic three-act dramatic structure we've referred to before.

❦ **The first act of a TV movie corresponds to the first act of the three-act dramatic structure.** In length they tend to run from twenty to twenty-five minutes. Those opening minutes will introduce us to the story and end with a strong hook that keeps the viewer locked to the screen.

The twenty to twenty-five minute length of the first act is also one means of ensuring that viewers will not channel surf during an early commercial break. Any other show they might choose to watch will already be well into its story at twenty minutes in.

It's also essential that the first commercial break ends on a note of suspense. Usually it involves our lead, a woman in her late thirties or early forties being forced to confront the dilemma that will propel the story. It's now that she learns her supposedly faithful husband is having an affair, or that her child has a terrible disease, or that she's being stalked by a vicious serial killer.

The second through fifth acts of a TV movie correspond to the second act of basic dramatic structure. These four segments together serve to complicate the situations our protagonist must face.

Our leading lady struggles to overcome the new crises as they arise. The next most critical act break comes between acts three and four, which is around the one-hour mark. Again, the purpose is to prevent the viewer from deciding to give up on the movie and switch to another station.

Another crisis further complicating the protagonist's struggles is inserted here. Maybe it's the discovery that the serial killer is in fact her own husband, or that the disease ravaging her child could be cured if only she can get him to the right specialist before it's too late. The basic point and purpose is simple. Hold the viewer through the commercials.

Clearly HBO and Showtime movies do not face this artificial restriction and are thus freer to have events flow more naturally. Good MOW writers learn to hit these points when they're in the outline stage.

Most of the other commercial breaks also occur at some point of tension or suspense, but it's never as critical as those already cited.

The last two TV acts correspond to the final act of the three-act structure. In Act Six we might reveal that the killer knows his wife is aware of his murderous activities and now he's begun to stalk her. The sixth act will also break on a point of high tension. This corresponds to the crisis that usually occurs in the middle of the last act of the three-act structure.

So here we break at the point where the killer is now stalking his wife. She's alone except for her wits and a cop who's befriended her. He's on his way to the rescue, but will he arrive in time?

The seventh act runs us through the final moments of suspense and ends with the demise of the killer, the recovery of the sick child, or the wife setting off on a new life away from her unfaithful husband.

A tag, if it occurs, ties up any loose ends.

Because their target audience is adult women, MOWs almost always start at nine o'clock, after kids are in bed, and run through until the 11:00 p.m. news. The local stations will generally pop in a promo for their news broadcast between the seventh act and the tag or credits roll. Once again, the news promo serves as its own tease for the next half hour.

❧ As with other types of television, the most common error an inexperienced writer can make is to be ignorant of the basic nature of MOWs. You must understand the style and subject matter of TV movies before attempting to write one. You must study the types of MOWs you want to emulate. Again, tape as many as you can. Learn their rhythms, act breaks, and tone.

After grasping structure, a writer must next learn to analyze the types of characters seen in most movies. Is the leading lady bad or good? Is she an active participant in determining her fate or is she a passive victim waiting for the hero to rescue her?

How much do we learn about our characters? Is there a lot of set-up time used, or does the story take right off? Are the roles designed to be glitzy and soap opera-ish, or are they real and intensely dramatic? Are they presented light-heartedly or with great seriousness?

After studying MOWs and understanding how characters are presented, it's vital to observe the patterns used to intensify conflicts.

When choosing a story to tell for an MOW, it's best to stick to the mainstream. Do the kind of stories you see being done, provided you have a natural feel for them.

Miniseries

Bill Greenblatt, president of Symphony Pictures, has produced and directed a variety of MOWs and features. He'd be among the first to

150

suggest that unlike other areas of television, the realm of the miniseries is almost exclusively left to the veteran writer. The principal reasons for this are clearly size, scope, and cost. Miniseries can range anywhere from four hours to twenty hours in length. The dramatic demands are usually beyond the skills of most new writers.

To break in, there are simpler ways than attempting to tackle two-hundred-plus page miniseries scripts on a spec basis.

Further, the simple reality is that most miniseries are based on best-selling novels of some stature that are too big to compress into two hours. The rights to such literary works are usually snatched up by aggressive producers long before these books hit the stores.

Most large studios either control publishing houses themselves or have contacts with large publishers that make them aware of big titles when they are still in the manuscript or galley stage. Rights are then acquired and deals are cut with the networks.

The range and diversity of miniseries vary as much as the books and original stories upon which they are based. There are few conventions here other than the fact that the story is not one that can be told well within two hours.

Generally, as with most thick and complex novels, there are several main characters and concurrent story lines. The events may be spread out over years, decades, or generations.

There are no set running times for miniseries, though most use up forty-eight minutes per hour for screen time with the remainder devoted to commercials and promotions. Scripts should be single-spaced. Time is measured at an average of one page per minute.

The running time and acts for a miniseries may vary considerably, but by and large, for each night that it runs, it follows a schedule similar to the seven acts of an MOW. The variations however are so numerous that it would be impossible to lay out a typical breakdown of acts.

Multiple story lines also serve to complicate any breakdown into the three-act structure. What does remain consistent with all miniseries, though, is that each night ends on a cliffhanger. This is the hook that brings viewers back night after night.

SAMPLE OF A SITCOM SCRIPT
(Notes on Format)

TV scripts are different from those of features. Aside from the format instructions below, note that scene locale designations, such as INT. BOWER KITCHEN - THE NEXT MORNING, are underlined. The same is the case with act breaks, such as ACT ONE and ACT TWO, which are underlined and placed at the top of a new page. (This is also done with TAGS and TEASERS if needed.) Parentheticals can be typed flush with the left margin in full caps, or they may be done in the same style as that of feature scripts. Parenthetical directions in TV scripts are double-spaced, however.

Settings (the number of typewriter characters, counting from the left-hand side of the page)

- 17   Left margin
- 25   Dialogue
- 38   Character Cue (name)
- 60   Right-hand margin (the right-hand margin should be about 2.5 to 3 inches)
- 72   Page number (in the top right-hand corner of the page)

Spacing

Use double spacing:

Between scene locale and narrative
From FADE IN to first scene locale
Between narrative and character cue (above dialogue). Narrative.
Between character's name and dialogue
Dialogue
Between speeches of characters

152

Length

A sitcom (half-hour) script should be approximately forty-five to fifty pages in length. Normally episodes are twenty-six minutes long.

Capitalization

Everything, *except dialogue and character list*, is in full caps.

SAMPLE OF SITCOM SCRIPT FORMAT

                                                              10.

ACT ONE

SCENE THREE

(Mary, Joseph)

INT. BOWER KITCHEN - THE NEXT MORNING

(JOSEPH, LOOKING DOWN, IS EATING BREAKFAST.

MARY, NOT LOOKING GREAT, ENTERS AND GOES TO

THE REFRIGERATOR. SHE SNEEZES AND BLOWS HER

NOSE.)

                    MARY

    Hi!

(SHE COUGHS.)

    Ready for a great day?

11.

                    JOSEPH

Mom, you don't sound good.

                    MARY

Just morning drip.

A little grapefruit juice will help.

(MARY OPENS REFRIGERATOR AND TAKES OUT A

BOTTLE OF GRAPEFRUIT JUICE, STARTS TO REACH

FOR A GLASS, BUT INSTEAD TAKES A SIP FROM

THE BOTTLE.)

Note: For submission of true stories, screenplays, manuscripts, and books for potential sale of film rights, see Chapter 23.

Chapter 8.

Writing Strategies

FEATURE SCREENPLAY

In any creative business one always strives to be better. In the movie business, as we mentioned before, development is where all projects end up, regardless of who is involved or what stage the project is at: idea, treatment, outline, manuscript, book, or screenplay. Also, we know that for the visual medium, we are working on a screenplay format. In this chapter we will introduce you to the world of script development and writing.

There are many books and teachers that are qualified to teach you the details of script writing. We highly recommend Dr. Linda Seger's *Making a Good Script Great* or Christopher Vogler's *The Writer's Journey*. We also suggest that you take as many workshops as possible, including those of Madeline DiMaggio, Michael Hauge, Robert McKee, Linda Seger, John Truby, Christopher Vogler, or Professor Richard Walter.

The rewriting process can be complex and lengthy, and we don't expect you to become a development expert just through reading this chapter. However, the quality of your projects' screenplays is crucial.

✎ **Melinda Jason, producer (*Body of Evidence, Eve of Destruction*), strongly believes that a brilliant script is the first and**

**foremost element in getting a project financed and/or green-
lighted.** To achieve such a level of perfection, the creative team has to
know the basic elements of screenwriting and rewriting.

**Michael Hauge, author of *Writing Screenplays That Sell*, feels
that "nine out of every ten film projects fail because they lack one
or more of the following essential elements: a clear, sympathetic
hero; a compelling visible objective for that hero to pursue; and
overwhelming obstacles which require immense courage."**

SCREENPLAY ELEMENTS

Now, we are going to guide you through our development system.

The form of a script is fixed by a time limit. The restriction of having
to tell a story within the allotted period of time initiates a framework
which begins the revision process. Writing does not have to be done
only one way, but having a logical plan to guide the writer's creativity
in a focused direction will facilitate the development process. Poetry,
the most creative application of language, also contains the most rigid
and codified structure manifested in the written word. So, perhaps
poetry should be taken as an example for us to follow.

Theme

The theme guides the characters' changes. The first thing that a
poem must do is say something, convey a message. What does that
mean? It means that the poem must be unified by a point of view. The
author has some perspective which he/she manages to communicate to
the reader. Like a poem, a script must have a perspective, or in other
words, a theme. An active theme encompasses some human experience,
something the viewer can incorporate into his/her scheme of the world.
Accompanying the universal human experience is a universal knowledge which the writer can describe in a single sentence. In more familiar

156

terms, the theme is the thought left with the audience or the moral of the story.

Genre
(Please refer to the genre charts that we provided in Chapter 5.)

Genre formats the story's structure. In screenwriting, genres fall into three classic categories: comedy, drama, and tragedy. Like poetic categories (epic, mock heroic, lyric, etc.), genres employ specific conventions. For example, if a writer chooses comedy, the script must be humorous, the characters somewhat exaggerated. Comedy generally depicts a sane human being in a crazy world, or a crazy human being in a sane world. The humor comes from the juxtaposition of opposites. Certain types of characters and dialogue suit each genre.

Log Line

A log line summarizes the story's content in two or three sentences and may be used not only to condense, but also to expand a reader's view of a script. The antagonist and protagonist should be mentioned along with highlights which summarize the story's beginning, middle, and end. In a creative log line, the highlights are well chosen and their description well phrased, to show the script to its best advantage. In adaptation or revision, the simplicity of a log line may guide the complexity of a script.

Ending

The ending dictates the direction of the film. Its function resembles that of logic in a poem. A poem must make sense and come to some conclusion. The best choice of words, the most exacting meter, the most imaginative metaphors cannot redeem a poem that doesn't make sense. For a movie to make sense, for all the scenes to lead up to some

157

conclusion, a script must have a logical ending. In fact, it helps to know the ending before beginning to write, for the ending assigns final meaning to every event which precedes it. Writing a script with foreknowledge of the ending allows the writer to create a sense of intentionality, a sense of fate.

FORM

Theme, genre, log line, and ending manifest themselves throughout a script. They may be tracked via the script's form. A script's form works in somewhat the same manner as a poem's form. **Form shapes the content.** In a poem, it dictates the placement of details through rhyme scheme, meter, and stanza structure.

For the purpose of discussion, consider the form of a sonnet. In the Elizabethan sonnet each line consists of iambic pentameter, ten syllables alternating strong and weak stress. The sixteen lines group into four stanzas. The first three stanzas, which are quatrains, consist of four lines each; the last stanza, a couplet, consists of two. The rhyme scheme focuses on the last syllable of each line. In each quatrain, the first and third lines rhyme and the second and fourth lines rhyme. The couplet rhymes as well.

Just as the parts of poetic form work together, the parts of a script also intertwine. **The original form for drama was prescribed by Aristotle. He defined unities — time, place, and action — which provided a structure** for the play. The drama was limited to a period of less than twenty-four hours and to a single setting. Aristotle's unities translate into the modern-day concept of story structure.

STORY STRUCTURE

Story structure governs the action of a film. Here another analogy may be of use. In a sense, a movie script is a potential voyage, a trip for the imagination, a vacation. If the details of the story comprise the scenery, then the central elements of story structure become the main sights. The elements of story structure can be divided into foreground and background. **Foreground elements** are obviously and immediately significant; their importance communicates itself at a single glance. They **include: hook, inciting incident, protagonist's plan, antagonist's plan, story points, climax, and resolution. Background elements** may be equally significant, but their significance develops for the audience over time, often through several incidents. Examples of background **include back story, links, and clock.**

FOREGROUND ELEMENTS

Hook

The hook acts as a signpost which **demarcates the beginning of the film.** It engages the audience's attention and interest.

Inciting Incident

The inciting incident is the very first event that gets the story going. It unsettles the status quo and **propels the character into pursuing a specific goal.** The initial event must be strong enough to push the story through to its conclusion. For the writer, the inciting incident foretells the climax or vice-versa, the climax foretells the inciting incident. Loss, for instance, is followed by recovery. Heartbreak is recouped by love. Wrongdoing receives punishment. Imprisonment warrants freedom. And the list of inciting incidents and climaxes goes on.

Protagonist's and Antagonist's Plans

The entire story affects the characters, but **the protagonist's plan and the antagonist's plan directly join the action of the plot with the formation of the main characters' identities.** The protagonist's and antagonist's plans, established early in the second act, involve everything the main characters say, feel, think, or do that influences what follows. **The plans work best when they involve several steps and allow for several obstacles** to face both protagonist and antagonist.

Story (Plot) Points

The main sights along the way to the climax are called plot points. Assuming that the script may be divided into three acts, the writer will optimally place the first plot point at the conclusion of the first act. The purpose of the first plot point, **Story Point A, is to present the protagonist's initial problem, the first obstacle to the desired goal.** In the second act, **Story Points B and C occur. Story Point B, the mid-plot point, presents a compounding problem which forces the protagonist to fight harder** in order to achieve the desired goal, while **Story Point C presents the ultimate complication.** Story Point C catapults the protagonist toward the climax, and is the last significant twist in the main plot.

In some sense a story point, or plot point, is simply a scaled down version of the climax. At a story point, the current situation changes. The action intensifies. Certain plot elements resolve and certain questions find answers. A sense of irresolution, however, continues until the climax is reached.

Climax

The best place to begin with plot, contrary to expectation, is near the end. The question to ask is this: What will be the climax of the script? There are three things to keep in mind as that question is answered. First, consider the desired ending, the genre, and the theme. Second, keep in mind that the climax readies the plot for resolution. Finally, remember that in order to optimally satisfy the audience, **the climax should have a higher energy level than any other moment.**

Inciting incident, story points, and climax are the greatest points of change. Circumstances and status quo shift around each of these actions. Once the intensity of the climax is known, other elements in the story structure can be modulated, presented in optimal order, and from the best possible perspective, in order to generate a build-up to the climax. Again, think of the analogy of a vacation. The writer is the tour guide. A perceptive tour guide will save the best sights for last.

Resolution/Balance

Resolution, the final element of story structure, **marks the end of a movie** and releases the audience's attention. It offers a certain finality which reassures the viewer. The protagonist is at a "new" level of balance. The hook and the resolution frame the story in a visual manner.

SUBPLOTS

The elements of story structure apply not only to the main plot but also to the subplots. Subplots have a shorter lifespan than main plots. They are of greatest significance in the second act where they sustain audience interest as the main plot develops. While subplots can start anywhere and end anywhere, they should merge and resolve with the main plot if they are of major significance. Finally, **subplots must have a beginning, middle and end to fully serve their purpose — developing the theme, the main story, and/or the characters.** An unfinished subplot detracts from a strong ending, a complete one provides support.

STORY STRUCTURE — ORDERING OF EVENTS
(See Story Structure chart on page 163.)

BACK STORY — The background of the characters and the situation up to the beginning of the script (to be revealed throughout the story).

HOOK	Visual event/information that secures one's attention and curiosity. [For the audience.]
INCITING INCIDENT	An event that impels the character into pursuing a specific goal.
CHAIN OF CONFLICT	Protagonist/Antagonist plans. Plotting is what the characters do, feel, think, or say that makes a difference to what comes afterwards.
STORY (PLOT) POINTS	Major events that create a change of direction in the story. They are turning points.
Story (Plot) Point A	Initial problem (what is at stake?).
Story (Plot) Point B	Compounding problem (what/who is forcing the protagonist to fight harder?).
Story (Plot) Point C	Ultimate complication.
CLOCK	Protagonist is faced with time limitations to reach final goal. Urgency to solve problem.
LINKS	Action points that give momentum and intensity to the story.
CLIMAX	The highest point of crisis or confrontation after which the conflict is over.
RESOLUTION	Should be a payoff of the initial problem.
BALANCE	Protagonist is at a "new" level of balance.

STORY STRUCTURE — ORDERING OF EVENTS

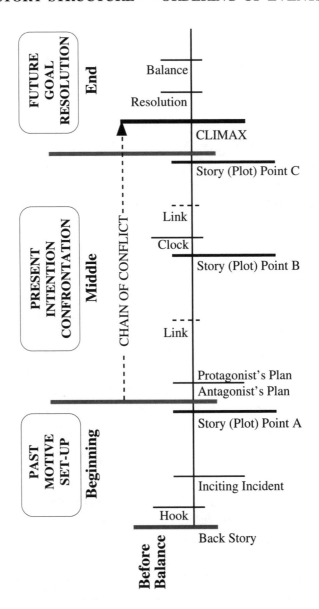

BACKGROUND ELEMENTS

Back story, links, and clock provide a setting against which the elements in the foreground (hook, inciting incident, protagonist's plan, antagonist's plan, story points, climax, and resolution) stand out.

Back Story

Back story may be a familiar term. It **consists of the sum of all events occurring before the beginning of the movie.** It concerns every single thing which has happened in the world of the film before the audience begins watching. Back story information is revealed throughout the movie as pieces of the past become relevant to the present.

Links

Links are another element of the script's scenic background. **Links involve details or actions that reappear during the movie and help move the story along.** The significance of the link reveals itself as the movie progresses. The function of the link is to provide unity; it may help to connect scenes together. Often links operate as extended visual metaphors or symbols. They can refer to past plot or character changes, and can foreshadow upcoming events.

Clock

The third element in the script's background is the **clock. This is another word for a time limit.** The clock may be introduced at any point. It indicates an upcoming end to the action, to the plot, to the movie. Once the clock starts ticking, the audience has been forewarned that at some point in the future they will encounter a resolution. The clock heightens the audience's interest by playing on a sense of anticipation. It offers an effective way of building toward a climax, but it necessitates an eventual payoff. At some point the clock must stop.

CHARACTER
(See Character Structure & Arc charts on pages 167, 168, 169.)

In addition to charting the development of the action, charting the development of the characters assists both in the adaptation of books to film and in script revision. While there are tangible components to a character's development, the concept of a character's evolution is more nebulous than the concept of a story's evolution. Dividing character growth into external and internal components simplifies the analysis. In a well-written script, the story structure intertwines with two other progressions, the character structure and the character arc. **Character structure deals with the external, while character arc concerns the internal. Character structure affects others, character arc affects the self.**

Character Structure

Character structure depicts outer change. It involves the given character's goal, his or her final external objective. **External change points delineate the character's path toward the goal.** They happen after story points (significant shifts in action) and/or after internal change points (significant shifts in emotion).

Character Arc

Character arc charts the internal change points. The overall progression of internal change is guided by the theme and motivated by the character's desire, an internal commitment and/or obsession that moves the character toward a goal. Because events precipitate human change, internal change points, like external ones, follow story points. Internal human changes, however, do not necessarily manifest externally. Changes in personality or emotion may not always be immediately evident, since human memory is capable of combining past, present, and future. Cause may be removed from effect.

Character Change Points

Consequently, a common problem in screenwriting is depicting character changes in a timely and credible fashion. Showing character change through visuals rather than through dialogue helps solve the problem. By developing character in tandem with story structure, the writer guarantees the visual evolution of characters. The action unfolds the characters' natures and reveals their conflicts. A typical scenario moves the protagonist from a low level of awareness to a high one. Consciousness increases with each story point. **The action at the story point leads to a revelation (new information). That leads to an internal change, which, in turn, leads to a character's reaction, an external change.** The pattern of character change need not apply to the climax. Around the climax, the level of consciousness may waver, dipping briefly to enhance the last rise. A high level of awareness typifies the subsequent resolution and balance, balance describing the protagonist's newfound internal and/or external equilibrium.

On the following pages, we provide charts to help you visualize both character structure and character arc.

On page 169, the main arc represents the changes that Richard Gere's character goes through in the movie *Pretty Woman*. At the beginning, Richard's character is at a low level of consciousness. All he cares about is himself and his business and all he wants is an "armpiece" that he can use for whatever and whenever. By mid-point as the story unfolds, Richard's character begins falling in love with Julia Roberts' character to the point that Richard cancels important meetings with his business associates, which is totally out of character. By the end of Act II, Richard is totally in love and he's at a higher level of consciousness. However, when the time comes for him to choose between saying good-bye or taking Julia, he descends to a lower level of consciousness and returns to his old self. To follow the right pattern of change for a character arc, Gere's character changes his mind and sends the limo driver to pick up Julia, completing his arc and achieving a higher level of consciousness, and of course, thrilling the audience.

CHARACTER CHANGE

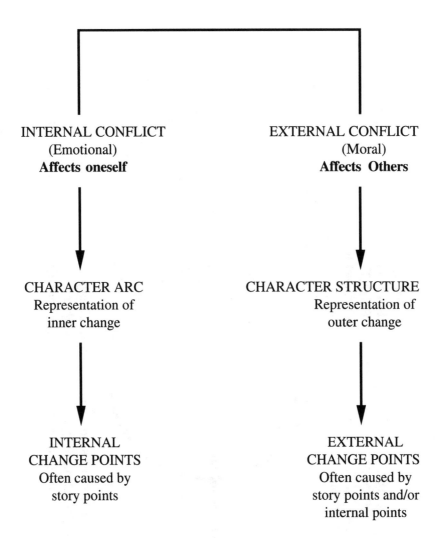

INTERNAL CONFLICT	EXTERNAL CONFLICT
(Emotional)	(Moral)
Affects oneself	**Affects Others**

CHARACTER ARC	CHARACTER STRUCTURE
Representation of	Representation of
inner change	outer change

INTERNAL	EXTERNAL
CHANGE POINTS	CHANGE POINTS
Often caused by	Often caused by
story points	story points and/or
	internal points

Note: Character change is strongest when shown visually instead of through dialogue.

PATTERN OF CHARACTER CHANGE

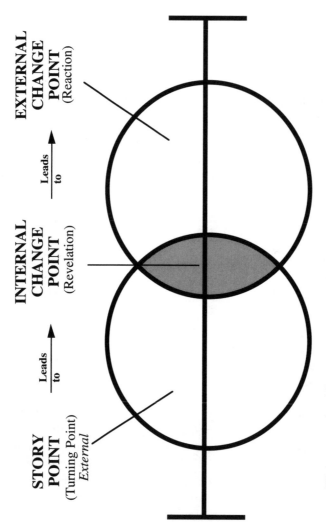

EXTERNAL CHANGE POINT (Reaction)

Leads to

INTERNAL CHANGE POINT (Revelation)

Leads to

STORY POINT (Turning Point) *External*

- The most significant character changes result from major action points.
- Reaction results from internal change.
- The pattern of character change sometimes does not apply to the climax.

© De Abreu & Associates

CHARACTER ARC GUIDELINES EXAMPLE

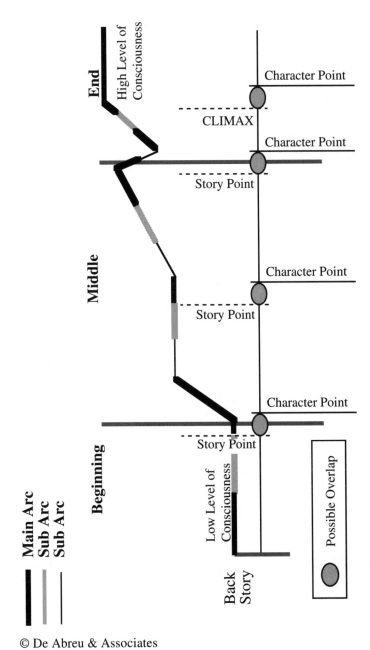

Main Arc
Sub Arc
Sub Arc

End
High Level of Consciousness

Character Point

CLIMAX

Character Point

Story Point

Middle

Character Point

Story Point

Character Point

Story Point

Beginning

Low Level of Consciousness

Back Story

Possible Overlap

• A Character Arc is created by the theme.
• A Character Point is a specific internal (only) change of emotion(s) that leads to an external reaction.
[The Main Arc represents Richard Gere's character in the movie *Pretty Woman*.]

© De Abreu & Associates

SUMMARY

What makes a story interesting is creativity, what makes it believable is form. A believable story is one that the audience can understand and relate to. It is a story that communicates. In classic Greek drama, the unities prescribed by Aristotle — unities of time, place, and action — worked to create verisimilitude, the illusion of reality. In film, story structure is an extension of Aristotle's unities. It is one key to creating an understandable script and a believable film.

The other key is character. It is human nature that people compare themselves to one another, and as a result, they compare themselves to the characters on screen. If a story is viewed as a model of human behavior, then the most effective story will contain familiar characters. In the oldest stories told, familiar character types combine with familiar story structures. Fairy-tale romances, tragic epics, heroic adventures — these are the stories that audiences recognize. **The challenge lies in using the familiar structures to create an inventive story.**

If the audience is familiar with a form, it will recognize intelligent deviations. **Then, as much can be gained from consciously defying a regular form as can be gained from following it.** Returning to the example of poetry, consider free verse in comparison to the sonnet. The sonnet is a well-established form with a specific structure. The free verse poem, on the other hand, contains an infinitely flexible form defined by the poem's content and natural intonation. The lines consist of varying lengths. The rhymes occur irregularly. Each free verse poem has a different structure.

Why bring up such anomalous types of poetic structure? Contemplate the notion of a free verse poem which mimics a sonnet. By drawing on an old structure to create a new one, the free verse poem has doubled its resources. It can draw from two vastly different intellectual landscapes to communicate its message. It would be as if one spectator standing on a mountain might, in a single instant, peruse both jungle and desert; a wealth of images and comparisons would present themselves. Like free verse, **a film may communicate by simultaneously building upon and destroying a familiar form.**

170

The real key then is not form itself, but how form is used. **Once understood, form is not a limitation, it is the framework for a house. It is something to build on, something to challenge individual creativity.** A successful writer is not only one who can give form to a brilliant idea, but also one who can create a brilliant form.

STORY BREAKDOWN — *GHOST*

We recommend that you rent the videotape of the movie *Ghost* before you go through this story breakdown. Seeing the movie will help you immensely to understand our development/rewriting strategies.

Theme

In one word or one sentence, express the underlying "universal" theme this script dramatizes. Why is this an important subject of philosophical, social, or political thought (i.e., love conquers all)?

Overcoming fear to live and love (fear of betrayal, success, failure, love, life, death), love conquers all, even death. (Eternal love.)

Genre

What is the genre and is it the best genre to support the theme, premise, and the story?

Ghost is an amazing mix of genres: Romance, comedy, drama, thriller, mystery, supernatural, action. The complexity of the genre mix works surprisingly well to support the complexity of the theme and story.

Log Line

Do we have a clear two- to three-sentence description of the story (TV Guide-type one-liners)?

After being killed for money by his best friend, a Wall Street broker has to overcome being a ghost to save the life of and prove his love for the woman he's left behind.

Story

Is the story rich enough and innovative enough for a movie?

Yes. The story is extremely rich and complex. While the ghost angle has been done many times before, the uniqueness of the execution of this genre makes the story feel fresh.

Is the story focused, with clear-cut cause and effect?

No. The story sometimes lacks focus, especially in the first act. While a cause and effect exists, we as audience have no idea what that is. Carl is taking actions (using MAC code to set up the money laundering, hiring Willy to get the book, etc.) which set the story in motion, but we're not clued in to that.

Are the characters the right characters to support the story?

Yes. The characters are good choices to support the story.

Does the story support the premise and theme?

Yes. The story supports the premise and theme.

Is the story big enough (or too big) for a full screenplay/script?

The story basically works because of the skill with which it's handled, but at times, the story feels a little too big for the movie.

Why will an audience respond to this story?

Many different types of audiences will respond to this story — because of the desire or need many of us have to believe in life after death and eternal love. It has humor, romance, action and special effects.

STORY STRUCTURE

Beginning, Act One

Back Story Relationship

What is the background of our characters and the situation up to the beginning of our story?

In the opening scenes where Sam, Mollie, and Carl break down the wall, we learn: Mollie and Sam are a couple moving into a new place, possibly living together for the first time. Carl is a good friend of them both. In the scene where Carl and Sam go to the office, we learn that Carl is materialistic and greedy, and that Sam has fear about his new account/presentation.

Hook
(Visual event/information that secures one's attention and curiosity.)
[For the audience.]

Does the opening scene(s) capture your attention and propel interest in the story to follow?

The hook is weak. Is it the under-credit sequence in the attic? This is a mysterious and intriguing opening, yet it doesn't grab the audience in any significant way. Is it the scene when Sam, Mollie, and Carl break down the wall? This shows the conflict of going from a known world into an unknown world. Yet neither is strong.

Inciting Incident
(An event that impels the character into pursuing a specific goal.)

Is the inciting incident big enough to force the protagonist to stop or fight to maintain his or her usual life?

Subplot (money) — Sam gives Carl his MAC code because money needs to be transferred (eight minutes into the movie). This action starts the story. Yet, notice how we as audience have no idea that this event is significant. Because we're not yet clued into the story, this action by Sam and Carl has little or no meaning.

Main Plot (romance) — Sam getting killed (twenty-one minutes in) is the inciting incident, because this is the first event that seemingly starts the movie. Also notice how the inciting incident of the subplot caused the inciting incident of the main plot.

Story Point (A)
(A major event that creates a change of direction in the story/initial problem. What is at stake?)

Does the question and/or problem that ends Act One require seventy-five to one hundred pages to play out?

Subplot (money) — After sorting through Sam's possessions, Carl tries to leave with the box containing the address book with the MAC code, but Mollie keeps the box. This forces Carl to take further action to get the MAC code.

Main Plot (romance) — Willy enters the apartment to look for the address book, and Mollie reenters. Willy is a threat to Mollie, and Sam realizes that something strange is going on. When Sam jumps through the door to follow Willy, he's jumping into Act Two.

STORY STRUCTURE
Middle, Act Two

Protagonist's Plan

Does the protagonist's course of action/plan require several steps which can encounter obstacles? What is at stake? Is it important enough?

Now that Willy has alerted Sam that something is going on, Sam has a plan: to find out what is happening and to protect Mollie. Mollie's safety is at stake.

Antagonist's Plan

Does the antagonist's plan present some of those obstacles?

Carl has a plan — to get the address book with the MAC code, then resolve the money laundering situation. The way the story is structured, though, we as audience aren't aware of his plan until much later in the script.

Protagonist's Confidant(e)/Friend

Does he/she complement or contrast the protagonist in a character-revealing fashion?

Oda Mae is Sam's confidante. She is a strong and effective contrast to Sam.

Antagonist's Confidant(e)/Friend

Does he/she raise the question of whose side he/she is really on? Do they add tension because of their rivalry with the antagonist, and thereby make a potential ally to the protagonist?

Willy is Carl's confidant. He is a purely functional character, a hit-man.

First Link

Is the link clearly set up?

The pennies. Sam and Mollie discover an Indian head penny in the attic in the opening scenes.

The cat. In the scene where Mollie, at the potter's wheel, talks out loud to Sam, the cat senses Sam and gets scared.

Control of actions. Sam, when on the subway, is thrown off the subway by another ghost, who then uses his power to break the glass window, showing a ghost can move things in the real world.

Second Link

Does the link continue to give momentum to the story?

The pennies. After Sam's death, Mollie lets the jar with the Indian head penny roll down the stairs, shattering, showing her loss of faith.

The cat. When Willy is in the apartment, Sam scares the cat into jumping at Willy, scratching his face.

Control of actions. When Carl makes a pass at Mollie, Sam gets so angry that he moves the picture off the table.

Third Link

Does the link payoff have impact?

The pennies. To prove to Mollie that he's real, Sam uses a penny, sliding it up the door and into Mollie's hand. She has regained her faith.

Control of actions. Sam returns to the subway, and learns how to channel his power into moving things, which he continues to use to link the entire third act to the rest of the script.

Mid-Story Point (B)
(Compounding problem.)

Does the protagonist's problem require a higher level of commitment due to higher stakes?

Subplot (money) — Mollie tells Carl she knows that a man named Willy is behind Sam's murder, alerting Carl that he needs to adjust his plan of action.

Main Plot (romance) — Sam, following Carl to Willy's place, discovers that Carl is behind his murder. Notice again how the mid-point of the subplot causes the mid-point of the main plot.

Clock

Is the story structured in such a way that we have a race against time for the protagonist to achieve his/her goal?

Subplot (money) — Carl makes a telephone call where he's instructed to deposit the money into Rita Miller's account and then withdraw it at 3:55 p.m. the next day. So, by 3:55, the money subplot will climax.

Main Plot (romance) — In Mollie's kitchen, Carl tells Sam that unless he gets the check back by 11:00 that evening, he'll return and kill Mollie. Now, Sam has only until 11:00 to save Mollie.

177

Story Point (C) • Kicking off Act Three
(Ultimate complication.)

Is the protagonist (and the possible antagonist) driven to go to an even higher level to accomplish the goal?

Subplot (money) — Carl discovers that the money is not in the account.

Main Plot (romance) — Carl threatens to kill Mollie if he doesn't get the check back. Again, the Story Point C of the subplot causes the Story Point C of the main plot.

STORY STRUCTURE
End, Act Three

Climax • Self-Understanding
(Moral/psychological.)

Is this the highest point of crisis and confrontation?

There are multiple climaxes which keep building, each stronger, until the final climax where Carl is killed by the broken window shard. Once Carl is killed, the money situation is resolved, the threat to Mollie and Oda Mae is over, and Sam can then leave the earthly world.

Resolution

Is the resolution visual/non-dialogue and a payoff to the opening scene(s)?

Sam and Mollie reaffirm their love for each other and "say" good-bye. Notice how this scene is almost completely non-verbal. Also, notice how the resolution is parallel to the opening scene — they both take place in an attic.

Balance

Is our protagonist leading a "new" level of balance?

Sam has moved on to a higher level of existence, entering heaven. Mollie, too, is at a higher level, now believing in the spiritual side.

SUBPLOT(S)

Structure

Do all the subplots have a beginning, middle, and end? (If they do not, they are not a subplot, but a complication.)

Subplot A (money) is extremely well-developed, almost as much as the main plot. **Subplot B** is Oda Mae's story of growing from being a fraud medium to a true-blue psychic.

Development

Does the subplot help develop the story, theme, or character?

Notice how the **Subplot A (money)** is integrally related to the **Main Plot (romance)**. In fact, the main plot could not function without it. Also notice how **Subplot B (Oda Mae)** is entwined with the main plot.

Resolution

Do the subplot(s) relate to the main story point, intersecting in the final act?

Notice how **Subplot A** is resolved almost simultaneously with the **Main Plot**.

CHARACTER

Protagonist's Goal • Final Objective

Is the protagonist's final objective defined? Is there only one from beginning to end? Is the protagonist's external desire a committed, obsessive drive?

Sam's objective is clearly defined, although he develops more than one single goal. Along the way, Sam decides that seeking revenge on Carl is something he's going to do, not only save Mollie.

Yes, Sam is completely committed to saving Mollie.

Protagonist's External Conflict
(Affects others.)

Is the protagonist's external problem interesting and complex, and will it allow the inner conflict to surface?

Sam's external problem is interesting and exciting — how to be dead and operate in the land of the living to save Mollie.

Protagonist's Internal Conflict
(Affects oneself.)

Is the protagonist's inner conflict illustrated through action?

Yes, Sam's inner problem is to learn how to express his love for Mollie and overcome his fear of living (and dying).

Protagonist's Friend

Is he/she similar to the main character without having the same moral need, or does he/she contrast with the main character yet have a similar moral need?

180

Sam and Oda Mae are completely different characters. Yet, they have the same external drive. Once Sam enlists Oda Mae, they are both trying to save Mollie, and later he saves both Mollie and Oda Mae.

Antagonist's Goal

Is the goal in conflict with the protagonist's goal?

Carl's external goal is to get the MAC code which will give him access to the money in the computer system. However, because of the way the plot and subplots interact, Carl's obtaining the money comes in conflict with Sam saving Mollie.

Antagonist's Desire

Is it clear and does it sufficiently directly oppose that of the protagonist?

Once Carl is revealed to be the antagonist, his desire is immediately clear. He acts from greed.

Antagonist's Friend

Are they motivated to remain with the antagonist for personal gain?

Willy is purely motivated by the money he is getting from Carl.

CHARACTER ARC

Character Back Story

Sam is living in his fear. He's scared to tell Mollie he loves her. He's scared about his meeting with the Japanese businessmen. He's scared about dying when he sees the plane crash on TV. He's scared of betrayal. He's scared his life is too good and something will go wrong.

181

Once he's a ghost, he's scared of being dead. He's scared of going through walls.

Character Change Point (Caused by Story Point A)

Does the character see the problem, and does he/she take a step forward to change it? Is it an unconscious or conscious choice?

Willy comes to the apartment to search for the address book and Mollie reenters. When Willy leaves the apartment, Sam overcomes his fear for the first time and bursts through the wall. Notice how an action point caused the character change point, and how the character change was presented visually.

Character Change Point (Caused by Story Point B)

Does the character start to see the effects of his/her problem and the value of change?

Sam follows Carl to Willy's apartment and discovers that Carl's greed is responsible for his death. This revelation creates a major emotional upheaval which transforms Sam's internal and external drive. His expression tells it all — Sam is disgusted, shocked, and horrified at the betrayal. An immediate reaction occurs when Sam tries to punch Carl as he enters the car (his fears have been confirmed).

Character Change Point (Caused by Story Point C)

Does the character decide it is not worth what it takes to change, and revert back to old behavior instead?

Between Story Point C and the reaction, there's no character change because there's no revelation. Because Sam is a purely good character he doesn't revert, because that would contradict his goodness. Because the story point is a continuance of Carl's evil, Sam does not need to

182

change. However, now the change occurs in the antagonist, Carl. Mollie reveals that Oda Mae has or had the money. Carl is extraordinarily upset and desperate. His reaction is to threaten Mollie's life, something he would never have considered before.

Character Change Point (Caused by Climax)

Does the character decide to change to achieve goal? Is it a conscious choice?

After Carl has been killed, Sam has completed his arc. He's moved through his fear. He's able to completely express his love for Mollie and lets go of his fear of death.

Characteristic of Change Points

Is change visual, that is, not told by others or through dialogue or exposition?

The character change is almost always portrayed visually, supported by the dialogue instead of defined by the dialogue.

DIALOGUE

Does it sound like people talking, not moralizing or joke-driven?

The dialogue is almost always believable. Yet in the final moments of the script, Sam's dialogue about taking the love inside with him is quite heavy-handed.

Is it character appropriate (i.e., no inappropriate witticism)?

The dialogue is for the most part appropriate to the characters.

Do characters have distinct, different voices from each other?

The voices of the characters are distinct and varied.

Is there an emotional subtext supporting each line?

Not all, but much of the dialogue has emotional subtext.

BUDGET

Is it economically feasible?

The official final budget apparently was around $26 million, a moderate budget for a studio picture.

Can we tell the same story, even though we may have to change some of the settings?

Yes. While New York is the perfect setting for the script, if necessary, the location could be changed to another city without sacrificing the story.

ELEMENTS

Casting

For the most part, the casting was effective. Perhaps Patrick Swayze was not believable as a Wall Street broker. Yet by casting against type, Sam became a fish out of water — a likable, very human guy who was somewhat out of place in the cold machinations of Wall Street. This casting choice helped to align the audience with Sam.

Director

Jerry Zucker was a solid directorial element. His ability to handle the diversity of genres while maintaining a strong emotional core for the movie was integral to its success.

Note: For information on script consultants, see Chapter 24.

184

Chapter 9.

Feature and Television Development

FEATURE DEVELOPMENT

In this chapter we will give you an overview of how the development process works. We will start with the feature process and later we will tackle television.

The development process is often referred to as "development hell." Every year, between twelve and fifteen thousand projects are in active development. However, yearly only about three hundred of those films get released by the majors, two hundred by independents, and another five hundred are never released theatrically. Still, as we told you, five hundred million dollars are invested in this process annually.

There are plenty of different ways that companies operate. According to Linda Seger, there are standard steps that most studios follow:

The first thing you should do when a buyer says, "We want it," is to get an agent or find an entertainment attorney. Most agents will be happy to negotiate a deal to earn their 10 percent. That agent can then help you turn this success into another.

After the deal is cut, the next step will be a "notes" session. The initial meeting may be about an hour or two. The participants will include the vice-president of the company, the creative director, and the producer, if there's a separate producer. There may be an assistant as well.

The development notes might be only a couple of pages and very generalized. Some may make sense to you and others may be awful. Expect a broad range of suggestions from, "Fix the second act to make it funnier," or, "On page 5 I think you have a typo," to, "Let's change the male to a female," or, "Let's set it in Beverly Hills instead of Detroit."

You may not like their notes, or you might think they're brilliant. And that's where the work begins.

You go home after that meeting with verbal and written notes, and begin to rewrite the script. The time it takes can vary and is normally specified in the contract. When finished, you send it back. Some executives will read it immediately; others may not get to it right away. So, you wait to get your second set of notes. At that point, you'll rewrite again. They may even take you off the project. If you're a new writer, they might bring another writer in. Don't be discouraged by this. It is very common, even for more experienced writers. What matters is that you've sold your first script. This will give you more clout the next time around.

With one of our Christopher Columbus Screenplay Discovery Awards scripts we were able to convince a studio to keep the original writer for two rewrites, but after that they decided to hire a seasoned writer to take over. Still, the new writer made over fifty thousand dollars. Not too bad.

According to Linda Seger, the buyers are often thinking of casting as soon as they see the script. One reason they may be interested is because they can figure out exactly who should be in it. For example, if it's at the studio, they might say, "Well, we have a deal with Bette Midler, we have to do two movies a year with her. This is perfect for her." Or they might have done their last movie with Tommy Lee Jones and say, "Gee, Tommy said to me, 'I want to work with you again.' "

Also, they may not even send the script around until it's rewritten and they're completely satisfied with it. An average number of rewrites is between three and five, but there are a lot of scripts that have had more. *Cape Fear* reportedly holds the record with twenty-three drafts. *Rhinestone* supposedly had seventeen drafts.

Writers are usually off the film when it starts shooting. Once in a rare while a writer might be brought onto the set if there are still things to be fixed.

During the filming of *The Fugitive,* the writer was on the set because they were writing as they were going. Most of the time they're not. Usually writers are allowed to be on the set, but most find it so boring they don't want to be.

You have to take every step of the process seriously, starting with the script. You have to recognize that if you don't have a script you have nothing. If you do not have a good script, you will not have a great movie. You must not have the attitude of, "They will fix it in the development process," or, "I'm sure the director/editor can make that work."

You must take everything in your script seriously. Examine your story and your theme. Make sure everything works. If you have a really good script to start with, they will not be able to do as much to ruin it because they'll realize as soon as they change one part the whole script falls apart.

Many people say, "Well, I don't have money to have someone help me with the script." That's the one place to put your money, in the script. Do not be penny wise and pound foolish. There are a lot of people who say, "Well, it's just a little independent film. Is it that important?" The answer is, absolutely.

When Linda worked on independent films, she saw how a small independent film made a career. They can make somebody. She's told people, "If you're doing a six-minute or a thirty-minute film, make sure that the script is terrific."

She recently consulted on a six-minute film. The producer was trying to break into the business through this little film. She had the attitude that "we're going to shoot this little thing." Linda said, "It's not a little thing. This is your opportunity. You must take this seriously."

And she thought about it. Linda consulted with her on the script to make it as good as it could be. She hired a directing consultant to make her directing as good as it could be and because she wants to be a producer, Linda told her, "Get your name as a producer on this." And she said, "Well someone else is the producer." Linda said, "Then you get your name as a co-producer, associate producer, executive producer. Get a producing credit on that six-minute film because that might be your way in. Don't say it's not important because it's only six minutes. What if it wins awards at film festivals and everyone's begging to know what else you have?"

TELEVISION DEVELOPMENT

If you were to consider "on-air" programs at the network as a string of freight cars carrying twenty-two hours of programming, then the development departments would be the locomotives that drive the train.

The reason is simple. With formerly three and now four networks competing head-to-head every hour of every night, there will always be one show that wins its ratings time slot and three that fail. As Ann Daniel, former senior vice-president of series development at ABC-TV, frequently pointed out, three-fourths of the prime-time schedule is filled with losers.

With advertisers paying top dollar for the opportunity to sponsor shows, there is a ceaseless battle for ratings. High ratings mean high revenues, poor ratings lead to weak revenues and eventual cancellation.

On average the networks replace nearly half their schedule every year. Two-thirds of the new shows appear each fall, with another third appearing somewhere during the mid-season, usually January through March.

Executives at the networks live and die by the success of their shows. When one fails, they must be ready with another to throw into the battlefield.

The result is a heavy emphasis on development and the endless search for the next hit show, or the next show that can at least deliver solid ratings, even if it doesn't always win its time slot.

In all fairness, a strong second-place finish rarely leads to a cancellation. Even against a blockbuster like *The Cosby Show* in the eighties, or *Roseanne* in the nineties, networks must program something and they do. The usual tactic is counter-programming, which we'll discuss later.

As we noted above, networks have somewhere between one hundred and two hundred new shows in development at any time. Only a half-dozen or fewer of those will make it on air and last a full season.

The odds are terrifying, the cost astronomical, and the risks to careers are enormous.

And logically one might ask, What exactly is development? Later on we'll give a detailed examination of each phase, including who the key players are and what the development cycles are.

❧ **Development at all the networks and, for that matter, at most major studios is divided into three departments: Drama, Comedy, and Movie of the Week.**

As noted, the forms are very different in conception and execution. Drama, again, focuses primarily on one-hour formats, Comedy on half-hour sitcom formats, and MOWs on two-hour blocks.

Long Form Development (Movies Made for Television)

In addition to programming comedies and dramas, the networks usually devote anywhere from four to six hours per week to regularly scheduled movies of the week and miniseries.

MOWs (movies of the week) tend to run in two-hour blocks, minis, in this day and age of economy, are usually four to six hours long. Once in a rare while a mini may jump to eight, ten, or twelve hours.

With each network airing anywhere from twenty to fifty original movies each year, development of these scripts is constant and intense. Usually the development ratio of scripts produced and aired to those developed and written is only 2.5 to one or 3 to one.

The long form departments are constantly supervising anywhere from 60 to 150 movie scripts.

Next we're going to describe the typical process a writer or new producer goes through in development. The guidelines we describe apply most to MOW development, but keep in mind that most of the advice we give also applies to the development of feature screenplays. Although some of the specifics vary, the same basic situations will occur. Let's assume that the studio or network bought your project.

THE DEVELOPMENT PROCESS

The Story Meeting

Your next encounter with the studio or the network will be at a story meeting. Granted everybody and their brother has already added their two cents to your original creation by this point, but now it's the studio or network's turn. After all, they're the ones footing the bill, and they have a fairly specific idea of what they want.

The good news is that as soon as you start working on the story, you're going to get your first check, according to WGA rules. Enjoy it, but don't spend it all at once. And never assume that just because you've gotten one project sold, all the rest of the ones in your file are going to be sold as well.

Never forget you've entered the domain of the self-employed freelancer. You'll get paid handsomely for what you sell, but you'll never have the weekly security of a paycheck again unless you end up on a show's staff or on a development deal — and even those are subject to major upheavals every season.

Before the big 6.8 earthquake in January 1994, Tom Towler (*Lonesome Dove: The Series*) used to joke that the life of a producer or writer in Hollywood is akin to living on an earthquake fault line. Everything looks great when you're working, but you never know or have advance warning of when a disaster may strike.

So, be as prepared as possible and don't squander your savings.

190

There may come a day, as it comes to some players in this town, when you may need them. However, think positive and hopefully you will just move forward without any setbacks.

Most writers we have worked with would concur with the following advice: ☜ **At this stage of your career listen carefully to what the network or studio says.**

When you're more established and financially secure, you'll have a better ability to modify their suggestions the way you sense they should be altered, but for now, just go along for the ride.

Remember, they are your employers and the question of whether or not your movie ends up being made is in their hands. Give them what they want and respect their opinions.

With you at the meeting will be your producer and studio executive. From now on all of you are married at the hip. Furthermore, you'll probably find that they control all communication with the studio or network.

☜ **Don't try to circumvent them or get into playing any form of office politics. You're too new to play these sorts of political games and emerge unscathed.**

For the time being, do what you do best; be creative and/or write. Suggestions coming from the various executives may not always make sense. Whether they do or not is not the question.

You got to this point because you're a talented writer or a new producer with a hot idea. They got to their positions because they're "players" in the Hollywood game.

☜ **Also, never cross, argue with, or undercut your studio executive or producer, especially in front of anyone else. Play the game with grace.**

Doing this will ultimately put you on the road to writing for a salary or producing your next picture.

Delivering the Story

After the meeting you'll probably huddle with your producer and studio executive to interpret the notes and figure out the best way to incorporate them into your story outline. This is a process that you're going to do repeatedly, so get used to it.

Your creative team will send you home to redraft the outline. You'll submit it to them when you're done, get a few more notes, make a few more changes, and when it's all done, your studio executive will send it to the studio or network executive for approval.

✿ **Never submit anything directly to the studio or network. Always go through your creative team. If you go around them, it will be seen as your being uncooperative, and this substantially reduces your chances of having your project succeed.**

You've just finished a polished version of your story outline. Your producer loves it, the studio loves it, and when you hear back from the network, you discover that they love it, too. Of course, they'll want a few minor changes, but as long as you promise to incorporate them into your first draft, you're free to move on.

Writing the First Draft

Now, we are treating you as if you are a writer, and maybe you are. But if you are not, we still want you to know all about the process. For the first time in months, you'll find yourself back in a realm you're used to (as a writer): sitting at home and writing the teleplay to a story you dreamed up ages ago.

Now is the time to let your creative juices flow without looking over your shoulder. No one is going to be there checking your every word — or are they? Many producers, especially with new writers, feel nervous about the writer's ability to give them what they really want. They may want you to fax over pages or use a modem so they can see what you're doing.

Our recommendation is to dodge them as best you can. Remember what we said earlier. Never show anyone anything but your best, most

192

polished version. Producers and executives are not mindreaders. They don't know what your thinking really is. They're only going to judge you by what's on the paper. If what you show them is rough, you're going to get treated roughly.

Keep in mind, too, that first draft delivery has nothing to do with what you may call your first draft. It may take you fifteen drafts to get it to a point where you think it's worth showing to anyone. If that's what it takes, then do that — provided you do deliver their "first draft" within the approximate time frame called for in the contract.

Know, too, that no one follows those time frames to the letter of the contract — unless there's real trouble, and that's pretty rare. And a quick note on contracts: You may be finished with your MOW and have it on the air before a fully fleshed-out contract is signed. Believe it or not, a lot of Hollywood business is conducted on the basis of a handshake and a one-page deal memo.

Let's go back to the concept of "first draft." And let's be real clear. It does not mean your first draft of a script. From a writer's point of view, it's the last draft, the one version you think accomplishes everything that's been set out in the outline and in note meetings to the very best of your ability.

❧ **Never take the attitude you can fix something in the official second draft. If your official first draft is not good enough, the creative team may lose confidence in your abilities, and you may never get authorization to move onto the next version. And even if you do move on, the loss of confidence may be so great that it dooms the project anyway.**

❧ Most people in Hollywood will tell you with great accuracy that **the only rule of this town is that there are no rules.** And we agree — but not entirely. If there is one rule in this town that you should never forget it's this: **Never present anything less than your best shot.**

Delivering the First Draft

So, you finally have this great polished "first draft," which you want to deliver to the network or the studio if it's a feature. You're ready to

have your producer or the studio tuck it in an envelope and send it out
— but not so fast . . .

And this is where it gets sticky. The producer and the studio
executive will both want to read it first. That's okay, but the odds are
that they're also going to find little flaws here and there that they're
going to want removed or altered before it goes out. Or they may be so
dissatisfied that they'll want a complete rewrite (i.e., a free draft).

But let's assume the draft is finished, you're happy, the producer and
studio are happy. However, they may (and most times they do) give
you more notes.

Getting Notes

Once more you'll return with your team to the studio or the network
offices. When you walk in you'll see one, two, or even three executives
sitting in the room with dog-eared copies of your script. Don't get
alarmed. Yet.

First, with whom do you meet? Usually it's the director of development for that department. This is the executive you sold the project to
in the first place.

Occasionally the vice-president of the department may also sit in.
His/her presence is neither a show of support for nor against your work.
Rather, it's a measure of the status of your creative team. If you walk
in with a major star attached, the VP will be there, if only to say hello.

On the other end of the spectrum will be the manager of development for the department. His/her function is to take notes of the notes
given and to learn the job of the director so that one day he/she can take
over that role.

Trade handshakes, bear hugs, kisses, whatever. When in Rome, do
as the Romans do.

**Again, listen carefully to all of their notes. In the room, be
rapt at attention, relaxed, and trade thoughts in a gentle and non-
confrontational manner.**

Remember that the more executives there are in a room, the more different opinions you may get. Go along with this. Later, in the quiet confidence of your producer's office, you can review the comments and figure out how you can work them into your story.

Rewriting the Second Draft

Rarely is rewriting the second draft as difficult as the first unless the network or studio is totally dissatisfied with what you've come up with. This happens on occasion. They pictured something totally different from what you delivered. Or they promised their boss something totally different from what you tried to deliver.

✒ Don't try to outguess their logic. Frequently it's beyond your knowing.

Just go ahead and rewrite. Try to incorporate their changes without destroying what you've written. However, they know what they want and you're being paid to give it to them.

Creatively you've got to try your best to serve everyone, including yourself. If something really doesn't ring true, you as the writer have the power to convince the executive that his or her idea does not work in this instance. Use diplomacy!

Polish Notes

After you've again delivered the best draft you can, and after your producer and studio have tinkered with it, it'll go back to the studio or network. Months will have passed since you first pitched the idea.

Circumstances change. Staff may have turned over. You may have a new director of development to work with. Or another studio or network will have beaten you to the punch with a similar story. Or the VP may send down notes that change the tone, because stories with that new tone seem to do well. There is no end to the turmoil that may surround your project that in fact has nothing to do with what's on the page.

195

These alterations in the creative landscape, however, are just as real and important, if not more so, than what you wrote. Again, go with the flow.

Listen to the notes. Don't complain. Smile and move ahead. You've gotten this far, so don't blow it.

Polishing the Draft

You'll polish the draft, which in practical terms means doing whatever is necessary to make it just what they want.

Your creative team will review it and now the waiting game begins. Will they pick it up to be shot?

Chapter 10.

Development Deals

There are all kinds of deals, but the most common are the **"housekeeping"** and/or **"first look"** deals. What this means is that the writer, director, or producer will have an office and a secretary. **The studio that they cut the deal with pays for the operating costs.** However, whatever projects they find, they must first introduce to that studio.

Production Companies

There are literally hundreds of independent production companies in Hollywood. They come in all shapes and sizes. Many sustain themselves with occasional feature or TV deals.

Some, such as Academy Entertainment, produce movies primarily to sell to video chains and stores, but will occasionally produce product for HBO, Showtime, or the networks. Others are financed by outsiders trying to break in.

Most independents are built around a team of successful producers, writers, actors, or a management team. Their clout arises out of past relationships, previous winning efforts, and their ability to attract funding and talent.

In features, a good example is Amblin Entertainment, Steven Spielberg's company, and his relationship with Universal Studios. In television, a good example is Steven Bochco's company. Bochco was the driving force behind the success of *Hill Street Blues* and *L.A. Law*. Another good example for TV is Witt-Thomas-Harris, the powers behind *The Golden Girls* and *Empty Nest*.

Powerful independents with strong track records usually have a close relationship with either a studio or network which provides a steady source of financial backing.

These deals shift from time to time as the fortunes of the independents rise and fall along with the studios and networks.

Producer and Development Deals

Next in line are the many freelance producer and writer development and production deals. In order to guarantee a steady supply of quality product to sell to the networks, studios and larger independents frequently cut deals with individual writers, producers, or teams.

Again, these deals are most typically given either to successful individuals with a proven track record or to former studio executives who believe they can branch out successfully on their own.

Deals are typically one to three years in length with various renewable options. In addition to salaries, these deals usually provide for a studio office and staff as well as access to funding for script options or purchases.

In TV a head writer of a hot show such as *Roseanne* or *Seinfeld* might typically be lured to another studio hoping to lock him or her up on an exclusive basis, in the hope that they'll be able to create the next hit show.

At any given time, major studios might have anywhere from ten to thirty such deals with writers, directors, or producers.

Development Deals

As noted above, successful producers and writers are frequently locked up by the studios or larger independents in the hope that they'll find the next *E.T.: The Extra-Terrestrial* or create the next hit series, or the big winner in the MOW or miniseries market.

198

Writers and producers in this category are almost always the ones who have paid their dues and have proven through previous hard work that they're capable of producing a potential hit.

Deals such as this are usually the most sought after in the business, guaranteeing significant financial security, and representing a serious commitment on the part of the studio to assist in their success.

Producers and writers in this realm generally earn in excess of six-figure incomes, with some deals topping a million per year. They're paid to do nothing more than sit and create the next hit.

Although the deal is a dream, the process of being in development is often difficult, tedious, and frustrating. The actual success rate is rather small, and clearly few writers, directors, or producers on such deals meet with success.

For the studios it's a way of hedging their bets. The more creative deals and teams you assemble, the better the chances are that one of them will come up with a monster hit.

For the creative teams, though, such deals are usually a race against time. Can I create, sell, and deliver a winner before the deal is up? It's easy to see that there are few successes and many failures.

In spite of these challenges, the development deal at its best represents one of the few opportunities for creative talent to do what they do best, create new and pure visions. It's an opportunity few ever turn down, and all try to make the most of it.

Chapter 11.

Feature Buyers

*"You must feel passionately about your project and...
submit, submit, submit, submit, submit."*

— **Arthur Hiller,**
Director
(Love Story, Outrageous Fortune)

W e are lucky to be part of the twentieth century. With the world becoming a global community and with technology's advances, the creative machinery more than ever needs projects. As you know, staggering amounts of money are spent yearly, searching for, acquiring, and developing projects.

Your project can be one of those selected to be acquired and to go into development. Of course the odds are against you, but it can happen.

The Christopher Columbus Screenplay Discovery Awards, in the last two years, has been able to sell the screenplays of two of the screenplay winners. The writers signed six-figure deals. Another winner was able to secure two writing assignments which brought him a five-figure deal.

Every other week we see in the trade papers, *The Hollywood Reporter* and *Daily Variety,* announcements of projects being bought:

"....estimated low six-figure sum against a mid-range six-figure...."

"Warner Bros. has purchased the spec script *Body Language* for $350,000 against $600,000 for Steven Spielberg to produce in a deal that closed over the weekend . . . ."

Ideas, manuscripts, books, and screenplays are bought every day in Hollywood, be it by major or minor studios, mainstream or small independent producers.

In this chapter we'll examine who the key buyers are and what types of projects are bought.

Which Studios and Production Companies Buy Original Projects?

Basically all studios and independent producers are looking for original projects. Everybody is in a rush to find that great story: the next *Star Wars, Sleepless in Seattle, The Terminator,* or *Forrest Gump.* They know that their careers will skyrocket or their bank accounts will bulge with cash if they are the ones to find it first.

The buyers are easy to identify. Access to them is where the problem normally lies. In this chapter we will tell you how you can gain direct access to them. But before we reveal that to you, let's go over who has the power to approve deals.

At the top of the studio system you have the president, then the executive vice-presidents, senior vice-presidents, vice-presidents of production and/or creative affairs, creative directors, and creative executives.

In a studio, the person with the power to green-light the making of a picture is normally only the president or chairman. However, vice-presidents can make their own calls and approve buying projects for development deals.

If it is a production company, normally it is the president or owner who has that power.

What all this means is that everybody on the ladder has to sell the projects to the next one up the line.

Feature Projects Bought and Sold

It's difficult to categorize what sells or doesn't sell. Overall it depends on who the buyers are.

As a rule, if it's Disney, you are not going to be able to sell them an erotic thriller. They want family-oriented movies.

If you are trying to sell a project to Robert Redford's production company, you know that the project should have an acting or directing part for him. Also, he likes meaningful projects. However, there are exceptions.

In another chapter we will give you selling strategies that will help you evaluate your approach to buyers.

Every year, we read over two thousand screenplays. It's hard to find a great original premise or concept together with high-quality writing. However, the criteria for buyers of projects may not have anything to do with "a great story" or "quality writing," but who wants what.

🗝 **Jorge Saralegui, vice-president of production at Twentieth Century Fox, feels that "the most important elements in selecting a project are concept, star potential, and story."**

🗝 According to other industry insiders, **those three elements are crucial.** Also, star potential includes directors. **A "hot" director is KEY in the moviemaking game nowadays.**

🗝 **Through the years we discovered that originality is very important.** Great examples of this are *Die Hard, RoboCop*, and *The Terminator*, among others, but really, what they buy is what they believe is going to succeed.

If the buyers make a wrong decision, they will be out the door. They can lose millions of dollars for their companies. It's easier to make no decisions than make ONE BAD DECISION. You might do the same. One needs more than just an original project or great writing. Luck, timing and the marketplace play a significant role.

As an example, last year we found a beautiful screenplay, *Freedom's*

Bride, by a new writer, Robert Blankenhorn. It is the story of the famous female pirate Anne Bonny. We got all excited, contacted a major literary agency and the studios, and made the submissions.

The story department of the literary agency called back saying that they couldn't help — "there are nine other Anne Bonny scripts out there."

The agency had just packaged a deal for producer Jon Peters to produce Anne Bonny's story. They attached writer Michael Cristofer (*The Witches of Eastwick*) to write the screenplay based on the book *Mistress of the Sea*. The point is:

🗝 **It is crucial to know what the buyers need and/or want. What projects do they feel are hot, what projects are the producers and stars with development deals looking for?**

🗝 **A quality project will get you noticed**, regardless. We were able to introduce the writer to an executive at Universal Studios. Other smaller producers have contacted him as well. So good writing and good projects do get recognized.

🗝 We don't want to discourage you. We are **not** saying that you should only find or develop projects that buyers want, because **those requests change constantly**.

🗝 **"Have passion for your project."**

Once again. The more information you have the easier it is to target your buyer.

Chapter 12.

Television Buyers

C onsidering that the development of new projects is the loco-
motive that drives the train, imagine then, the enormous
amount of resources in Hollywood devoted to the pursuit of
the next great hit.

Here we will examine who the key buyers and sellers in the
television development game are, what types of shows are bought for
the prime-time schedule, what the buying and selling seasons are, how
an idea is sold and developed, and why shows are purchased to go on
the air.

Who Produces Shows to Sell to the Buyers?

Television is an ever-changing marketplace defined by the networks
and cable. Consider, for example, that the average network programs
approximately twenty-two hours a week for an average of twenty-two
to twenty-six weeks a year. This translates loosely into between 450
and 575 hours a year. Consider that a significant portion of those hours
is filled by half-hour sitcoms, resulting in a need for perhaps as many
as 630 to 800 or more individual scripts.

➤ **With four major networks now operating, that number
quadruples to between 2,500 and 3,200 individual scripts. Factor
in the new and ever-growing cable channels that are in need of
fresh product, and that total may grow to 4,000 to 5,000 scripts a**

year. Five thousand scripts means five thousand transactions between buyers and sellers. **It also means five thousand opportunities for success.** What we're going to do in this section is identify who the principal television buyers are in Hollywood, what production entities serve as middleman suppliers, who the basic sellers of product are, and who the facilitators, agents, managers, etc., are that aid in the sale of scripts.

Which Broadcast Outlets Buy Original Programming?

From the formative days of television in the 1950s, and right on through the seventies, three powers decided what entertainment programs were aired throughout the nation during prime time. Those powers were the big three broadcast networks, NBC, ABC, and CBS.

The networks were the ultimate buyers. Only those entertainment programs they purchased made it to the air. If you had a script, a story, or a show to sell, your options were severely limited.

That universe began to shift and move in the late seventies with the introduction of cable outlets. Cable became a new means of reaching television consumers, and as the cable outlets matured, they, too, sought original materials to be produced and aired. The growth of cable increased rapidly in the eighties, and continues to expand in the nineties.

The outlook for the future includes an ever-expanding cable universe with more channels seeking ever more diverse types of programming. This expansion requires a constantly growing supply of original shows and scripts.

Many media analysts predict a world of five hundred or more stations in the relatively near future. Whether this comes to pass is not as important as the notion that regardless of how big cable gets, it is decidedly going to continue to expand.

Right now that expansion is moving ahead at a breathtaking pace. New channels are coming online every year. So, remember, **more outlets represent more opportunity.** And your task is to seek out opportunities to sell your work.

Let's take a quick look at who the buyers are.

First, the ultimate buyers of scripts are the broadcast and cable networks.

To the outsider it might seem that these are the places to go to to sell your work. And at first glance, that would appear to be the case.

The reality of the Hollywood marketplace is far more complicated. There is an intricate web of middlemen and relationships that funnel scripts, shows, and projects to the networks.

The common term for these middlemen is "suppliers." First there are the major studios, including Columbia, TriStar, Warner Bros., Disney, Paramount, Twentieth Century Fox, Universal, and MGM. Next are the larger production companies such as Castle Rock, Hearst, Republic, Spelling, Viacom, Cannell, and Carsey-Werner.

Additionally, there are a host of smaller successful production companies and producer teams. Some of these are essentially writers or writer-producer teams with successful track records who have become entrepreneurial enough to cut their own network deals.

Many deals are also packaged or assembled by the major talent agencies and management companies.

Types of Television Programming Bought and Sold

In order for an aspiring producer or writer to succeed in Hollywood, it's vital to understand and be familiar with the types of shows that are on the air. Too many neophytes try to come up with new ideas or concepts that are outside the forms used in television and then they wonder why they fail.

Other would-be innovators learn what the demands of broadcasting are and then take the existing forms and expand on them. It is this second group that more often than not succeeds.

Also, to get work in television, the primary avenue for writers is **to create sample scripts, commonly called spec scripts**, i.e., scripts done on speculation by the writer in the hope that they might sell.

To create a strong spec script, you must fit it into one of the existing formats commonly used in TV.

What follows is a basic description of the primary types of programming created for TV.

Original entertainment programming for most networks and a fair percentage of the newer cable entities is broken into two parts, Prime Time and Daytime.

Daytime programmers at the networks usually handle administrative responsibility for all soap operas, game shows, after-school specials and, on occasion, late-night programming.

Prime time is designated as 8:00 p.m. to 11:00 p.m., Monday through Saturday, and 7:00 p.m. through 11:00 p.m. on Sundays.

Let's look at what goes on in each area and what opportunities exist for producers and writers.

DAYTIME

As we noted above, the three principal areas covered by daytime programmers are soap operas, game shows, and after-school specials.

Soap Operas

By far soaps provide the greatest opportunity and employment for writers and producers in daytime work. Soaps are one of the oldest staples of TV, with roots that go back to the days of radio.

At any given time there are anywhere from nine to twelve soap operas on the three networks. As Ken Corday, executive producer of *Days of Our Lives*, points out, soaps are written by teams of writers in a somewhat unique format.

Employment and wages are covered by the Writers Guild contract and staff positions are fairly lucrative.

Senior staffers and writer-producers generally lay out long-term story arcs for each of the characters. Arcs can last several weeks, months, or even years.

Mid-level staff writers will then write out the story lines for all of the episodes. Keep in mind that soaps are broadcast five days a week, fifty-two weeks a year. Production is done at a fast and furious pace.

Once the story lines are composed, a separate team of dialogue writers fill in the characters' actual speeches. The approach is akin to a factory assembly line, with each member of the team having a specific task.

Usually shows have five dialogue writers. One will handle Monday's episodes, the next Tuesday's, and so forth.

Periodically new writers are auditioned for soaps with an assignment to write a typical episode based on the existing story line. These sample episodes, rarely, if ever, make it on the air, but they are used to judge a writer's ability to learn the various characters, their speech patterns, and their styles.

When a show finds a new writer who can emulate the style for the existing characters and add something special to their work, they're sometimes given an additional opportunity to do an on-air script. If that's up to snuff, they're considered for full-time work.

Dialogue writers usually work at home and are expected to turn out a typical hour-long episode in less than a week's time, week in and week out.

Aspiring soap writers need to be thoroughly familiar with the genre, have a real love and feel for its rhythms, and be willing to work as part of a team on their small section of any given script.

Game Shows

Game shows are a unique aspect of the industry. Their creation and production fall outside all the typical guild rules and it's not an area we'll cover in this book.

After-School Specials

These dramas are essentially one-hour movies produced and aired on a somewhat irregular basis by the three major networks.

They are generally designed to be for teenagers. They focus on problems often faced in adolescence.

The dramatic requirement for these shows is normally that the problems faced and resolved are to be handled by the teens in the story. Typically they might deal with date rape, teen pregnancy, interracial dating, drug use, or dealing with handicaps.

Although budgets for these tend to be miniscule, usually close to guild minimums (called "scale") for actors, writers, and directors, the tough dramatic nature of the stories often allows them to be a showcase for the talents of the participants.

Frequently, writers and producers who have created strong after-school stories have gone on to win daytime Emmys. These awards then become stepping-stones to careers as MOW or series producers and writers. When Howard Jay Smith worked with Bill Greenblatt and Jeff Auerbach at Embassy TV, their after-school special *Babies Having Babies* won several Emmys. The awards definitely boosted their careers.

🦒 **Because of the low wages, veterans generally shy away from this realm, which makes it a good area for new talent to break in and demonstrate their skills.**

PRIME TIME

The twenty-two hours a week of programming during prime time is the heart and soul of the networks. And despite their ongoing challenge from cable, the networks still heavily dominate this realm.

Although the senior executives of the networks are responsible for the final scheduling of all prime-time shows, the day-to-day administrative and creative work is handled by three distinct divisions. Within those divisions are additional sub-units, but let's look first at the basic set-up.

🦒 The three units are **Current Programming, Development, and Long Form**.

Current is responsible for overseeing all existing on-the-air series programs, such as *Roseanne* or *Seinfeld*.

209

The development team is responsible for overseeing the creation of all new series, the most common product of which is the pilot or sample show.

☜ The long form units oversee the creation of MOWs (movies of the week) and miniseries.

Note that we specifically state that these departments oversee the creation of their products. They do not do the actual writing or producing of the shows. That is handled by independent production companies or studios.

The one exception to this, and an area that is hotly under debate, are shows created by sub-units of the network, which are, in effect, wholly owned production units.

For example, ABC has ABC Productions and ABC Circle Films, the latter of which was responsible for the eighties' hit, *Moonlighting*. NBC has NBC Productions, and CBS has its own "in-house" unit as well.

Normally networks do not actually own the shows they air. They pay a license fee to production companies for the right to air shows twice.

Previously, federal rules allowed the networks to own up to two hours a week of their own programs, hence the in-house units. Changes recently implemented in these rules are beginning to send economic shock waves through the production community.

If networks can own more of their own shows, then production companies will share in a smaller segment of the economic pie. For smaller production companies this is a potential disaster.

Current Programming

The current program departments at the networks have oversight responsibility for all of the regularly occurring series shows, with the exception of those produced by the news departments, such as *60 Minutes* or *20/20*.

The three areas of prime concern are the half-hour comedies, the hour-long dramas, and the new wave of reality shows such as *Cops*.

Network executives are assigned to each show. They monitor the development of story ideas, scripts, casting, filming, and editing. The actual work of running the show, however, is left in the hands of the production team hired by the studio or production company for that series.

Sitcoms are generally a half hour in length and more often than not are shot on videotape before a live audience. Classic examples of this are *Roseanne* and *Home Improvement*. Examples of sitcoms shot on film are *Murphy Brown* and *Seinfeld*. On occasion as the franchise of the show requires, episodes are done on film on location or on soundstages, such as with *M.A.S.H.* The choice of whether to use videotape or film in producing a show is a creative decision usually made by the producing team at the inception of the project. Film, for example, without getting too technical, is usually of higher quality than tape. Tape, however, is cheaper and easier to use and edit.

Actual half-hour episodes run about twenty-four minutes, the other six minutes being allotted to commercials, public service spots, and network promotions.

Most series shoot between twenty-two and twenty-four episodes per year, the exact number being determined by the network orders.

Drama shows, such as *L.A. Law* or *Northern Exposure*, are shot on location and soundstages on film without the benefit of a live audience. Script length comes to some forty-eight minutes.

Because the shooting of hour-long dramas is more complex and time-consuming than their half-hour cousins, twenty-two episodes is usually the most that can be handled in a given season.

Reality shows take a variety of formats, with their most common denominator being their relatively low cost.

Some, such as *Cops*, are shot live, with a camera crew following police in action. Segments are then edited down to fit the half-hour format. Other types are reenactments of actual crime stories with actors portraying the cops and criminal suspects. Only in the latter are writers employed to write scripts based on actual crime stories.

News shows, such as *20/20* or *60 Minutes*, are produced by the news divisions of the networks. Rarely do they provide opportunities for creative writers or dramatists. They're handled by news journalists and are generally produced out of New York.

Arnie Friedman (*In the Line of Duty*), a producer of true life news stories, often tries first to develop his ideas for the prime-time news shows. The attention the stories draw then enables him to pitch and sell the ideas as a TV or feature movie.

Miniseries

During the era of shrinking budgets, the big event miniseries, such as *Roots*, *The Winds of War*, or *Amerika*, have vanished in favor of smaller four-hour and six-hour projects. Jackie Collins' novels are typical of the types of work now dominating miniseries fare. Books like these have a large built-in following. They can attract an audience and, more importantly, they can attract stars for the leading roles.

Big projects mean big investments and that gets risky. Production of *Scarlett*, the continuation of the *Gone With the Wind* saga, is expected to cost nearly twice the dollar amount per hour as the typical MOW or mini. The only way these costs can be recouped is through overseas TV and film sales, and through domestic video sales. Even so, it's a risky proposition. If the project flounders and gets a poor critical reception, future earnings will be jeopardized in the ancillary markets.

✿ **Most miniseries, even the smaller four- and six-hour ones, are generally conceived of as event programming. They're reserved for the sweeps months: November, February, and May.** Ratings achieved during sweeps months help establish advertising rates and future revenues. Networks struggle mightily during these periods to boost their overall ratings as much as possible. One tool is clearly the miniseries.

Gaining the extra ratings is considered so important that the networks will pour considerable funds into creating and promoting a big event project. Unlike the one week devoted to pushing an MOW, promotion for minis may last two weeks or more, depending on the size and scope of the investment.

For *Scarlett*, promotion takes place at each step along the way. Open casting sessions were held seemingly everywhere for new faces to play the leads. This attracted all of the tabloids, print and TV, to a feeding frenzy over who would play Scarlett and Rhett. In the end RHI Entertainment settled for two well-known and established actors, Joanne Whalley-Kilmer and Timothy Dalton.

As airdates near, the publicists for these event programs vie with each other to get coverage in all the trade and Sunday TV magazines. Such additional promotional help is considered vital to getting a large audience.

By scripting a tale adapted from a best-seller such as *Lonesome Dove*, the networks ensure that as many people as possible will be aware in advance of the saga to be presented and will want to tune in to see it unfold on the small screen.

Again, although the bulk of all miniseries come from the big three networks, we're seeing more of them on cable. According to Betsy Newman, a vice-president at Turner Network Television, Turner's *Gettysburg* was originally designed to be a TNT miniseries, but was given a theatrical push at the last moment. It aired on TNT after it was sent to the home video market.

Chapter 13.

Schedule of Purchasing Prices

FEATURES AND TELEVISION

Typically a small production company may strike a variation on one of two types of deals, **the option** or the **"if-come"** memo. **Options usually apply to either an existing property, book, screenplay, or real-life personal story, while "if-come's" are usually for an original treatment or story idea.**

An option works this way. In exchange for a nominal sum of money, usually five hundred to a thousand dollars, you grant the production entity the right to shop your material around for a specified period of time.

Should they strike a studio or network deal, the producer will then have the right to call in the option by paying you a pre-specified amount for the full rights. The purchase price may go as high as four million dollars for a completed screenplay. However, a sum between one hundred and five hundred thousand dollars is more likely.

If the producer is able to raise independent (non-studio/network) financing for the picture, the screenplay purchase price may be as low as five thousand dollars.

Options are most commonly set for six months or a year, with a second year renewable for another pre-specified and nominal sum. No one gets rich off of options, but it is a common first step to seeing

214

outside material make it into Hollywood.

"If-come" deals are somewhat similar but no money is exchanged unless the project or the services of a writer are sold to a solid buyer.

❧ **"If-come"** is shorthand for **"If we're able to sell this project to a buyer, then all the fees specified in our contract will come into your hands."**

Most of these contracts are covered by basic Writers Guild minimums. They're so commonplace that actual contracts specifying all contingencies are rarely used.

Often what you'll see is a one-page deal memo. The time and cost of executing full contracts on what is essentially a speculative endeavor would cause this town to grind to a halt.

Now we are going to introduce you to the Writers Guild minimums. Keep in mind that many of the deals in Hollywood are made between non-Guild writers and non-signatory producers. Therefore, any deal is possible, including "no money down." The key is to evaluate the overall benefits of doing business with certain entities. Be careful, however, if you can't check references on those people that you intend to do business with. We highly suggest extreme caution on "no money down" deals.

RANGE OF WRITERS' FEES

The *Schedule of Minimums* is a book published by the Writers Guild of America (WGA), in which the Guild indicates the minimum payment a writer can expect for his/her work. The following tables show some of the "flat deal" figures — ones that would apply to a writer who has not previously been employed in TV, radio, or film. The *Schedule of Minimums* is available from the WGA for $1.

The rates provided show a low-end figure and a high-end figure. These figures are based on the entire production budget. A low budget would be less than $2.5 million, and a high budget would be one that is $2.5 million or higher. The figures are given for the periods of May 2, 1993, through May 1, 1994, and May 2, 1994, through May 1, 1995.

Motion Pictures — Employment, Flat Deals

	5/2/93–5/1/94		5/2/94–5/1/95	
	Low	High	Low	High
Original Screenplay including treatment	$36,479	$68,425	$37,938	$71,162
Installments—				
—Delivery of treatment	16,530	27,372	17,191	28,467
—Delivery of first-draft screenplay	14,366	27,372	14,941	28,467
—Delivery of final-draft screenplay	5,583	13,681	5,806	14,228
Original Screenplay excluding treatment and sale of original screenplay	$24,514	$50,176	$25,495	$52,183
Installments—				
—Delivery of first-draft screenplay	18,931	36,495	19,689	37,955
—Delivery of final-draft screenplay	5,583	13,681	5,806	14,228
Additional compensation for story included in screenplay	4,565	9,123	4,748	9,488
Story or treatment	$11,970	$18,248	$12,449	$18,978
Original treatment	$16,530	$27,372	$17,191	$28,467
First-Draft Screenplay with or without option for final-draft screenplay				
—First-draft screenplay	$14,366	$27,372	$14,941	$28,467
—Final-draft screenplay	9,574	18,248	9,957	18,978
Rewrite of screenplay	11,970	18,248	12,449	18,978
Polish of screenplay	5,987	9,123	6,226	9,488

Television Network Prime Time — 30 Minutes

	5/2/93-5/1/94	5/2/94-5/1/95
Story	$ 4,816	$ 5,009
Teleplay	10,365	10,780

Installments—
—First draft: 60% of agreed compensation but not less than 90% of minimum.
—Final draft: Balance of agreed compensation.

Story and teleplay	$ 14,450	$ 15,028

Installments—
—Story: 30% of agreed compensation.
—First-draft teleplay: 40% of agreed compensation or the difference between the story installment and 90% of minimum, whichever is greater.
Final-draft teleplay: Balance of agreed compensation.

Network Prime Time — 60 Minutes

	5/2/93-5/1/94	5/2/94-5/1/95
Story	$ 8,478	$ 8,817
Teleplay	13,981	14,540

Installments—
—First draft: 60% of agreed compensation but not less than 90% of minimum.
—Final draft: Balance of agreed compensation.

Story and teleplay	$ 21,251	$ 22,101

217

Installments—
—Story: 30% of agreed compensation.
—First-draft teleplay: 40% of agreed compensation or the difference between the story installment and 90% of minimum, whichever is greater.
Final-draft teleplay: Balance of agreed compensation.

Network Prime Time — 120 Minutes, Non-Episodic

	5/2/93-5/1/94	5/2/94-5/1/95
Story	$16,511	$17,171
Teleplay	28,205	29,333

Installments—
—First draft: 60% of agreed compensation but not less than 90% of minimum.
—Final draft: Balance of agreed compensation.

Story and teleplay	$42,999	$44,719

Installments—
—Story: 30% of agreed compensation.
—First-draft teleplay: 40% of agreed compensation or the difference between the story installment and 90% of minimum, whichever is greater.
Final-draft teleplay: Balance of agreed compensation.

(Source: Writers Guild of America West)

MAJOR SCREENPLAY SALES
(1991 – 1994)

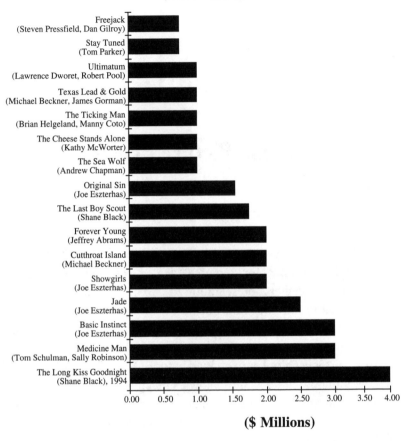

($ Millions)

(Sources: Brookfield Communications, *The Hollywood Reporter*, *Los Angeles Times*)

Book Sales

In addition to spec screenplays, the film rights to novels, especially those of popular writers such as Tom Clancy (*Clear and Present Danger*) and John Grisham, can command seven-figure amounts. The feature film rights to Grisham's first novel, *A Time to Kill*, for example, sold for a record $6 million, according to *Variety*.

219

Chapter 14.

Motion Picture Players

STUDIOS AND MAJOR PRODUCTION COMPANIES

W e know that you are eager to find someone to write a treatment for your great idea, or learn how you should put together a presentation to introduce your story to a producer or studio. Or you want to find out whom to contact regarding potential financing for your screenplay. Or you just want to know which buyer to contact.

As Christopher Vogler mentioned before, ⚷ **you have to be patient**. It is very important for you to know as much as possible about all the facets of this business, even if you are only interested in a certain area. The more you know, the easier it will be to understand the dynamics of selling your project.

⚷ **Information is one of the major keys to opening the doors.** Fortunes can be lost or won in the stock market according to what information one is able to acquire or not. Governments spend billions of dollars yearly collecting information. They know that the more information you have, the more powerful you will be. We know that some of you are movie buffs and know all about the studios and networks; still keep on reading step by step. It is important to know who is who in the game.

Remember, ⚷ **knowledge is power**.

220

THE STUDIOS

In Hollywood's heyday, there were seven major studios, the "big five" — Metro-Goldwyn-Mayer, Paramount, RKO, Twentieth Century Fox, and Warner Bros. — and the "little two" — Columbia and Universal. Most of these studios grew out of smaller companies formed in the early days of filmmaking. With the exception of RKO, which ceased production in 1953, the studios are still going strong today. Not included in that group was The Walt Disney Company which began as an animation studio in the 1920s, and which has since become an entertainment giant. Most of the major studios, or their parent companies, have branched out over the years to embrace television and cable production, publishing, recording, and home video distribution.

Metro-Goldwyn-Mayer

The name Metro-Goldwyn-Mayer came about when Loew's, Inc., a film exhibition company founded and run by Marcus Loew, acquired Metro Pictures Corporation in 1920, the Goldwyn Company in 1924, and soon afterward Louis B. Mayer Pictures, as well as the services of Louis B. Mayer and Irving Thalberg.

For many years MGM was considered the leader in the industry and described itself with the publicity motto that it had "more stars than there are in heaven." Those stars included Greta Garbo, Clark Gable, Lionel Barrymore, Joan Crawford, William Powell, Jean Harlow, Spencer Tracy, Judy Garland, Mickey Rooney, Nelson Eddy, Jeanette MacDonald, and Laurel and Hardy, to name a few.

MGM purchased United Artists in 1981 and became the MGM/UA Entertainment Co. in 1983. In 1986 Turner Broadcasting purchased MGM/UA Entertainment and then sold off much of it and reorganized what was left. Pathe Communications' acquisition of the company in 1990 was followed by a battle for control between Pathe and Credit Lyonnais and the auctioning off of the company to Credit Lyonnais in 1992.

In connection with the Pathe merger, Pathe's principal subsidiaries, Pathe Entertainment, Inc., and Cannon Entertainment, Inc., became wholly owned subsidiaries of MGM.

MGM and MGM/UA releases of note include *Ben-Hur*, *Anna Christie*, *Grand Hotel*, *The Thin Man*, *Mutiny on the Bounty*, *Goodbye, Mr. Chips*, *The Wizard of Oz*, *Gone With the Wind* (produced by David O. Selznick but released by MGM), *Dr. Zhivago*, *Network*, *Moonstruck*, and *A Fish Called Wanda*.

Hampered in recent years by the above-mentioned series of buyouts, it is just now beginning to reestablish itself as a full-scale production entity. In the fall of 1992 the company decided to redirect its activities related to television programming and to focus on specials, reality shows, and series produced for cable and first-run syndication. In the 1992–93 television season, MGM had one prime-time network series, *In the Heat of the Night*, airing on CBS.

United Artists was created in 1919 by four of the biggest names in silent film history — Mary Pickford, Douglas Fairbanks, Charlie Chaplin, and D.W. Griffith. Over the years, management and control of the company shifted back and forth. The Arthur Krim management company gained 100 percent ownership in 1956 and went public in 1957. In the 1950s United Artists began what is common practice today — financing films made by independent producers. In 1967 UA became a subsidiary of Transamerica Corp. until it was sold to MGM in 1981.

Some of UA's better-known films include *Broken Blossoms*, *Way Down East*, *Hell's Angels*, *Scarface*, *Marty*, *West Side Story*, *In the Heat of the Night*, *Midnight Cowboy*, *One Flew Over the Cuckoo's Nest*, *Rocky*, *Annie Hall*, *Rain Man*, and all of the James Bond films and Woody Allen films through the 1970s. UA's film history also includes its multimillion-dollar disaster, *Heaven's Gate*.

MGM 1993 Film Revenues

(in millions)

	Title	Gross
1.	Benny & Joon	$23.3
2.	Untamed Heart	18.8
3.	Body of Evidence	13.8
4.	Undercover Blues	12.2
5.	The Meteor Man	8.0
6.	Fatal Instinct	7.8
7.	Son of the Pink Panther	2.4
8.	Rich in Love	2.0
9.	The Lover	1.1
10.	Six Degrees of Separation	0.5
11.	Flight of the Innocent	-0.1
12.	Dangerous Game	-0.1
		$89.7

(Sources: *The Hollywood Reporter*, Standard & Poor's *Industry Surveys*, Motion Picture Association of America)

Paramount Pictures

Paramount Pictures Corporation was founded in 1914 by W.W. Hodkinson and, through various mergers and acquisitions, was built upon a number of other companies, including Adolph Zukor's Famous Players Film Company and the Jesse L. Lasky Feature Players Company, which became Famous Players-Lasky Corporation in 1916.

Between 1927 and 1949, the company's name changed numerous times. In 1949 it was split into two companies: Paramount Pictures Corporation and United Paramount Theatres, Inc. Paramount merged with Gulf & Western in 1966 and became Paramount Communications, Inc., in 1989. In 1994, Viacom succeeded in its bid to acquire Paramount.

Paramount experimented with 3-D in 1953 and introduced VistaVision

223

in 1954. This was to compete with CinemaScope, which was being pushed by Twentieth Century Fox. The first VistaVision film was *White Christmas*, and another was Cecil B. DeMille's remake of *The Ten Commandments*.

Among Paramount's first great stars was Mary Pickford, who had worked for Famous Players.

Over the years, the studio was known by and large for producing family entertainment with such stars as Rudolph Valentino, Maurice Chevalier, Bob Hope, Bing Crosby, Dorothy Lamour, Claudette Colbert, and the Marx Brothers.

Some of the company's notable films include *The Sheik*, the Bob Hope–Bing Crosby *Road* films, *Going My Way*, *The Greatest Show on Earth*, *Love Story*, *The Godfather*, *Saturday Night Fever*, *Grease*, the *Star Trek* films, the Indiana Jones films, *Fatal Attraction*, *Top Gun*, *Beverly Hills Cop*, *The Addams Family*, and *Wayne's World*.

Paramount's television programs have had across-the-board success in hour, half-hour, and long form. The studio has also had great success in selling syndicated programs, such as the *Star Trek* spin-offs, and in developing movies for the USA Network, which it co-owns with Universal/MCA, and which now includes USA's new cable network, the Sci-Fi Channel.

Paramount's television group includes Wilshire Court Productions, which produces feature films, principally for cable. Some of the group's television programs include *Wings* and *Star Trek: The Next Generation*. Past Paramount successes include *Cheers*, *Happy Days*, and *Laverne & Shirley*.

In addition to its filmed entertainment activities, Paramount is involved in publishing, sports, and recreation. Paramount Publishing includes Simon & Schuster, Pocket Books, and Prentice Hall, among others.

Paramount also owns Madison Square Garden, the New York Knickerbockers (basketball) and the New York Rangers (hockey).

Paramount 1993 Film Revenues
(in millions)

	Title	Gross
1.	The Firm	$158.4
2.	Indecent Proposal	105.6
3.	Addams Family Values	44.6
4.	Wayne's World 2	38.9
5.	Sliver	36.2
6.	Coneheads	21.1
7.	Fire in the Sky	20.0
8.	Flesh and Bone	9.5
9.	Searching for Bobby Fischer	7.3
10.	The Temp	6.3
11.	Leap of Faith	6.1
12.	The Thing Called Love	1.0
13.	What's Eating Gilbert Grape	0.3
14.	Bopha!	0.2
15.	It's All True	0.1
		$455.6

(Sources: *The Hollywood Reporter*, Standard & Poor's *Industry Surveys*, Motion Picture Association of America)

Sony Pictures

Sony Pictures Entertainment, owned by the Sony Corporation of Japan, is comprised of two semi-autonomous units, Columbia and TriStar. They focus on all aspects of film and television production, including hour series, half-hour comedies, and TV movies.

In total, Sony Pictures Motion Picture Group includes Columbia Pictures, TriStar Pictures, Triumph Releasing, Sony Pictures Classics, and Columbia TriStar Film Distributors International. The Television Group includes Columbia Pictures Television, TriStar Television, Columbia Pictures Television Distribution, Merv Griffin Enterprises,

225

and Columbia TriStar International Television. Sony's Television Group has started the Game Show Channel with the help of United Satellite Video Group. Other Sony Pictures subsidiaries are Columbia TriStar Home Video, Loews Theatre Management Co., and Sony Pictures Studios.

Columbia Pictures

Columbia Pictures started in 1920 with the creation of the CBC Films Sales Co., which was run by brothers Harry and Jack Cohn and by Joe Brandt. In 1924, not long after the company's successful release of its first feature-length film, it was renamed Columbia Pictures. Harry Cohn eventually wielded most of the power as president of the company. Columbia released many "B" pictures, many of them shot on its eight-acre ranch in Burbank, along with some "A" film releases.

In 1951, Columbia formed Screen Gems to produce television programs and commercials, and it became the first company to produce films specifically for television. In 1982, Columbia was purchased by Coca-Cola, which formed a separate production company, TriStar Pictures, in conjunction with Home Box Office and CBS. TriStar was later made a unit of Columbia Pictures. In 1989, the company was acquired by the Sony Corporation of Japan for $3.4 billion and is now a part of Sony Pictures Entertainment, Inc.

Columbia's first big artistic success came with director Frank Capra's comedy, *It Happened One Night* (1934), which won five Academy Awards. In addition to other Capra comedies, Columbia's film releases have included *The Jolson Story, Born Yesterday, From Here to Eternity, On the Waterfront, The Bridge on the River Kwai, Lawrence of Arabia, A Man for All Seasons, Guess Who's Coming to Dinner?, Easy Rider, Close Encounters of the Third Kind, Kramer vs. Kramer, Tootsie, Ghostbusters, Bram Stoker's Dracula,* and *In the Line of Fire.*

Columbia 1993 Film Revenues
(in millions)

	Title	Gross
1.	In the Line of Fire	$102.3
2.	Groundhog Day	70.9
3.	A Few Good Men	64.1
4.	Last Action Hero	50.1
5.	Malice	45.1
6.	The Age of Innocence	31.5
7.	Poetic Justice	27.6
8.	My Life	25.8
9.	Striking Distance	23.8
10.	Nowhere to Run	22.1
11.	The Remains of the Day	16.8
12.	Geronimo	15.2
13.	Needful Things	15.1
14.	Amos & Andrew	9.7
15.	Lost in Yonkers	9.2
16.	A River Runs Through It	8.6
17.	Hexed	2.7
18.	Calendar Girl	2.6
19.	El Mariachi	1.9
20.	Josh and S.A.M.	1.5
21.	Bram Stoker's Dracula	0.4
22.	The Pickle	0.1
		————
		$547.1

(Sources: *The Hollywood Reporter*, Standard & Poor's *Industry Surveys*, Motion Picture Association of America)

Columbia Pictures Television

Columbia's television arm is a presence in prime time and daytime. The division's programs include *Married . . . with Children*, *Days of Our Lives*, and *The Young and the Restless*.

Sony Pictures Classics

A newer division of the company **created to focus on films like** *Indochine* and *Howards End.*

TriStar Pictures

In 1982, after the Coca-Cola Company's purchase of Columbia Pictures, Coca-Cola, Home Box Office, and CBS formed TriStar Pictures as a separate production company. TriStar was later made a unit of Columbia Pictures, and is now a division of Sony Pictures.

TriStar film releases include *The Natural*, *Rambo*, *First Blood Part II*, *Rambo III*, *Total Recall*, *Basic Instinct*, *Sleepless in Seattle*, and *Philadelphia.*

TriStar 1993 Film Revenues
(in millions)

	Title	Gross
1.	Sleepless in Seattle	$126.3
2.	Cliffhanger	84.1
3.	Rudy	21.5
4.	Sniper	18.6
5.	Weekend at Bernie's II	12.8
6.	So I Married an Axe Murderer	11.6
7.	Manhattan Murder Mystery	11.2
8.	Look Who's Talking Now	10.0
9.	Chaplin	9.1
10.	Mr. Jones	8.3
11.	Candyman	0.5
12.	Philadelphia	0.5
13.	Wilder Napalm	0.1
		$314.6

(Sources: *The Hollywood Reporter*, Standard & Poor's *Industry Surveys*, Motion Picture Association of America)

TriStar Television

An example of one of TriStar Television's programs is the NBC situation comedy *Mad About You.*

Twentieth Century Fox

The beginnings of Twentieth Century Fox trace back to William Fox who worked with various companies in the early nickelodeon days of film and then founded the Fox Film Corporation in 1915. In the late 1920s, Fox pioneered the Movietone sound-on-film process. In 1935 the Fox Film Corporation merged with Twentieth Century Pictures, run by Joseph M. Schenk, to become the Twentieth Century-Fox Film Corporation. The merger resulted in Darryl F. Zanuck's joining the company as a vice-president. Fox merged with a Marvin Davis company in 1981 and was subsequently sold to Australian publishing tycoon Rupert Murdoch, head of The News Corporation. This resulted in the formation of Fox, Inc., which includes Twentieth Century Fox Film Corporation, Fox Television Studios, Inc., and the Fox Broadcasting Company. In 1989, the name changed again to Fox Film Corporation, with a greater emphasis on motion picture production.

Fox's stars have included Theda Bara, Shirley Temple, Alice Faye, Don Ameche, Betty Grable, Marilyn Monroe, and some of its best-known film releases have included *Drums Along the Mohawk, What Price Glory?, The Grapes of Wrath, How Green Was My Valley, The Ox-Bow Incident, Gentleman's Agreement, The Robe, There's No Business Like Show Business, South Pacific, The Diary of Anne Frank, Cleopatra, The Sound of Music, The Towering Inferno* (made with Warner), *The Poseidon Adventure*, the *Star Wars* trilogy, *Aliens, Die Hard, Sleeping with the Enemy, Home Alone*, and *Mrs. Doubtfire.*

Twentieth Century Fox has sold heavily in all areas to the other networks and also produces significant amounts of material for its own Fox Network.

Twentieth Century Fox 1993 Film Revenues
(in millions)

	Title	Gross
1.	Mrs. Doubtfire	$123.2
2.	Rising Sun	62.5
3.	Rookie of the Year	53.2
4.	The Good Son	44.4
5.	The Beverly Hillbillies	41.5
6.	Hot Shots! Part Deux	38.6
7.	Robin Hood: Men in Tights	35.3
8.	The Sandlot	31.7
9.	Home Alone 2	26.9
10.	Used People	15.8
11.	The Vanishing	13.5
12.	Hoffa	7.7
13.	Once Upon a Forest	6.2
14.	Best of the Best II	6.1
15.	Hear No Evil	5.2
16.	Jack the Bear	4.7
17.	Toys	3.2
18.	Only the Strong	3.0
19.	Freaked	nil
20.	The Abyss (re-release)	nil
		$522.7

(Sources: *The Hollywood Reporter*, Standard & Poor's *Industry Surveys*, Motion Picture Association of America)

Universal Pictures

Carl Laemmle, an exhibitor who became a producer, founded Universal in 1912. Universal is credited with starting the "star system" by hiring Florence Lawrence for a thousand dollars a week and giving her the billing of "Queen of the Screen." The company set up a studio at Sunset and Gower in Hollywood but soon after moved to its present site, Universal City, on the San Fernando Valley side of the Hollywood Hills near Burbank.

Early stars with Universal included Wallace Reid, Lon Chaney, Rudolph Valentino, and Boris Karloff. The company also established the careers of Deanna Durbin, Abbott and Costello, Donald O'Connor, and many others. Even so, the studio was long referred to as one of the "little two" (the other being Columbia Pictures), producing many low-budget co-features, including gangster films, horror films, westerns, serials, and comedies.

In 1946, the company eliminated the production of those "B" pictures, following a merger with International Pictures Corp. In 1952, Decca Records became Universal's controlling stockholder. In 1962, MCA, Inc., acquired and consolidated both companies, making Universal Pictures the theatrical film division of MCA.

In 1990, Matsushita Electrical Company of Japan purchased MCA. That same year, a fire damaged much of Universal's backlot and did damage to its popular tourist attraction, Universal Studios Hollywood Backlot Tour.

Universal's film releases over the years have included *The Hunchback of Notre Dame*, *All Quiet on the Western Front*, *Dracula*, *Frankenstein*, *Destry Rides Again*, *Spartacus*, the Doris Day–Rock Hudson romantic comedies, *Charade*, *Earthquake*, *Jaws*, *Airport*, *E.T.: The Extra-Terrestrial*, the *Back to the Future* series, *Twins*, *Field of Dreams*, *Born on the Fourth of July*, and *Jurassic Park*.

Universal produces across the television broadcast spectrum, including cable and syndication. As noted, it co-owns the USA Network with Paramount.

Universal 1993 Film Revenues
(in millions)

	Title	Gross
1.	Jurassic Park	$339.4
2.	Scent of a Woman	61.7
3.	Dragon: The Bruce Lee Story	35.0
4.	Carlito's Way	34.1
5.	Hard Target	31.7
6.	Beethoven's 2nd	31.5
7.	Cop and a Half	31.2
8.	CB4	17.7
9.	Heart and Souls	16.5
10.	Judgment Night	12.1
11.	Mad Dog and Glory	10.7
12.	Army of Darkness	10.5
13.	Matinee	8.9
14.	We're Back!	8.0
15.	Lorenzo's Oil	7.0
16.	The Real McCoy	6.3
17.	Schindler's List	6.0
18.	Splitting Heirs	3.2
19.	Trespass	3.0
20.	In the Name of the Father	0.1
		$674.6

(Sources: *The Hollywood Reporter*, Standard & Poor's *Industry Surveys*, Motion Picture Association of America)

The Walt Disney Company

Walt Disney and his brother Roy arrived in Hollywood in 1923 and started an animation studio in the back of a real estate office. In 1928, Disney's most famous cartoon character, Mickey Mouse, was introduced (with Walt Disney himself providing Mickey's voice). Donald

Duck appeared in 1936. Disney's cartoons were distributed through Columbia Pictures, then United Artists, and finally RKO, for whom Disney produced *Snow White and the Seven Dwarfs* in 1937, Disney's first feature-length animated film.

In 1953 Disney broke with RKO and formed its own distribution company, Buena Vista. Between 1939 and 1953, Disney released many of its now famous and classic animated films: *Pinocchio, Fantasia, Dumbo, Bambi, Cinderella, Alice in Wonderland*, and *Peter Pan*.

In the 1950s, the company branched out into live-action films, introduced the enormously popular *Mickey Mouse Club* and *Davy Crockett* series on television, and opened Disneyland in Anaheim, California, while continuing to release quality animated features such as *Lady and the Tramp* (1953) and *Sleeping Beauty* (1959).

The company's growth has led to the creation of Disney World and Epcot Center in Florida, Tokyo Disneyland and Euro Disney theme parks, *Disney's Wonderful World*, the longest-running network series in television history, and the creation of The Disney Channel on cable television.

Other films of note over the years have included *Treasure Island, Old Yeller, Mary Poppins, The Absent-Minded Professor*, and recent animated films such as *The Little Mermaid, Beauty and the Beast, Aladdin*, and *The Lion King*.

Walt Disney won a record thirty Academy Awards for his work.

Disney's filmed entertainment subsidiaries include Buena Vista Television (syndication), The Disney Channel, Hollywood Pictures, KCAL-TV – Los Angeles, Touchstone Pictures, Touchstone Television, Walt Disney Pictures, Walt Disney Television, and Miramax.

The company also owns *Discover* magazine, Hollywood Records, and Walt Disney Records.

Buena Vista 1993 Film Revenues
(in millions)

	Title	Gross
1.	Aladdin	$102.6
2.	Cool Runnings	61.9
3.	The Three Musketeers	49.2
4.	The Nightmare Before Christmas	49.1
5.	Homeward Bound	41.6
6.	Snow White (re-release)	41.3
7.	Sister Act 2	41.0
8.	Hocus Pocus	39.3
9.	What's Love Got to Do With It	38.9
10.	Son-in-Law	36.4
11.	Alive	36.3
12.	The Joy Luck Club	31.5
13.	The Adventures of Huck Finn	23.9
14.	The Program	23.0
15.	Guilty As Sin	22.7
16.	Tombstone	22.5
17.	The Super Mario Bros.	20.8
18.	Another Stakeout	20.1
19.	Born Yesterday	17.8
20.	Indian Summer	14.7
21.	A Far Off Place	12.9
22.	Life with Mikey	12.3
23.	The Distinguished Gentleman	8.2
24.	Aspen Extreme	7.9
25.	The Cemetery Club	5.6
26.	Swing Kids	5.4
27.	Bound By Honor	4.1
28.	Father Hood	3.3
29.	My Boyfriend's Back	3.2
30.	The Muppet Christmas Carol	2.6
31.	The Mighty Ducks	2.5
32.	Money for Nothing	1.0
33.	Consenting Adults	0.2
34.	Captain Ron	0.2
		$804.0

(Sources: *The Hollywood Reporter*, Standard & Poor's *Industry Surveys*, Motion Picture Association of America)

Hollywood Pictures

In 1990, Disney created Hollywood Pictures and began the company with the successful release of *Arachnophobia*. Another highly successful film for the company was *The Hand That Rocks the Cradle*.

Touchstone Pictures

After the deaths of Walt Disney in 1966 and his brother Roy in 1971, no member of the family was at the helm until Ron Miller, Walt's son-in-law was made chief executive in 1983. Miller created Touchstone Pictures to widen the scope of Disney's film endeavors, without tarnishing its family image. Some of Touchstone's films have included *Splash, Pretty Woman, Three Men and a Baby, Sister Act*, and *Dick Tracy*.

Touchstone Television and Walt Disney Television

Disney was far less successful than its rivals in selling to the networks in the past, but recently it has come on like gangbusters, trailing only Warner Bros. in on-air shows. Its major focus ❧ **has been on half-hour comedies and long form**.

Network television programs from Touchstone and Walt Disney Television have included *The Golden Girls, Empty Nest, Nurses*, and *Home Improvement.*

Also, through its Disney Channel sub-unit, the studio produces a variety of shows for this wholly owned cable outlet.

Warner Bros.

Warner Bros. Pictures, Inc., was formed by four brothers who started in Pennsylvania in 1905 with the Cascade Theatre, a nickel-odeon. In 1913 the brothers, Harry M., Sam, Albert, and Jack, branched out into production with Warner Features, and incorporated as Warner Bros. in 1923. That year they released fourteen pictures, including the first of the Rin-Tin-Tin series, which was scripted by Darryl F. Zanuck, who later became production chief under Jack Warner, the studio's head.

Warner pioneered sound research, introducing a sound-on-disc process called Vitaphone, which premiered in 1926. The success of their initial sound efforts led the studio to produce *The Jazz Singer,* with Al Jolson, released in 1927. Though not a full-sound feature, the film was a sensation and revolutionized the industry. Warner put the sound to good use with its musicals of the thirties, such as *42nd Street* and the *Gold Diggers* series. Warner also did well in the same era with its popular gangster films, starring James Cagney, Edward G. Robinson, and Humphrey Bogart.

Some of Warner's well-known releases over the past thirty years have included *My Fair Lady, Who's Afraid of Virginia Woolf?, Superman, The Exorcist, All the President's Men, Batman,* the *Lethal Weapon* series, *Gremlins, Robin Hood: Prince of Thieves, JFK, Unforgiven, The Bodyguard,* and *The Fugitive.*

Warner Bros. is also famous for its **theatrical cartoons**, now seen primarily on television and video. The company's most famous cartoon and best-loved character is Bugs Bunny.

Warner's television series include *Murphy Brown, Life Goes On,* and *Room for Two,* and the company has launched WB, the fifth television broadcast network.

Time, Inc., acquired the company in 1989, creating Time Warner, Inc. In addition to Warner Bros., Time Warner includes all of Time, Inc.'s publishing activities (*Time, Sports Illustrated, People, Entertainment Weekly, Fortune, Life* and other publications, Time-Life Books, Book-of-the-Month Club, Warner Books, Little, Brown and other publishing operations) as well as Home Box Office, Cinemax, HBO Video, and American Television and Communications Corp. Other subsidiaries include DC Comics, Lorimar, and Lorimar Telepictures (*Knots Landing, Perfect Strangers, Full House, Sisters, I'll Fly Away, Time Trax*).

Like Sony, Warner has a full slate of production and is the leader in production of TV series, more than twice that of its nearest competitor.

Warner Bros. 1993 Film Revenues

(in millions)

	Title	Gross
1.	The Fugitive	$179.4
2.	Free Willy	77.7
3.	Dave	63.3
4.	The Pelican Brief	60.5
5.	Demolition Man	56.5
6.	Dennis the Menace	51.3
7.	Sommersby	50.1
8.	Made in America	45.2
9.	Falling Down	40.9
10.	The Bodyguard	33.7
11.	The Secret Garden	31.2
12.	Point of No Return	30.0
13.	A Perfect World	29.0
14.	Unforgiven	26.2
15.	The Man Without a Face	24.8
16.	Forever Young	22.5
17.	Grumpy Old Men	17.3
18.	The Crush	13.6
19.	True Romance	12.3
20.	Boiling Point	10.1
21.	Fearless	6.9
22.	Batman: Mask	4.3
23.	This Boy's Life	4.1
24.	Under Siege	3.9
25.	Malcolm X	3.3
26.	Mr. Wonderful	3.1
27.	Airborne	2.9
28.	Passenger 57	2.6
29.	The Nutcracker	2.0
30.	M. Butterfly	1.5
31.	Heaven and Earth	1.3
32.	Pure Country	0.8
33.	Wrestling Ernest Hemingway	0.1
34.	Saint of Fort Washington	0.1
35.	That Night	nil
		$912.5

(Sources: *The Hollywood Reporter*, Standard & Poor's *Industry Surveys*, Motion Picture Association of America)

MAJOR PRODUCTION COMPANIES

Carolco Pictures

Carolco and LIVE Entertainment, a subsidiary, are engaged in production, acquisition, and distribution of feature films, television and video programming and related entertainment software. In 1992 the company produced *Cliffhanger* (released in 1993) and the biographical film *Chaplin.*

Other subsidiaries of the company include Carolco International, The Vista Organization Partnership, The Vista Organization, Carolco Television, and Carolco Studios.

Castle Rock Entertainment

Castle Rock was created in 1987 by Rob Reiner and four former executives of Norman Lear's Embassy Communications. Castle Rock has had its greatest success in producing features. Among others, the company produced the film *A Few Good Men.*

In TV its focus has remained until now on 🗝 **half-hour sitcoms**, including the wildly successful *Seinfeld.*

Castle Rock was recently purchased by Turner Entertainment. As a subdivision of Turner, it's expected that Castle Rock will begin to branch out into other areas of programming, including hour format and long form projects.

Miramax Film Corp.

Miramax was started in 1981 by brothers Harvey and Bob Weinstein, who had run an old movie house in Buffalo, New York, after college, before they began buying and distributing movies. Miramax has been known mostly for its emphasis on 🗝 **foreign language and art films.**

The company's films have included *The Crying Game, Truth or Dare, The Grifters, Cinema Paradiso, sex, lies, and videotape, Tie Me Up! Tie Me Down*, and Academy Award–winning *The Piano.* In May 1993, the Walt Disney Company acquired Miramax.

238

Miramax 1993 Film Revenues
(in millions)

	Title	Gross
1.	The Crying Game	$58.1
2.	Like Water for Chocolate	19.6
3.	The Piano	17.1
4.	Strictly Ballroom	11.6
5.	Children of the Corn II	7.0
6.	Fortress	6.7
7.	Into the West	4.8
8.	Passion Fish	4.7
9.	Farewell My Concubine	3.6
10.	Tom and Jerry — The Movie	3.5
11.	Map of the Human Heart	2.8
12.	The Night We Never Met	1.9
13.	Enchanted April	1.5
14.	Reservoir Dogs	1.0
15.	The Opposite Sex	0.7
16.	The Snapper	0.6
17.	Deception	0.6
18.	Especially on Sunday	0.5
19.	Just Another Girl on the IRT	0.5
20.	El Cid (re-release)	0.3
21.	House of Cards	0.3
22.	Ethan Frome	0.3
23.	Blue	0.2
24.	Benefit of the Doubt	0.1
		———
		$148.0

(Sources: *The Hollywood Reporter*, Standard & Poor's *Industry Surveys*, MPAA)

New Line Cinema

In the early 1990s, New Line was the leading independent producer and distributor of theatrical motion pictures in the United States, with a 50 percent market share of all independent releases, and 3 percent of the total market. Now it is known ✎ **for some famous and successful slasher/horror films**, though when CEO Robert Shaye started the company in 1967, he was distributing films to college campuses. In 1983, it successfully released *A Nightmare on Elm Street,* followed by the sequels centered on character Freddy Krueger. In 1990, it released *Teenage Mutant Ninja Turtles*, the highest-grossing picture ever released by an independent producer. Other film releases include *The Lawnmower Man* and *Poison Ivy.* In 1990, it created **Fine Line Features to produce artistic films** and entered the television market by acquiring an interest in RHI Entertainment, an independent producer of MOWs and miniseries for television. In 1991, New Line bought the home video and foreign distribution rights to productions of Castle Rock Entertainment. In 1993, Turner Broadcasting bought New Line.

New Line 1993 Film Revenues
(in millions)

	Title	Gross
1.	Teenage Mutant Ninja Turtles III	$42.3
2.	National Lampoon's Loaded Weapon 1	28.0
3.	Menace II Society	27.8
4.	Jason Goes to Hell	15.6
5.	Who's the Man?	11.3
6.	Man's Best Friend	10.6
7.	Gettysburg	9.0
8.	Damage	7.2
9.	Three of Hearts	5.5
10.	Surf Ninjas	5.0
11.	Mr. Nanny	4.2
12.	Short Cuts	4.0
13.	Wide Sargasso Sea	1.4
14.	Excessive Force	1.2
15.	The Player	0.6
16.	Glengarry Glen Ross	0.4
17.	Waterland	0.1
18.	Naked	-0.1
		———
		$174.1

(Sources: *The Hollywood Reporter*, Standard & Poor's *Industry Surveys*, MPAA)

Orion Pictures

Orion Pictures, based in the Century City area of Los Angeles, began as Filmways, Inc., which changed its name in 1982 to Orion Pictures Corporation. In 1988 the Metromedia Company acquired control of Orion Pictures, and by doing so, kept it out of the hands of Viacom, Inc. In December 1991, Orion filed a Chapter 11 bankruptcy. According to the company, financially disappointing motion picture releases and lower home video sales were among the reasons for its financial troubles.

Orion produces and distributes its own films and those of others for theatrical, television, and video distribution. Since 1982 it has released more than 100 films, including *First Blood*, *Dances with Wolves*, and *The Silence of the Lambs*.

A subsidiary, Orion Productions, also produces motion pictures. Other subsidiaries include the Orion Classics Division, which distributes foreign films and English language films, such as *Babette's Feast*, *Au Revoir Les Enfants*, and *Cyrano de Bergerac*.

Republic Pictures

Republic Pictures was originally best known in the forties and fifties as a producer, before becoming a syndicator of low-budget Westerns. Republic has had some limited successes with TV series. ✆ **Their greatest accomplishments have been in TV movie production**.

They are controlled by Blockbuster Entertainment and have merged with fellow independent, Spelling Productions. The expectation is that they will branch off into a variety of other production areas.

Republic relies heavily on its home video arm to support its overhead costs.

MARKET STUDY OVERVIEW

The charts on the following pages will give you an overview of the market reflecting box office grosses and distributor market shares.

241

The U.S. theatrical film box office receipts in 1993 reached a record high of $5.2 billion. The top grossing film was Universal's *Jurassic Park*, released on June 11 and earning $339.4 million by the year's end. Warner Bros., however, which had five films (including *The Fugitive*) in the top twenty, led the industry in market share in 1993, for the third year in a row. In 1993 eight films grossed $100 million or more.

Top 10 Grossing Films of 1993
(in millions)

	Title	Distributor	Gross
1.	Jurassic Park	Universal	$339
2.	The Fugitive	Warner Bros.	179
3.	The Firm	Paramount	158
4.	Sleepless in Seattle	TriStar	126
5.	Mrs. Doubtfire	Fox	123
6.	Indecent Proposal	Paramount	106
7.	Aladdin	Buena Vista	103
8.	In The Line Of Fire	Columbia	102
9.	Cliffhanger	TriStar	84
10.	Free Willy	Warner Bros.	78
			$1,398

Top 10 Grossing Films of 1992
(in millions)

	Title	Distributor	Gross
1.	Batman Returns	Warner Bros.	$163
2.	Home Alone 2	Fox	146
3.	Lethal Weapon 3	Warner Bros.	145
4.	Sister Act	Buena Vista	140
5.	Wayne's World	Paramount	121
6.	Basic Instinct	TriStar	118
7.	Aladdin	Buena Vista	115
8.	A League of Their Own	Columbia	107
9.	The Bodyguard	Warner Bros.	89
10.	The Hand That Rocks the Cradle	Buena Vista	88
			$1,232

(Sources: *The Hollywood Reporter*, Standard & Poor's *Industry Surveys*, MPAA)

MARKET SHARES OF MAJOR DISTRIBUTORS, 1992-1993
1993 MARKET SHARES

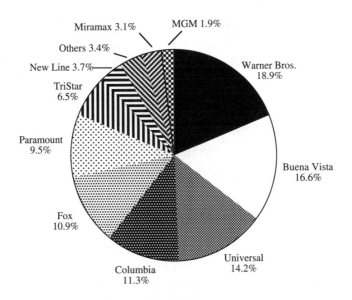

1992 MARKET SHARES

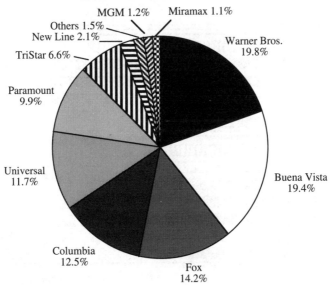

(Sources: *Los Angeles Times,* Standard & Poor's *Industry Surveys*, MPAA)

243

MARKET SHARES OF MOVIE DISTRIBUTORS
Feature Films

(Market share is the % of total market sales or revenues for a product or service.)

Distributor	1993 Share (%)	#Pix	Rank	1992 Share (%)	#Pix	Rank	1991 Share (%)	#Pix	Rank
Warner Bros.	18.9	35	1	19.8	28	1	13.9	28	1
Buena Vista	16.6	34	2	19.4	27	2	13.7	23	2
Universal	14.2	21	3	11.7	22	5	11.0	23	5
Columbia	11.3	22	4	12.5	19	4	9.1	14	7
Fox	10.9	21	5	14.2	24	3	11.6	20	4
Paramount	9.5	14	6	9.9	20	6	12.0	21	3
TriStar	6.5	13	7	6.6	11	7	10.9	13	6
New Line	3.7	27	8	2.1	15	8	4.0	18	9
Miramax	3.1	24	9	1.1	20	10	1.4	20	11
MGM	1.9	12	10	1.2	9	9	2.3	16	10
Others	3.4			1.5			10.1		

Note: Orion ranked 8th in 1991 (9 pictures, 8.5% share).

DOMESTIC BOX OFFICE REVENUE GROWTH, 1980-1993
(in billions)

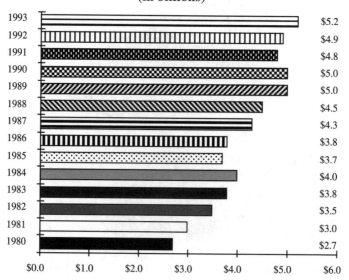

(Sources: Standard & Poor's *Industry Surveys*, MPAA)

244

You can see clearly how much money is made in this business. Impressive.

With films like *The Lion King* and *Forrest Gump*, 1994 was a record-breaking year for box office receipts. According to *Variety*, the box office totals as of August 1994 were $3.08 billion compared with $3.03 billion and $2.83 billion for the same period in 1993 and 1992, respectively. The top seven films of summer 1994 and their estimated grosses projected through the Labor Day weekend were:

Top 7 Feature Film Box Office Receipts
Summer 1994 through Labor Day
(in millions)

Title	Distributor	Gross
The Lion King	Buena Vista	$260
Forrest Gump	Paramount	225
The Flintstones	Universal	130
True Lies	Fox	130
Speed	Fox	115
Clear and Present Danger	Paramount	100
The Mask	New Line	100

(Source: *Los Angeles Times*)

✦ **The tables allow you to analyze what types of movies sold the most.** These figures should give you a good idea of what's going on.

You must always realize, however, that today's trends can be totally different. The figures we give are for the past. ✦ **It's very important that you keep updated.**

There are three major sources of trade information that we recommend you **subscribe to —** *The Hollywood Reporter, Daily Variety* **and** *Weekly Variety.* Everybody in the entertainment industry reads them. **It's a must.** Other good sources are *Premiere, Entertainment Weekly,* and *Movieline.* If you can't afford them, read them at your library. Otherwise, **at least subscribe to** *The Hollywood Reporter;* the *Reporter* covers both television and motion picture news.

Chapter 15.

Television Players

NETWORKS, CABLE, AND PRODUCTION COMPANIES

The three major networks that once dominated television are ABC, NBC, and CBS. Though their influence has declined since the mid-eighties, they're still the big boys on the block and wield enormous power and influence.

A decade ago they controlled perhaps 75 percent of all programs watched during prime time. Now their share hovers around the 50 percent mark. That percentage is expected to decline even more as the marketplace is further fragmented.

The upside for producers, writers, agents, and executives is that as the network market share declines, more venues spring up that provide outlets for scripts.

There is, however, a downside to this fragmentation that everyone must be aware of. Because the networks control less of the audience, they also control less of the advertising revenue. Decreases in revenue have forced the networks to seek ways of cutting costs. And the way they cut costs is to reduce the amount of programming they develop on a speculative basis. And clearly, as the networks develop or invest less, they will employ fewer producers and writers.

Recently, there's been a new player on the network block, Fox-TV. Fox began in the mid-eighties as a group of independent stations banding together in a loose confederation to share programming developed especially for them. Over the last decade they've increased their total on-air hours to the point where they compete head-to-head with the other three networks seven days a week. Their market share has also increased each year to the point where several of their shows regularly land in the top ten ratings winners each week.

Both Warner and Paramount have started new networks: The WB Network and the Paramount Network, respectively.

ABC

ABC began as an offshoot of RCA's Blue Network in 1943. For much of its early history, it was in third place among the networks, although it aired some popular and long-running programming over the years, including *Ozzie and Harriet*, *Make Room for Daddy*, *Wyatt Earp*, *77 Sunset Strip*, *Maverick*, *The Fugitive*, *American Bandstand*, *Disneyland*, *The Mickey Mouse Club*, *The Lawrence Welk Show*, and ABC Sports' *Wide World of Sports* (followed later with the success of *Monday Night Football*).

In an effort to survive and to compete with the other networks, ABC was responsible for some of the major changes in television, including bringing the Hollywood film studios into television production, an important factor in the switch from live television to film. ABC also opened programming to participation advertising, which spelled the end to program sponsorships.

In 1976, ABC jumped to first place with the help of Fred Silverman and shows like *Love Boat*, *Happy Days*, *Charlie's Angels*, and *Three's Company*. More recent hits have included *Moonlighting*, *Roseanne*, *NYPD Blue*, and *Home Improvement*. In 1984, ABC bought the ESPN cable network, and in 1986 ABC was itself acquired by Capital Cities for $3.5 billion.

ABC's Television Network Group includes ABC Entertainment, ABC Productions, ABC Early Morning and Late Night Entertainment, ABC News, ABC/Kane Productions (non-fiction films), ABC Sports and Daytime Entertainment, ABC Children's Programming and the

ABC Television Network. The Broadcast Group includes ABC's radio networks and TV stations, its video and cable enterprises (ESPN, Arts & Entertainment, the Lifetime Channel [co-ownership with the Hearst Corp.], and others), and the company has a strong publishing group, which includes seven newspapers, among them the *Fort Worth Star-Telegram* and the *Kansas City Star*, numerous magazines, including *Los Angeles* magazine, the Chilton guides, *W*, *Women's Wear Daily*, and *Institutional Investor*, among others.

CBS

In 1929 William Paley bought control of the Columbia Broadcasting radio network, which evolved into the CBS television network. From 1955 to 1968, CBS was number one in the ratings and was regarded as the most glamorous and prestigious of the networks, as well as a network with high production values.

The network was a leader in daytime and Saturday morning programming. CBS also maintained a high reputation for news coverage, particularly with the help of Edward R. Murrow and Walter Cronkite.

Other successful CBS programs have included *Playhouse 90*, *I Love Lucy*, *The Honeymooners*, *The Ed Sullivan Show*, *The Dick Van Dyke Show*, *Mayberry R.F.D.*, *The Beverly Hillbillies*, *The Mary Tyler Moore Show*, *All in the Family*, *Kojak*, *Murder, She Wrote*, *Cagney and Lacey*, and *Murphy Brown*.

Over the years the company bought and sold other companies, including cable companies it was forced to divest, which resulted in the formation of Viacom in 1970. In 1982, CBS and Twentieth Century Fox Video formed CBS/Fox, and CBS helped to form TriStar Pictures in 1983. Among other ventures, CBS sold Fawcett Books and CBS Records in the 1980s; the latter was bought by Sony. In 1985, Loews Corporation, whose CEO is Laurence Tisch, began buying CBS stock. Tisch is now the chairman, president, and CEO of CBS.

The Broadcast Group at CBS includes CBS Enterprises, CBS Video, CBS Entertainment, CBS News, CBS Radio, CBS Sports, and the CBS Television Stations.

Fox Broadcasting

Fox Broadcasting got its start when Rupert Murdoch (head of News Corp., which owns Twentieth Century Fox) bought several major TV stations from Metromedia.

The network itself was launched under Barry Diller's leadership in the late 1980s, and Fox Broadcasting succeeded in creating the fourth television network, starting in 1987 with programming in prime time two nights a week.

The network has grown with the success of such popular shows as *The Simpsons, Married . . . with Children, 21 Jump Street, In Living Color,* and *Beverly Hills 90210.*

NBC

NBC started as RCA's radio and television subsidiary. RCA (Radio Corporation of America) was founded in the 1920s by General Electric, Westinghouse, and AT&T, but GE sold its RCA holdings in 1930 due to an antitrust ruling. In 1986, GE purchased RCA, including NBC, for $6.4 billion.

For most of its history, NBC has run second among the networks but it has also been highly innovative. NBC introduced the morning and late-night talk shows, *Today* and *Tonight* (hosted successfully by Johnny Carson for thirty years), *Saturday Night Live,* the Sunday press conference (*Meet the Press*) and many other broadcasting innovations. NBC was also the first network to push color broadcasting, airing all of its programs in color, in part because RCA's color broadcasting system won out over its competitors in the early 1950s.

Early in its history, NBC did well with variety shows (Bob Hope, Milton Berle, Red Skelton), movies, adventure dramas, event programming, and news coverage.

✎ **In recent years it has also achieved great success with its prime-time sitcoms,** such as the *The Cosby Show, The Golden Girls,* and *Empty Nest.*

PBS

The Public Broadcasting Service was formed in 1969 by the Corporation for Public Broadcasting and later organized to focus on an orientation to local stations, rather than complete and central control from Washington.

The service is funded by federal funding, private and corporate/foundation contributions, and program underwriting.

❧ **PBS has a strong focus on educational and children's programming** (*Sesame Street* and *Mister Rogers' Neighborhood*, for example) as well as fine arts, history, and drama — *Live from Lincoln Center, Masterpiece Theatre* and *The Civil War* series — and acclaimed news programs, such as the *MacNeil/Lehrer News Hour*.

CABLE OUTLETS

Cable outlets were originally designed to provide niche programming, that is, specialized programming for small slices of the market.

Although this is still somewhat the case, cable programming moves closer and closer to the mainstream. It's becoming increasingly difficult to distinguish what's carried on the networks versus what's on cable.

There are even some cases of shows being carried both by cable and the networks.

A&E (Arts and Entertainment Network)

In the early 1980s, ABC and the Hearst Corporation founded the ARTS Network as a co-venture. In February 1984, they created the Arts & Entertainment Network when ARTS obtained the programming of the Entertainment Channel, one of the unsuccessful attempts in the eighties by other companies to create cable channels focused on cultural programming.

A&E went on to great success, largely by providing a diverse range of programming, from ✎ **"highbrow" fine-arts programming to lighter fare such as** *An Evening at the Improv.*

The Disney Channel

The Disney Channel is controlled by Walt Disney Studios and is geared toward family entertainment. It was launched by Disney in 1983.

Its programming is a mix of classic movies with a general family appeal, as well as new series and movies created especially for the channel.

✎ Disney is particularly fond of generating projects **that have a classic or timeless feel to them. It will take well-known material or literary characters and create new adventures** around them.

HBO (Home Box Office)

The HBO cable network was founded by Time, Inc. (now a part of Time Warner, Inc.) in the early seventies, and HBO, or Home Box Office, was initially conceived of as a channel that would bring feature movies, movies originally shown in theaters, to individual homes in their original uncut versions. HBO launched a companion service, Cinemax, in 1980.

For years, network television broadcast theatrical movies, but in order to fit two-hour time slots and commercial breaks, these films were routinely edited. Furthermore, many films' sexual and violent content had to be altered to air on network TV. Because it is a pay service offered only to subscribers, HBO is able to offer movies in their original format.

When the advent of the VCR fueled the home video market in the mid-eighties, HBO began to create its own original movies. It tended to choose controversial subject matter not normally seen in theaters or on broadcast television.

More recently, they've begun to offer series programming, or

☜ **what are essentially adult sitcoms with a harder or more sexual content.**

Ironically, as HBO has drawn viewers away from broadcast TV, the networks have responded by trying to increase the adult content of their own programs.

Among the top recent HBO hit original movies are *And the Band Played On*, *Barbarians at the Gate*, and *Stalin*. Series hits include *The Larry Sanders Show* and *Dream On*.

One division of the company, HBO Independent Productions, produces network series. Another division produces motion pictures and other programs for broadcast on HBO or by others. HBO subsidiaries include Film Management, Kremlin Productions, Simba Productions, WAC Productions, and Running Mates, Inc.

Lifetime

Lifetime is known as the woman's channel. ☜ **Its mandate is to produce or air programs of interest to women.**

The network was launched in 1984 and was co-owned by Capital Cities/ABC, Hearst, and Viacom until 1994, when Viacom sold its interest in Lifetime to ABC and Hearst. Its shows were originally a mix of documentaries, health programs, syndicated TV series that appealed to women, and original programming. Now the health programs are gone and original material is beginning to dominate.

Lifetime has produced a variety of series and movies and will only continue to do more.

For the moment it is still heavily invested in reruns of female-appeal shows such as *thirtysomething* and *Moonlighting*.

MTV

MTV, or Music Television, and its sister station, VH-1, have their roots in the music video explosion of the early eighties. MTV was launched in 1981.

They've gone from broadcasting an endless stream of music videos

252

to an eclectic mix of programming designed to appeal to teens and young adults.

They'll feature off-the-wall game shows, animated projects with a hip edge, as well as their own version of newscasts.

MTV and VH-1 are part of MTV Networks, a division of Viacom.

Nickelodeon

Nickelodeon, which was introduced in 1979, and its prime-time segment, Nick-at-Nite, began as children's programming and have gradually expanded with family fare.

Much of the prime-time programming has consisted of reruns of classic sitcoms from the fifties and sixties. Recently they, too, have begun creating original material.

Of particular interest are some of their new animated series such as *Rugrats, Doug,* and *Ren and Stimpy.*

Nickelodeon and Nick-at-Nite are also a part of MTV Networks, a division of Viacom.

Showtime/The Movie Channel

Launched in 1983, Showtime and The Movie Channel have been described by some as Viacom's response to HBO, which is controlled by Time Warner. Both cable channels are now a part of Showtime Networks, a division of Viacom. They, too, started with a heavy diet of theatrical features as the focus of their schedule.

Now they have added their own original movies with fare that is more controversial, more risque, and more adult than that traditionally handled by the networks.

Stylish thrillers such as *Acting on Impulse*, as well as their original anthology *Fallen Angels,* have given the channel a film noir feel.

Turner Broadcasting System

Ted Turner bought Rice Broadcasting, a small Atlanta TV station in 1970, and formed Turner Communications Corporation, then, later in the seventies, created "superstation" WTBS which was broadcast via cable by satellite. In 1980, Turner launched the Cable News Network (CNN) to provide round-the-clock news coverage. In 1982 he also created the Headline News channel, to compete with the Satellite News Channel from ABC-Westinghouse. (He bought out SNC in 1983.) Turner's purchase of MGM/UA for $1.7 billion in 1986 (which he soon sold) almost ruined him financially, but his acquisition of the MGM film library served as the backbone of Turner Network Television (TNT). In recent years, Turner has acquired Hanna-Barbera (shortly after which it debuted the Cartoon Network), New Line Cinema, and Castle Rock Entertainment.

TNT (Turner Network Television)

TNT, or Turner Network Television, came alive in the mid-eighties as part of Ted Turner's efforts to create and expand his media empire.

TNT airs a mix of classic movies from the old MGM/UA library and new films especially created for cable. TNT also tends to create films not traditionally seen in theaters or on broadcast TV.

Unlike HBO, though, TNT is part of basic cable in many parts of the country. Not being a pay service, explicit sexual content and violence are limited.

☙ TNT movies tend to be star driven. That is, in order to get one off the ground, production companies usually need to attach at least one big name star and preferably a feature name at that.

A typical original movie is *Zelda*, a story about author F. Scott Fitzgerald and his flapper wife. Another is *The Good Old Boys*, starring Tommy Lee Jones, Sissy Spacek, and Sam Shepard.

254

USA Network

The USA cable network was begun in the late 1970s as a partnership of Madison Square Garden and UA-Columbia Cablevision.

It became the USA Network in 1980, and is now a joint venture of Paramount and Universal that specializes in action-adventure programs, many of which are drawn from the two studios' libraries. USA recently started the Sci-Fi Channel.

Many one-hour series previously aired on the networks have found a home here in reruns. Original series programming also occurs for both movies and series.

☙ Murder and crime are the prime topics for original USA movies.

Typical reruns might be *Murder, She Wrote* or *Major Dad*. Original programs that air first on the network, then rerun frequently, are *Silk Stalkings* and *Swamp Thing*.

MAJOR TELEVISION PRODUCTION COMPANIES
(Due to space limitations, we haven't included all major independent production companies in this chapter.)

Stephen J. Cannell Productions

Stephen J. Cannell began as the writer and producer of numerous action TV shows, such as *The Rockford Files* and *Baretta*. His company has developed into a powerful mini-major on the back of its trademark one-hour action shows. Some of Cannell's other programs include *The A-Team, Hunter, 21 Jump Street, Stingray, Hardcastle and McCormick,* and *Wiseguy*.

As network tastes and budgets changed, Cannell moved into production for Fox-TV, **☙ syndication, and late night. It also produces TV movies and miniseries**.

255

Carsey-Werner Company

Carsey-Werner rose to the top of the comedy world on the back of its extraordinarily successful *The Cosby Show* and the powerhouse *Roseanne*. Their concentration has been almost entirely on 🐾 **half-hour development.**

The founders, Marcy Carsey and Tom Werner, came up the ranks as executives at ABC before moving on to becoming among the most successful producers of all time.

Hearst Entertainment

Hearst Entertainment, a division of the Hearst Corporation, has concentrated almost 🐾 **exclusively on TV movies and miniseries. Many of its deals are talent driven**, that is to say it has production deals with major TV stars for the various broadcast networks.

In order, however, to lessen their dependence on ever-shrinking network budgets, independents such as Hearst often rely on repackaging their MOWs as features for overseas distribution or for the ever-expanding home video market. These additional sources of revenue allow them to make up the difference in production costs and to cover their overhead.

Spelling Entertainment Group

Spelling Entertainment is a result of Aaron Spelling's phenomenal success as an independent producer in the seventies and eighties.

Spelling Television (formerly Aaron Spelling Productions) has produced such series as *Beverly Hills 90210, Melrose Place, Love Boat, Dynasty, Matt Houston, Fantasy Island, Charlie's Angels,* and *Hart to Hart.*

In an exclusive deal with ABC during the eighties, Spelling's shows, such as *Dynasty* and *Charlie's Angels,* dominated nearly a third of its programming. The company's focus was primarily on the one-hour format with occasional forays into long form and features. Present

256

strategy centers around such youth-oriented programming as *Beverly Hills 90210.*

The company also produces films for theatrical release. Spelling Entertainment acquired Laurel Entertainment in 1989, which has been engaged in the development and production of first-run syndicated series and theatrical feature films. Spelling generally arranges financing and distribution through a major studio or other third party.

Now controlled by Blockbuster in a merger with Republic, it's expected that the new configuration will branch out into a variety of programming formats.

Viacom

Viacom was initially formed by CBS as Viacom International after the FCC ruled that TV networks could not own cable systems and TV stations in the same market.

In the seventies, Viacom bought several cable systems; then, with Teleprompter in 1978, formed Showtime, one of the first subscription TV services. Viacom bought out Teleprompter in 1982. In 1983, Viacom and Warner/Amex combined Showtime with The Movie Channel to form the Showtime Networks. In 1986, Viacom obtained controlling interest in Showtime as well as acquiring the MTV Networks, including the MTV Channel, which started in 1981. The MTV Networks also include Nickelodeon/Nick-at-Nite, and VH-1. Viacom's greatest strength is in the cable world due to its ownership of properties such as MTV and VH-1.

Viacom has been a small player in network production, concentrating on long form efforts. It has produced series, such as *Matlock*, for network television, and syndicates TV programming (in 1988, it sold the rerun syndication rights to *The Cosby Show* for more than $515 million). In 1990, Viacom began producing movies for theatrical distribution abroad and broadcast over its cable networks. Its Viacom Pictures division develops and produces films that premiere on Showtime and the Movie Channel. Viacom Productions produces TV series and other prime-time network TV programs, and Viacom New

257

Media focuses on interactive software.

In 1994, Viacom was successful in its bid to acquire Paramount Communications. The merger with Paramount makes it the second-largest media corporation, trailing only Time Warner in size and scope.

By now we hope that you have a better understanding of the differences between motion pictures and television/cable programming. Once again we have given you some facts for you to analyze. Each company has its own needs and tastes. When you are ready to sell your project you must be current with what the buyers want. Otherwise, if you send your project to the wrong buyer, it doesn't matter how great your story is, they simply won't buy it.

❧ **It's crucial that you know what type of projects your buyer is looking for.**

The following charts will give you an idea of the massive amounts of money that are generated by the television market, both domestic and foreign, and will graphically illustrate the size of the television industry and revenue growth in terms of syndication.

Note: All of the major movie studios have television divisions. We included information on those divisions in the previous chapter. In addition to referring to the studio and production company descriptions, see also Columbia Pictures Television on page 227, TriStar Television on page 229, Touchstone Television on page 235, and Walt Disney Television on page 235.

DOMESTIC SYNDICATION REVENUE GROWTH, 1989-1994

(in billions)

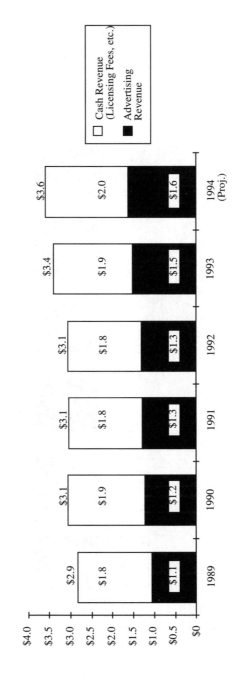

Cash Revenue (Licensing Fees, etc.)

Advertising Revenue

	1989	1990	1991	1992	1993	1994 (Proj.)
Total	$2.9	$3.1	$3.1	$3.1	$3.4	$3.6
Cash Revenue	$1.8	$1.9	$1.8	$1.8	$1.9	$2.0
Advertising Revenue	$1.1	$1.2	$1.3	$1.3	$1.5	$1.6

(Sources: Wilkofsky Gruen Associates, Advertiser Syndicated Television Association)

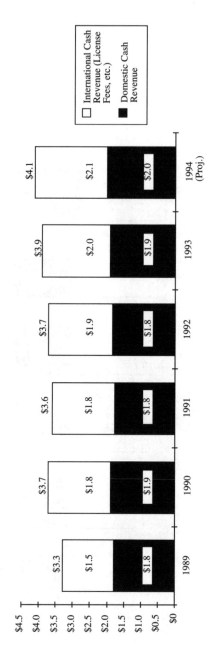

WORLDWIDE SYNDICATION REVENUE GROWTH, 1989-1994

(in billions)

□ International Cash Revenue (License Fees, etc.)

■ Domestic Cash Revenue

	1989	1990	1991	1992	1993	1994 (Proj.)
Total	$3.3	$3.7	$3.6	$3.7	$3.9	$4.1
International Cash Revenue	$1.5	$1.8	$1.8	$1.9	$2.0	$2.1
Domestic Cash Revenue	$1.8	$1.9	$1.8	$1.8	$1.9	$2.0

(Source: Wilkofsky Gruen Associates)

260

Chapter 16.

The Agencies

Agents and agencies come in many shapes and sizes, from the sole entrepreneur to the giants. The three most powerful agencies in the business are Creative Artists Agency (CAA), International Creative Management (ICM), and William Morris Agency (WMA).

As the power base of the networks and studios gradually became weakened and fragmented over the years, the strength of the large agencies has continued to fill the vacuum.

There are hundreds of agents and agencies in Hollywood that get involved in one form or another in the development of features and television shows.

Much good and bad has been written and spoken about agents, particularly of late. Their role has expanded and their clout has grown considerably.

They normally make 10 percent of their client's earnings, but with the packaging game, they can charge packaging fees that are not regulated.

Packaging agencies will frequently bring together the key elements of a show — the writer, producer, star, and director — as a package, and sell the show to a studio or network.

Agents can represent writers, directors, actors, producers, as well as many small and mid-sized production companies.

Of particular concern to producers and writers are literary agents and packaging agents.

☙ **Literary agents'** primary function is to represent writers. On a practical basis they serve as a kind of filter. Most executives at production companies will only deal with writers who have an agent, and most agents will only represent writers with a deal or a successful track record. It's a bit of a Catch-22.

Suffice for the moment to say that because of the sheer number of scripts that are written and circulated each year, it's impossible for any executive or company to read or even review anything more than a small percentage of what's out there.

Agents serve as the studio or development executive's first line of defense against the onslaught of scripts which roll into town each year. By giving a particular writer or script their stamp of approval, agents limit, and to some extent control, the number of scripts that make it to the studios.

Most studios, production companies, and networks are also frequent targets of lawsuits from individuals claiming that their ideas or scripts were ripped off or stolen. To cut down on these nuisance suits, most companies will only read material from agents. Rarely is material accepted from the outside.

The trick, as we said before, is to exploit these exceptions and ultimately find ways either to get around the barriers or make the system work on your behalf.

One way to do this is to get yourself an agent. And to do that you must have something they believe they can sell. Never forget that this is a business. As producers and writers you have the creative power to make something of value. If you can spot and secure a great story, or write well, you can attract the attention of a literary agent.

Just as you are trying to break in, so too are young or new agents trying to become established. They're always on the prowl for the next hot new talent. Convince them that they've discovered just that in your material and you're on your way.

Most aspiring agents start out in the mailroom of one of the major agencies and then work their way up the ladder by becoming an assistant to a full agent. These are the people you want to meet at this point in their career. Just like you, they're hungry and looking for that special project that will launch their career. Let it be yours and you'll have a supporter for life.

At their best, literary agents will circulate your story or script to the right people, people who have the ability to see that your story gets made.

A good agent will get you to the right people and negotiate a deal for a 10 percent commission.

❧ **Packaging agents** serve a somewhat similar function, but operate on a grander scale. They work at the larger agencies, which have a sizable stable of talent, that is, writers, directors, actors, and producers as their clients. They try to assemble the key elements for a production and assist in the sale of a project to the studios or networks as an entire package.

For this they charge a packaging fee for the life of the production rather than assessing a fee to the individual clients involved. The networks or the studios are then responsible for paying the commission.

In some sense, packaging agents function at this stage almost like producers, in that they're assembling the deal, putting the key elements together, and seeing that it's sold or financed.

Richard Weitz, an up-and-coming TV agent at ICM, notes that the big agencies are always looking to create opportunities for all of their clients. Furthermore, if they officially package the deal, they'll earn a commission based on the full budget of the show. This can be significantly more than individual commissions earned.

And since, in effect, it makes them a profit participant, they function almost as de facto producers. They'll marry up writer, director, producer, or talent teams and use their clout to bring a project to a studio or network.

If you're able to establish relationships with agents or agencies, they will be only too eager to help you sell material and set up deals. After all, that's the sole reason they exist.

➤ **An agent, that is the right agent, can be like a key opening up doors for a new writer or seller. But the only way to get an agent is to have samples or spec scripts or the rights to a "great project" that they believe are so superior to what's already out there, that they can sell it.**

Remember that agents are pure business people. They live off the deal. They're not counselors or advisors or script readers or literary consultants. They're salesmen and saleswomen who will take their best shot at a product they think they can move in the marketplace.

➤ All too often **if agents hear too much negative feedback** or the sledding goes uphill in their attempt to push a project, **they'll drop it fast.** They haven't got the time. This is not a negative assessment, it's a simple fact of life, one that is all too often overlooked by newcomers and veterans alike.

Chapter 17.

The Big Picture

For you to better understand the overall process, we are going to describe the five different steps of filmmaking from concept to screen: Each of these stages would require full chapters for us to be able to discuss them thoroughly. However, our intent is not to go into details but to give you an overall view of the full cycle.

DEVELOPMENT
PRE-PRODUCTION
PRODUCTION
POST-PRODUCTION
DISTRIBUTION

Development

In the development stage, an idea, concept, story, or literary material is acquired, either outright, through an option, or by hiring a writer to create original material. **For every forty scripts developed by studios, only one actually reaches the screen.**

Pre-Production

The production company selects (if not selected during the development stage) a director, actors and actresses, creates a budget, and secures the necessary financing. Pre-production activities are usually more extensive than the development process. In certain cases, commitments with talent must be made to keep them available for the picture.

Production — Principal Photography

Principal photography generally takes from eight to twelve weeks to complete.

Problems with permits, unions, weather conditions, or artistic changes that require reshooting scenes can seriously delay the scheduled completion of the picture. These delays can substantially increase production costs. ♔ **An experienced line producer is crucial.**

Post-Production

The post-production stage includes editing and sound effects (mixing of dialogue, scoring, and music). **It's the last chance to fix or improve the picture.**

♔ **A great editor can literally save or make a picture.** Master prints are delivered. With new technologies this phase is becoming even more crucial than ever (e.g., *Jurassic Park*, *In the Line of Fire,* and *Forrest Gump*).

Distribution of a Motion Picture

You can have a great movie, but ♔ **if nobody wants to distribute it, you are in trouble.** The movie's revenues are derived from worldwide licensing, both domestic and foreign.

Distributors' Basic Services

- **Advertising**

  Publicity & promotional materials — print & electronic media

266

- **Distribution**

  Duplicate prints & distribute them to theaters

  Monitor & collect revenue from the theaters

↜ **Distributors receive between 35 and 60 percent of total box office receipts** over the entire initial theatrical release.

Theaters keep the remaining 40 to 65 percent. The theater operator will also retain the revenue from the sale of popcorn/candy and drinks.

REVENUE STREAM

There are six main sources of distribution revenues:

(1)   Theatrical exhibition
- United States
- Foreign

(2)   Home Video

(3)   Cable & Pay TV
- Pay-per-view
- Video/movie on demand
- Pay cable – HBO, Showtime, Cinemax, etc.
- Basic cable
- Satellite

(4)   Television networks and local stations — Syndication

(5)   Non-theatrical exhibition (airlines, hotels, armed forces)

(6)   **Ancillary rights** (books, soundtracks/CD's, and miscellaneous merchandise).

• **U.S. theatrical receipts** are received 90 percent in the first year and 10 percent in the second year.

• **Foreign theatrical receipts** are received 40 percent in the first year, 50 percent in the second year, and 10 percent in the third year.

• **Home video royalties** are normally received 80 percent in the first year and 20 percent at a later date.

• **Pay and cable license fees** are received 65 percent in the third year, 25 percent in the fourth year, and 10 percent in the fifth year following theatrical release.

• **Syndicated domestic television receipts** are normally received in the fourth, fifth, and sixth years after theatrical release if there are no network television licenses, and the sixth, seventh, and eighth years if there are network licenses.

THEATRICAL   DISTRIBUTION

United States Theatrical Distribution

The total income earned from U.S. theatrical exhibition has declined with most pictures because of the increasing importance of cable and pay television, home video, and other ancillary markets.

☙ **It is very important for a picture to open theatrically in the U.S.** Its box office performance, or just the mere fact that it played in U.S. theaters, elevates the perceived value of the movie in other countries.

Foreign Theatrical Distribution

Today foreign theatrical markets are very important. **Distribution is usually done by local or regional distributors. Their fees vary between 35 percent and 40 percent.**

✤ There are risks associated with foreign distribution, the main ones being:

- Government quotas.

- Restrictions on the amounts of money that are allowed to be sent to the United States.

Home Video Rights

The United States video market has experienced a decline in the past several years. The "buyouts" by major corporations have upgraded the sophistication of the buyers.

Also, the possibility of **five hundred television channels and the cable pay-per-view — video or movie on demand —** service will force this market to possibly **go through an even greater decline.**

Films are released on home video six to nine months after initial U.S. theatrical release of the picture.

Pay cable (HBO, Showtime, Cinemax, etc.) and home video entities are continuously competing to acquire the same movies. They will not broadcast the same film, so it's important to be the first one to get it.

TELEVISION DISTRIBUTION

Cable and Pay Television

Pay television rights include rights granted to pay cable, pay-per-view, satellite, and other services paid for by subscribers.

Cable and pay TV networks license pictures for broadcast commencing six to twelve months after initial domestic theatrical release.

269

United States Television Distribution

Television rights are normally licensed first to pay television for a period following home video release, thereafter to network television, then to pay television again, and later syndicated to independent stations.

Network Television

In the U. S., network rights are granted mainly to ABC, CBS, NBC, and Fox. They license movies for a limited number of broadcasts during a period that usually commences two to three years after a motion picture's initial theatrical release.

Television Syndication

Distributors license the right to broadcast a feature film on local television stations in the U.S., normally starting five years after initial theatrical release of the picture.

Foreign Television Syndication

As we mentioned before, the importance of foreign markets has been increasing and should continue to grow. The distribution process is the same as the one that applies to the United States.

Ancillary Markets

The licensing rights of merchandise based on the movie characters can bring fortunes to those who retain those rights — books, games, posters, toys, and soundtracks/CD's among others.

In 1993, eighty-eight American films were among the top one hundred highest-grossing theatrical releases worldwide, according to Standard & Poor's *Industry Surveys. Jurassic Park* was number one, with $530 million in foreign sales out of a total of $868 million in ticket sales, followed by *The Fugitive* ($179 foreign/$349 total), *Aladdin* ($185 foreign/$303 total), and *The Bodyguard* ($248 foreign/$293 total). Some films, such as *Last Action Hero* and *Cliffhanger*, earned more overseas than they did in the United States.

As you can see, a motion picture can bring revenues from many different sources. It can make people rich. At the same time, the process is very complex.

Don't worry about being an expert on all the different phases that a picture goes through. However, by understanding how the whole process works, you will be better equipped to achieve your final goal.

❧ According to *Variety*, the summer of 1994 was remarkable at the box office, **including eight $100 million films in the theaters.** The table below shows the revenues and market shares for the major distributors.

TOP BOX OFFICE MARKET SHARES, SUMMER 1994
Domestic Box Office through August 25, 1994
(in millions)

Distributor	Gross	% Share
Buena Vista	$422.6	22.4 %
Paramount	351.7	18.6
Fox	257.5	13.6
Universal	235.1	12.4
Warner Bros.	208.9	11.1
Columbia	128.6	6.8
New Line	93.1	4.9
MGM	49.4	2.6
Miramax	42.7	2.3
TriStar	39.0	2.1
Gramercy	18.7	1.0
Others	41.8	2.2
	$1,889.1	100.0 %

On the next pages, the charts and table give an indication of the strength of foreign sales, based on worldwide theater rentals.

DOMESTIC VERSUS FOREIGN DISTRIBUTOR REVENUE
(in billions)

Year	Domestic Revenue*	Foreign Revenue*
1984	$1.3	$0.7
1985	1.1	0.6
1986	1.2	0.8
1987	1.2	0.9
1988	1.4	1.0
1989	1.8	1.3
1990	1.8	1.7
1991	1.8	1.4
1992	2.0	1.4
1993	2.0	2.0

* Theatrical rentals of distributors

(Sources: Standard & Poor's *Industry Surveys*, MPEA)

1993 TOP FOREIGN MARKETS FOR U.S. FILMS
(Rentals are in U.S. dollar values in millions of dollars)

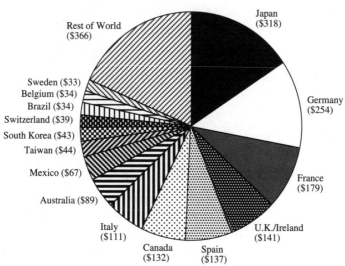

(Sources: *The Hollywood Reporter*, Standard & Poor's *Industry Surveys*)

FOREIGN FILM RENTALS, 1993
TOP FOREIGN MARKET REVENUE
(in billions)

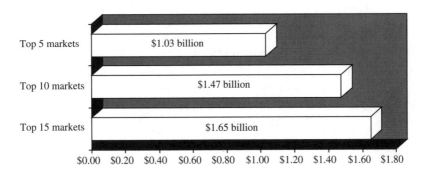

(Sources: *The Hollywood Reporter*, Standard & Poor's *Industry Surveys*, Motion Picture Export Association of America)

U.S. AND FOREIGN FILM RENTALS
1988 - 1993
(%)

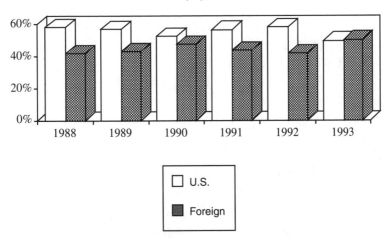

(Sources: *The Hollywood Reporter*, Standard & Poor's *Industry Surveys*, Motion Picture Export Association of America)

273

Chapter 18.

Motion Picture Selling Strategies

STUDIO AND MAJOR PRODUCTION COMPANY BUYERS

Once again let's identify who the buyers are, so we can start planning our strategies. The executive lineup at most of the major studios and production companies closely mimics those of the networks with several notable exceptions.

There are presidents, vice-presidents, directors, and managers of development, and at the very bottom the readers or story analysts.

Whereas the network is a buyer of property, the studio, in addition to being a buyer, is also a producer, seller, and syndicator of product.

Studio executives must be good producers and salespeople.

Because their job is more difficult, studio executives tend to earn more than their counterparts at the networks.

The failure rate is also very high, though, and the average term of office of a studio executive is scarcely three years.

Hollywood is not much for job security. And such insecurity breeds a combination of caution, fear, and a maddening desire to find the next great talent that can turn out a hit. It's the caution that this fear produces that is the new producer's or writer's worst enemy. No one will talk to you because you are untried and untested.

➤ **It is that maddening desire to find the next genius, however,**

274

that can be your greatest ally. If someone in a position of power believes you're the next Steven Spielberg, George Lucas, Steven Bochco, or Stephen Cannell, they'll roll out the red carpet to Spago, Chasen's, or Le Dome and the other hot Hollywood restaurants until they've signed you to a deal.

❧ **What you should know about the studio executives is that the power to buy and work with talent usually resides at the vice-president's level as opposed to the director level at the network. It's the old status game.**

A VP walking into the network is perceived as having greater stature than the network director. And when you're trying to sell, you need every edge you can get.

Although all of this varies considerably depending on the quality of persons who inhabit each position, the whole situation reminds one of "grade inflation" in many colleges today, where everyone doing adequate work receives an "A" and those who are weak earn a "B."

The United States has one president and one vice-president to govern in excess of 250 million people. A major studio, such as Warner or Paramount, may have a dozen of each title with every variation in the book added to them.

Flip through a typical directory and you'll see endless senior VPs, executive VPs, senior executive VPs, and just plain old vice-presidents of every imaginable subdivision.

One friend, recently taking over his boss's former slot at Warner, was at pains to explain to his family back east that, yes, even though he was going from being president of one division to a senior corporate vice-president, he was being promoted and not demoted. Go figure.

❧ What you need to know as the new seller, writer, or producer in town is this: If you meet with a studio manager or director, **they rarely have the power to say yes.** And many producers and writers consider meeting with such executives a waste of time. **It's not. It's just a long-term investment in your future.**

✎ Remember always that **today's director of development at Paramount might just turn out to be tomorrow's vice-president at Warner Bros.**

Independent Production Companies

The most significant differences between independent and major production companies are size and financial resources.

A major, such as the Samuel Goldwyn Company, has over the course of time amassed a solid library of films that can generate and sustain enormous resources which can be used to cut deals — development deals with producers, writers, and actors.

Most independents rarely have these deep pockets to fall back on. Their existence is more precarious, their staff sizes are smaller, with a much less significant degree of specialization. Whereas a Castle Rock or Republic Pictures may have different development executives for drama, comedy, and long form, at most smaller companies all of these functions are in the hands of one or two people, and they're most often the owner/producer/writer of the firm.

✎ **These smaller companies live and die by the deals they cut. They need to be both cautious and aggressive.**

They must stay within the mainstream yet at the same time find something fresh and original.

If a smaller company is headed by a writer, the chances are slim or none that they'll go outside to find creative talent. A writer heading his or her own firm is usually interested in creating and protecting their own material as a producer.

✎ **Companies headed by producers, however, are always looking for outside material and writers who can deliver. Very frequently they can be an excellent place to pitch projects to, particularly if you have an exceptional project or talent that has begun to be recognized by the creative community.**

Often the best way into a small production company is through agents who are able to direct the right type of project to the most suitable producer.

What these small companies, or "IndieProds," as they're nicknamed, offer, however, is rarely cash in hand. Few have the fiscal resources to pay outsiders for work. What they do offer, though, is entree and credibility. That entree can be translated into a network or studio deal.

꙰ Freelance Producers

Everyone in Hollywood is a producer, or so it seems. And it's true that thousands of people in town have some experience producing something, be it a thirty-second radio spot in the Texas Panhandle, or an Emmy Award–winning series. Don't be fooled by titles. Check the credentials of anyone claiming to be a producer who wants to make a deal with you.

꙰ On the other hand, there are hundreds of legitimate independent producers who do have real entree to studios and networks and can help create deals. They need you as much as you need them.

But how can you tell the difference between the good guys and the bad? You can't. What can you rely on? Your instincts, word of mouth, references, credits, cash, or a deal memo up-front.

꙰ Keep in mind that independents with a studio deal are in a far better position to help than those without, but even this is not a sign of either legitimacy or illegitimacy.

To make it in the film industry you're going to have to invest time and energy on speculation. That's the only way to create a script or project worthy of a sale.

In order to cut a deal at any level you've got to have something of value to offer. If you do and can prove it, your chances of success are that much greater; if you can't, you'll fail.

☙ ☙ ☙ READERS AND STORY EDITORS

There are two other players in the development game whose role is frequently overlooked, which is a shame because they are incredibly important and collectively wield an enormous amount of clout. These are the readers and story editors who are employed by most production companies and studios.

Their roles are similar; however, readers tend to be part-time freelancers and story editors tend to be full-time employees.

Who are they? What do they do? And why are they so important?

Hollywood is awash in scripts. The Writers Guild estimates that some thirty thousand scripts belonging to non-members are registered each year by their service alone. That's a lot of paper. And someone's got to read it.

The reality is that most producers, studios, agencies, and networks are buried under a daily landslide of incoming scripts. This is in addition to their own ongoing projects in all phases of development. And what goes in has got to be read and covered by someone. That task falls on the reader or story editor.

Most readers are either writers trying to earn cash on the side to support themselves or aspiring studio executives looking for a foot in the door. Story editors are usually the latter. They're people with some experience and training who are anxious to move up the administrative ranks.

Their primary task is to read every script that comes in and then write what is known as "coverage" for the senior executives to review. The onslaught of books and scripts coming in makes it impossible for executives to read more than the smallest fraction of what's out there.

Most senior executives don't ever read, unless they have to put time in on a script they're actively involved with. What they will look at, or better yet, glance at, is coverage.

Years ago, when Howard first started looking for a job, any job in Hollywood, he met with the former head of Twentieth Century Fox. When Howard asked if he'd be willing to read his spec script, he replied politely that when he ran Fox, he was accused of never reading the scripts of movies he green-lighted. "Why," he said, "should I start now?"

☙ Coverage, in a nutshell, is a three- to five-page critical summary of a script that analyzes its potential for the marketplace for that particular production company.

Ninety-nine percent of the time the recommendation is to "pass." And pass does not mean approval, it means to pass over or reject a script.

Why do so many scripts get passed over? Because most production entities can only create a handful of projects at any one time, everything is thrown back out the door.

☙ Why then are readers so important? Because the one time in a hundred that they recommend a script, everyone stops and takes notice. It's akin to finding a diamond in a coal mine.

☙ ☙ ☙ Writing to get past the reader is the first important hurdle to surmount when you enter the Hollywood wars. It's not a guarantee of success, it's merely the opening of the door to the next obstacle. But if the door doesn't open, you're back on the street.

On the other hand, don't get discouraged if you receive a pass. Your script has been evaluated on the basis of whether or not it's right for the studio or production company or agency you submitted it to, and no one else.

Try again, and keep trying until you succeed or you discover that what they've been saying about your script is right. Persistence pays off.

☙ If you pay attention to everything in this book, have creative talent, and apply yourself, you will be the one producer or writer in a hundred who gets his or her project past the reader.

SELLING DO'S AND DON'TS

Like most successful people in any business, you are going to have to use your common sense. ❧ The major questions that you have to ask yourself are: Who would buy my project? What studio? What producers? What stars? What directors? That's called **"target marketing."**

A lot of aspiring producers in this town try to sell their projects to whoever is willing to listen; after months and even years of invested time, most of those types of "shotgun approach" deals never happen. ❧ Do not use the **"shotgun approach." Use the "target market approach."**

PRODUCERS VERSUS STUDIOS

❧ ❧ **Do not send your project directly to a studio. If you do so, it will be a serious mistake.**

Most frequently when scripts are given directly to studio executives, those scripts are passed along to the story departments. Whatever comments the story editors or readers make are logged into their computer database. That means that if at a later time you come back with a major star or director attached, the studio executive will ask the story department to search in its computerized data bank to see if that project has been submitted before, and if so, to retrieve the old story analysis of your project.

If they find out that you have submitted the script or story in the past and that the studio passed on it, it will be much harder to sell to the executive, since they have to be convinced that they should reverse their original rejection.

It doesn't matter if you have a friend who knows the vice-president or the secretary to the president of the studio or whomever — be aware that that executive will send your project to the studio's story department for evaluation, and whatever the reader/story analyst decided the first time around will stick to your dream project for life at that studio.

280

Resubmitting to Studios and/or to Major Producers

Now here is a little secret that can help you in case you decide to introduce it to the studios and you were successful in doing so, although the responses were negative.

If you rewrote your screenplay or added great new elements (a star, a major director, etc.), then to protect you from the studio's retrieval of the old evaluation, you should change the following: The name of your screenplay/project, the names of your major characters, and the number of pages of your screenplay.

Now, **we are not suggesting that you deceive your potential buyer;** what we are trying to do is to help your revised project get a fair evaluation.

If you DO NOT rewrite it extensively and DO NOT ADD any major elements, DO NOT use this marketing strategy.

If the buyers find out that you are trying to deceive them, you will have lost one of the few sources available. After all, there are only eight major studios. Don't add more barriers to your odds of achieving your final goal. No matter what is said about Hollywood, there are a lot of honest people in the business and they don't appreciate being deceived.

Honesty and hard work never fail; it will just be a matter of time before you, too, hopefully, are able to touch your wall of success.

We strongly suggest that you **DO NOT try to reach the studios directly**, but instead, **try to attach yourself to an established producer.**
It is very difficult to get a project into the hands of a studio executive if it doesn't come from an accepted agent, attorney, star, or reputable director.

281

TARGET MARKET — BUYERS BY GENRE

If you are new in this business, we want to discourage you from playing independent producer.

If you are able to stimulate the interest of a major producer in your project, you are halfway there. Still, there are no guarantees until the movie is released to the theaters.

We could tell you some stories about movies that were green-lighted and ready to go, when suddenly something happened — financial problems, or the director dropped out, or whatever — and the project was dropped and put in turnaround (turnaround is the term used for a project that the studio decides no longer to continue developing).

A recent case is the megabucks movie by Carolco with Arnold Schwarzenegger titled *Crusaders*. They were already building the sets. Suddenly . . . pink slips to all those involved in pre-production. That was a shock for a lot of people.

Nonetheless, think positive. Hope that if you get a green light on your project, none of those problems arise.

Misdirected Approach

Do not send your project to the Zucker brothers if it's a dramatic story. On the other side of the spectrum, do not send a screwball comedy to Oliver Stone.

Make sure that your project reaches the hands of a potential buyer that is known for certain types of genres.

Yes, sometimes producers or directors make movies that are not exactly the genre of the projects that they normally have made in the past, but you don't want to take the chance of being the exception. We are here to cut down your odds.

To assist you in improving your odds, we are providing the following lists of feature film producers, categorized by genre.

FEATURE PRODUCERS BY GENRE

Feature Action Producers

Alphaville
Arnold Kopelson Prods.
Daybreak Prods.
Donner/Shuler-Donner Prods.
Edward R. Pressman Film Corp.
The IndieProd Company
Kennedy-Marshall Co.
Knickerbocker Films
Lee Rich Prods.

Lightstorm Entertainment
Neufeld/Rehme Prods.
Renaissance Pictures
Silver Pictures
Simpson-Bruckheimer Films
Stub Prods.
Trilogy Entertainment Group
Turman-Foster Co.
The Zanuck Co.

Feature Comedy Producers

Avnet-Kerner Co.
Donner/Shuler-Donner Prods.
Gladden Entertainment
The Haft-Nasatir Co.
Imagine Entertainment
The Jonathan Krane Group
The Koch Co.
La Luna Entertainment
Laura Ziskin Prods.
Laurence Mark Prods.
Mike's Movies
Morgan Creek Prods.
Red Wagon Prods.

Renfield Prods.
Robert Shapiro Prods.
Sandollar Prods.
Scott Rudin Prods.
Shadow Catcher Entertainment
Snapdragon Films, Inc.
Stampede Entertainment
Steel Pictures
The Steve Tisch Co.
Todman-Simon Prods.
Turman-Foster Co.
Z.M. Prods.

Feature Drama Producers

Alphaville
Arnold Kopelson Prods.
Barnstorm Films
Bregman/Baer Prods.
Daybreak Prods.
Di Novi Pictures
Douglas/Reuther Prods.
Edward R. Pressman Film Corp.
Edward S. Feldman Co.
Gladden Entertainment
The Haft-Nasatir Co.
The IndieProd Co.
Jones Entertainment Group
Kennedy-Marshall Co.
Knickerbocker Films
The Koch Co.
La Luna Entertainment
Laura Ziskin Prods.
Laurence Mark Prods.
Longbow Prods.

The Manhattan Project Ltd.
Marstar Prods.
Neufeld/Rehme Prods.
Pacific Western Prods.
Red Wagon Prods.
Richard Roth Prods.
Robert Greenwald Prods.
Robert Shapiro Prods.
Sandollar Prods.
Sanford/Pillsbury Prods.
Scott Rudin Prods.
Spring Creek Prods.
The Steve Tisch Co.
TFG Entertainment
Trilogy Entertainment Group
Turman-Foster Co.
Two Roads Prods., Inc.
Winkler Films
Wizan Film Properties, Inc.
The Zanuck Co.

Feature Historical Producers

Alphaville
Avnet-Kerner Co.
Donner/Shuler-Donner Prods.

Robert Shapiro Prods.
Trilogy Entertainment Group

Feature Horror Producers

Dark Horse Entertainment
Kennedy-Marshall Co.

Red Wagon Prods.
Renfield Prods.

284

Feature Sci-Fi Producers

The IndieProd Co.
Lightstorm Entertainment
Pacific Western Prods.

Renaissance Pictures
Renfield Prods.

Feature Thriller Producers

Bregman/Baer Prods.
Dark Horse Entertainment
Daybreak Prods.
Gary Lucchesi Prods.
The Koch Co.

Laurence Mark Prods.
Robert Lawrence Prods.
Roven-Cavallo Entertainment
Ruben/Robinson Prods.
Storyline Prods.

☙ Do your homework. If it is a director you want to approach for your story, contact the **Directors Guild of America and get their directory of members**. If it is a writer, get the **Writers Guild of America directory of members**. If it is a producer, get the *Hollywood Creative Directory.* These publications tell you what types of movies those directors, writers, or producers have made in the past. The guild directories will also give you the names of their agents.

Just be aware that when you contact agents, be it by telephone or letter, they may not get back to you immediately, and they may sometimes take weeks before they return your call or respond to your letter. They are very busy and they normally answer their calls on a priority basis.

☙ When they call you back, be brief and precise. Make sure you are ready to tell them why you called and what you have to offer. Tell them your story log line and any other elements (finances, actor attached, director attached, etc.) that you may have already attached to your project.

Whatever their answer is, accept it for now, but before you hang up ☙ ☙ **always ask if they are looking for something in particular for their client.**

If you are lucky and they tell you what they are looking for, you know what to submit next time around. However, their needs change frequently, so when you're ready to send it to them, they may no longer be interested.

If you get more elements attached to your project, you can always go back and let them know about your progress.

🖋 🖋 DO NOT CONTACT OR SEND YOUR PROJECT TO THE WRONG BUYER. IT'S A TOTAL WASTE OF TIME.

INDEPENDENT PRODUCING

We have discussed the strategies to sell to studios or major producers; however, most newcomers normally go the "independent producer" route. This means that they try to find financing and attach all the possible elements (actors, directors, etc.) to make it happen.

In this book we are not going to get into the details of how to raise financing to make a movie — we are concentrating on assisting you in selling your project.

If you are interested in becoming a producer, there is an organization called the American Film Market that organizes a yearly film market convention for independent producers (just like the Milano film market in Italy and the Cannes Film Festival and market in France) here in the U.S. You should contact them and get the list of the production and distribution companies that will be exhibiting their films.

🖋 These markets attract film buyers from all over the world. They normally buy finished projects, meaning produced movies. However, they also try to presell future movies.

🖋 They do it by getting commitments from **stars with international box office power** and they make a very appealing big poster, as if the movie had already been made. Those posters showing the commitment of bankable stars allow the distributors to entice the buyers to place advance orders.

If they are successful, they use all the advance orders from established exhibitors or regional distributors as collateral to raise the needed financing for the movie to be produced.

Again we do not recommend that you select this approach. If nobody knows who you are, or if you have not produced a movie, no distributor will be willing to represent your project.

❧ The real key for independent producing with international financing by using presales rests on the star that you are able to get a letter of intent or a firm commitment from to do your film, if it ever becomes a reality.

In case you decide to give it a shot as an independent producer and don't follow our strategies for newcomers, the following are lists of actors and actresses who have international star power.

❧ ❧ ❧ HOW THE STARS RATE WORLDWIDE

According to *The Hollywood Reporter*, stars are ranked in the industry in terms of their worldwide appeal and whether their names alone can bring about a foreign presale of a feature film. Following are their groupings based on their international box office power.

A+ • They Definitely Get the Movie Made
(In alphabetical order)

Sean Connery	Mel Gibson
Kevin Costner	Michelle Pfeiffer
Tom Cruise	Julia Roberts
Clint Eastwood	Arnold Schwarzenegger
Harrison Ford	Robin Williams

A • They Probably Get the Movie Made

Alec Baldwin	Kenneth Branagh
Kim Basinger	Macaulay Culkin
Warren Beatty	Geena Davis

Daniel Day-Lewis
Robert De Niro
Gerard Depardieu
Danny DeVito
Michael Douglas
Jodie Foster
Richard Gere
Whoopi Goldberg
Tom Hanks
Dustin Hoffman
Tommy Lee Jones
Demi Moore
Eddie Murphy
Jack Nicholson

Al Pacino
Robert Redford
Keanu Reeves
Meg Ryan
Winona Ryder
Steven Seagal
Sylvester Stallone
Sharon Stone
Barbra Streisand
Meryl Streep
Jean-Claude Van Damme
Denzel Washington
Sigourney Weaver
Bruce Willis

B+ • They May Get the Movie Made; Another Element* Is Needed (*financing, screenplay, distribution deal, etc.)

Woody Allen
Marlon Brando
Jeff Bridges
Glenn Close
Billy Crystal
Johnny Depp
Michael J. Fox
Gene Hackman
Goldie Hawn
Whitney Houston
Holly Hunter

Anjelica Huston
Jeremy Irons
Michael Keaton
Steve Martin
Bill Murray
Liam Neeson
Paul Newman
Nick Nolte
Kurt Russell
Emma Thompson

B • They Require a "Hot" Director and Other Element Attached

Isabelle Adjani
Alan Alda
Patricia Arquette
Richard Attenborough

Dan Aykroyd
Kevin Bacon
Billy Baldwin
Antonio Banderas

288

Ellen Barkin	Ralph Fiennes
Angela Bassett	Albert Finney
Annette Bening	Larry Fishburne
Tom Berenger	Bridget Fonda
Candice Bergen	Jane Fonda
Juliette Binoche	Morgan Freeman
Beau Bridges	Andy Garcia
Matthew Broderick	Danny Glover
Charles Bronson	Jeff Goldblum
Mel Brooks	Hugh Grant
James Caan	Melanie Griffith
Nicolas Cage	Linda Hamilton
Michael Caine	Daryl Hannah
Helena Bonham Carter	Woody Harrelson
Dana Carvey	Rutger Hauer
Chevy Chase	Katharine Hepburn
Joan Chen	Barbara Hershey
Cher	Hulk Hogan
John Cleese	Paul Hogan
Jamie Lee Curtis	Dennis Hopper
Willem Dafoe	Bob Hoskins
Timothy Dalton	Isabelle Huppert
Ted Danson	William Hurt
Judy Davis	Don Johnson
Rebecca De Mornay	Raul Julia
Catherine Deneuve	Diane Keaton
Laura Dern	Harvey Keitel
Leonardo DiCaprio	Nicole Kidman
Matt Dillon	Val Kilmer
Kirk Douglas	Ben Kingsley
Robert Downey Jr.	Kevin Kline
Richard Dreyfuss	Christopher Lambert
Robert Duvall	Jessica Lange
Emilio Estevez	Spike Lee
Sally Field	Juliette Lewis

Ray Liotta
John Lithgow
Dolph Lundgren
Andie MacDowell
Kyle MacLachlan
Shirley MacLaine
Madonna
John Malkovich
Mary Stuart Masterson
Mary E. Mastrantonio
Walter Matthau
Matthew Modine
Rick Moranis
Sam Neill
Leslie Nielsen
Chuck Norris
Gary Oldman
Lena Olin
Sean Penn
Rosie Perez
Joe Pesci
Brad Pitt
Sidney Poitier
Dennis Quaid

Stephen Rea
Alan Rickman
Tim Robbins
Isabella Rossellini
Mickey Rourke
Susan Sarandon
Greta Scacchi
Tom Selleck
Charlie Sheen
Christian Slater
Wesley Snipes
Madeleine Stowe
Kiefer Sutherland
Patrick Swayze
Elizabeth Taylor
Uma Thurman
Marisa Tomei
John Travolta
Kathleen Turner
John Turturro
Mario Van Peebles
Christopher Walken
Debra Winger
James Woods

Note: These lists change yearly.

HOOKING TO A PRODUCER

Let's explore our recommendation that you try to have an established producer option, buy, or even partner with you.

Developing the Concept

Any good producer with experience is going to know the market-

290

place far better than you. He or she will be up to date on what the studios are buying, when they're open for pitches, and what particular quirks of casting they may be after.

Consider yourself lucky. You've hooked up with someone who not only likes you and your idea, but who also has valuable knowledge of what else might be necessary to make it fly.

You'll probably have a few meetings to discuss changes in story and character. Be open to these ideas; don't be bullheaded, stubborn, or think you know better — even if you're convinced you do. You're still creating a product to sell and you need every bit of help you can get.

🐦 **Try to be amiable,** even when you feel you have important ideas to bring up. **Collaborate to the best of your ability.**

The goal is to refine your pitch, story, and presentation to sell it at the next level. Depending on the producer's clout or the nature of the project, they may want to try to interest a star in the piece and to build a package.

🐦 **Producers live and die by their sales. Everything a smart producer does is designed to enhance the package.** Go with the flow. Be patient, but play out your role with smarts and strength.

Once everybody is happy with the revised story, collectively you'll probably work out a new pitch. At this stage, the producers take over.

The Sales Pitch to Studios or Major Production Companies

Using their knowledge of the industry, the producers will attempt to set up pitch meetings with studio executives.

When they find a receptive ear, it's time to go in. This time around the producer will call the shots as to how the project is presented. You go along and do your part.

As before, there are two possibilities. A quick pass, or a thoughtful maybe. You wait and finally a week or two later the answer comes back. Yes, they want to move ahead. Great! Now it's time for the deal.

Cutting the Deal

The producer, studio, and you will be signed to a deal. For you as a new producer or writer, having a major studio standing behind you is a significant show of support.

Even though there's nothing on the table yet, you're definitely showing potential. It's time to get an agent.

Ask around; find out who other writers or producers like. Get a few referrals and call them up. Tell them you're trying to set up a deal with Studio X and need help.

🗝 **Many agents will offer to handle this for you** — it's usually rather simple — without actually signing you as a client. That's okay. You're still trying to get your foot in the door, and you'll need to take any opening that's there.

The agent will negotiate the deal for you. For writers it's typically something that's set at "scale" plus 10 percent. In other words, if you eventually sell the idea to the studios or network, you'll get the WGA minimum plus 10 percent to cover the agent's commission. For a first deal, it's not bad. Don't balk. A bird in the hand is worth two in the bush.

If you're a new producer, the numbers vary and it's much more difficult to pin down real dollars.

Many factors are involved, particularly since you may have other, more senior producers attached.

🗝 Our advice is **not to worry about the money this first time around. Getting the project made is far more important.** Worry about money on your next project. By then, you'll be the one with clout.

With luck or something special in your background or unique to the project, the agent may be able to negotiate for more, but don't hold your breath waiting. You're still an untested entity.

Redeveloping the Idea

Once the deal is closed, you and your producer will be sitting back down with the studio executives to once more refine the project. The studio brings with it extra clout and contacts. It may be able to attract a powerful piece of talent to attach to the project.

Once again, the best advice is to go with the flow. What you have may be a far cry from your original concept, but odds are it'll have a far better chance of success. Allow each of your collaborators to contribute to the project with their tools and skills.

In the business of filmmaking, projects sometimes take years before they are ever made. A perfect example is producer Wendy Finerman's movie, *Forrest Gump*. Even though she's a respected producer and her husband is the head of a studio, it took her nine long years to make the movie. So, when your opportunity comes, don't blow it. Enjoy the ride.

To end this chapter we are going to introduce you to one of Hollywood's most distinguished directors and producers, Robert Wise, and his philosophy on how to succeed in this business.

🦒 THE 3 P's

"Regardless of how you try to enter our business, there are 3 P's to abide by: 🦒 **passion, patience, perseverance**.

"Passion is number one. Start with the passion you feel for your project. If you have a project that you want to get going, you must have all three 'P's' to make it work.

"Once I had a project where I had an option on a book for four and a half years. All that time I tried to get it made, I kept at it because I had a passion for the story, and then the patience and perseverance to keep at it until it finally came together."

— **Robert Wise,**
Director
(The Sound of Music, West Side Story,
Star Trek: The Motion Picture)

293

Chapter 19.

Television Selling Strategies

THE NETWORK EXECUTIVES WHO BUY PRODUCT

T he hierarchy of power and authority varies slightly from network to network, but there are some consistent patterns. At the top are the presidents of the entertainment divisions, as well as senior executive vice-presidents of various allied divisions. Their role in the development process is to oversee the final selection of product that will air. They rarely get involved in the daily decisions.

The day-to-day work of buying ideas and scripts, and of working with writers, producers, and production companies, is left to the vice-presidents, directors, and managers of development.

Again, the patterns of management vary from network to network and from time to time, but a typical model is this:

A vice-president or senior vice-president oversees all prime-time programming development. Under that individual there will traditionally be vice-presidents of comedy, drama, and long form development. Below these VPs are usually anywhere from one to six directors and a corresponding number of managers.

What do they all do and who has the power to buy product?

Let's start at the bottom. Managers are mid-level executives with some prior experience in development, story-editing, producing, or agenting. Their primary function is to assist the directors and vice-presidents while being groomed for eventual promotion.

They read freelance submissions, meet with newer, younger, less established talent, agents, producers, and writers. They attend most story meetings and pitch sessions, take the notes, and contribute creative input.

Their unwritten goal is to network, establish positive relationships with the creative community, seek out as-yet-undiscovered talent, and show the aggressiveness and creativity that will lead them up the corporate ladder.

If you're starting out in Hollywood, they're great people to get to know. While lacking in real power, managers are on the power track and will, if they're good, rise through the ranks. If they get to know you and your work, there's a good chance they'll take you along for the ride to the top.

If you look over the resumes of nearly every major studio or network mogul, you'll find they started in either the mailroom of a major talent agency or they passed through the manager's slot at a TV network. The friends they made then are the associates they carry with them for the rest of their careers.

During Howard's first week at ABC in 1985, he was given on-the-job training by the departing manager of drama series development, Donald DeLine. Donald is now president of production at Walt Disney and Touchstone Pictures.

Immediately above the managers in the hierarchy are the directors of development. Directors are the real workhorses. Most of the time they have the authority to buy with some slight overseeing from the vice-presidents.

A good director knows the players in the creative community, from agents to talent to writers. And more importantly, they're known to the community at large. They will buy off a pitch from a credible writer or producer and then work with them for up to a year and a half to see the project through all phases of development.

Depending on the department, the strength of the network, and the trust given to them by superiors, the directors may shepherd as many as fifty projects at any one time.

Most have no social life outside work. Their job is a twenty-four-hours-a-day, seven-days-a-week pressure cooker of meetings, readings, and greetings. They've got to know and be in touch with more information than any one human can possibly manage, yet somehow they juggle it all.

The stress level is high. In Hollywood you're only as good as your current success; your last one isn't good enough. And the directors work in the trenches, fighting the good fight, against long odds, even longer hours, and a never-ending wave of competition.

Above the directors are the vice-presidents of the division who take a more supervisory role on most projects. They can and will do everything a director does while also courting the "A" level talent in town.

To people trying to break in, they are almost totally inaccessible. Their days and nights are filled with an endless stream of meetings, industry-related social functions, and endless hours of reading scripts and reviewing film dailies of projects being shot.

Because the pressure to succeed is unrelenting for executives in these positions, studio and network executives invariably turn to the producers, writers, actors, directors, and agents they know and trust to create projects that have a chance to succeed.

How did they get to meet, know, and work with these people? The answers are simple. They came up the ranks together, worked together under intense pressure, and came to rely upon each other for support.

❧ **The key for newcomers looking for long-term success is not to jump hastily into the middle of the pack, but rather to begin to cultivate the types of friendships and business relationships that will eventually provide an endless source of opportunities.**

Hollywood is really very much a small town. Your boss today may be your coworker or assistant tomorrow. Everyone knows or knows of everyone else. The biggest single activity is networking, that is, getting to know other players in the game, and offering them something of value.

❧ A final note about the networks. Because they are the buyers, executives get to meet and deal with everyone in town. Even the lowest ranking manager at the network will be introduced to the most powerful players in the city.

This creates unlimited opportunity for those capable of capitalizing on it. Consequently, positions at the studios and networks are jobs that most people would sell their mothers to obtain.

Network executives are not there to create a big fortune for themselves unless they make it to the uppermost ranks. They're there for the chance to wield power and influence, and to find future opportunities.

Most successful network executives move on to a studio or become independent producers.

Again, whether it's a Marcy Carsey, who created *The Cosby Show* and became a millionaire, or a Barry Diller, who ran Paramount and Fox before leading the moves to buy out Paramount and CBS through his holdings at QVC, check their resumes.

On the television side, the means necessary for pushing an original screenplay for an MOW are difficult enough, and the route is almost always through a producer or production company that has already generated some clout.

✎ If a production entity with clout gets behind your project, their clout becomes yours.

Pitching

✎ Keep in mind that your goal is to sell your idea as quickly, stylishly, and with as much pop and sizzle as you can manage. **Before you walk out the door to pitch it to anyone, make sure you know what you're doing.**

Think about the typical thirty-second commercial on TV for almost any product. In half a minute advertisers have gotten across the essence of a product they want us to buy. And we do. No one says you've got to pitch your idea in thirty seconds, but the lesson worth learning is that you've got to do it as efficiently and powerfully as you can in order to capture a customer. If you're not enthusiastic about your story, no one else will be either.

Say you've got six ideas. You've worked out the details of each of them to the tune of maybe four or five pages apiece. Some work well, others don't. Pick out the best of the lot. One, two, but no more than three.

❧ Save the others in an idea file. You might want to trot them out someday, but not today. No one is going to listen to six pitches in a row, nor can you honestly demonstrate enthusiasm for all six. Go with the best.

❧ Work with the other three. **Create interesting, compelling characters to flesh out your stories.** Expand your notes until you know as much about your material as possible.

Don't worry about a formal treatment. This round of notes is for you and your eyes alone. Never show rough drafts of an idea to anyone. Rough drafts are just that: rough. You know what you want, but it's not on paper. No one you show a rough to is ever going to know what's in your head that's going to make it sing, so don't waste your time.

When you've got it fully worked out, copy your notes over, then proceed to hone down a really tight treatment that captures the dramatic highlights into two to five pages maximum. If you need help writing, by all means get it.

❧ Try to place yourself in the position of a buyer. What is there about your idea that's going to hook them right away? The last thing you want to happen is to walk into a room to present your ideas and the next thing you know is that the executive or producer you're facing has a glaze of boredom over his or her eyes.

As distasteful as the notion is, keep in mind that your prime responsibility after creating a story is to become a salesperson. The best idea will go nowhere if you can't sell it.

Once you've created your perfect treatment, put it away. Practice presenting your idea without the benefit of the written word. Do not memorize what you have written, but rather, become so totally familiar with it that you can present it to anyone at the drop of a hat.

Think about conversations you've had with people in the past that have just rambled on and on versus those that have really hooked you. What was it that kept your attention? Does your idea have the same power?

When you're convinced it does and that you can present it wonderfully, then and only then are you ready to take it outside the walls of your house.

❧ Once you've got an appointment to pitch, remember to have your tools in hand. What are they? **First, you've got to have your pitch in your head. Second, you should keep a clean copy of your treatment tucked away in your briefcase. Third, if you're a writer, be sure you've got a brilliant sample script that shows off your writing skills for the type of movie or project you're pitching.**

If you've only got a sample sitcom in your portfolio and you're pitching a heavy melodrama, forget it. It won't fly. The script need not be for the idea you're presenting — though on very rare occasions that does work. It needs to show off your ability to work in the format you're trying to sell.

Once armed, you take the meeting. You verbally present your best idea. Sell it with every ounce of conviction you've got, and one of two things will happen: They'll either like it or they won't.

Notice, we didn't say buy it. That rarely happens in the room. If they don't like it, you might try to trot out one or two of your other ideas. Maybe one will go.

But let's say they do like it. You'll probably be told they'll get back to you in a few days. They might ask if you've got something in writing, and if they do, you give them your polished treatment. If they ask for something else you've written, give them your sample script.

❧ **Go home and wait until they call you back. While you're waiting, try to figure out whom else you might pitch to.**

If word comes back, and for this example we're going to presume that it does, that they want your idea, great!

Before anything else happens, you'll probably be asked to sign off on an if-come deal or an option. Don't hold out for big money because there isn't any yet. What you're basically after is a working relationship that's capable of taking your idea to the next level.

The relationship may also be no more than a handshake at this stage. That's okay too if you're dealing with reputable people.

Ultimately all the minimum wages on a TV movie are set by the Writers Guild of America contract. If you sell it to the network, don't worry, you'll get paid handsomely for your efforts. But right now you're still miles away from that goal, so don't blow it by becoming greedy, paranoid, or even overly cautious. There's a lot more work to do before you can move on.

Pitching to the Networks

Depending on the subject matter and style of the project, you'll have a limited number of places to finally sell the project. There are the four networks and a half-dozen cable outlets.

For creative or financial reasons some of the outlets may be ruled out immediately. If, for example, ABC's got something similar in development, they won't see you. And if Fox is full, they won't see you. And if the project seems too much like a broadcast TV movie, HBO won't see you either.

The studio executives know all of this and they'll pick the best shots first.

Development Seasons — When Is Product Bought and Sold?

If you're interested in getting a new show on the air for the upcoming fall season, that's great. Except for one small problem. You're about two years late. The creation of a new show is a slow and tedious process.

At the networks the fall development cycle begins anywhere from

300

sixteen to twenty-one months in advance for drama series and a year to eighteen months for comedy series.

The opening salvo of the development cycle at the network is referred to as "pitching season." Or, you'll hear people say that the network is "open for pitching." Anytime between, say, January and early summer, the networks will schedule meetings with those people they're anxious to work with.

The scheduling varies considerably because at the same time network staffs are taking pitches for next year's shows, they are also overseeing the production of this year's pilots. During the weeks when there is heavy work to be done on the new pilots, no pitches are taken.

During pitch season, network executives take hundreds of meetings and hear thousands of ideas for shows. From that overwhelming pool they might commission anywhere from 60 to 120 scripts.

After a pitch is accepted, writers generally spend the next three to six months engaged in writing outlines and the two drafts and a polish called for in most contracts.

From November through January, the networks evaluate the final drafts and select ten to fifteen drama scripts and a similar number of comedy scripts to actually film as pilots.

Filming begins on the different projects between January and late March or early April. Once everything is completed, the networks each schedule the equivalent of "Pilot Week." This is a period of time when all the completed works are screened for all of the senior network executives, including the chief executive officer, chairman of the board, and all the presidents of all the major divisions.

After everything has been screened, the senior staff members retreat to the corporate headquarters in New York to plan their fall schedule. They're followed there by all the studio heads, top agents, and producers who will lobby for their shows and clients.

By mid-May, the networks make their choices and plan their tentative schedules. The shows they're most interested in are given "pick up" orders, usually for six, nine, twelve, or twenty-two episodes.

By July or August, the show staffs are set. The first few episodes are written and shot. Come September or October they hit the air.

301

The Mid-Season Cycle

The notion of having mid-season replacements ready is one that's imbedded in concrete. The networks are always prepared for the worst. They know they're always going to need new shows to fill weaknesses in the schedule.

Since most mid-season shows begin airing between January and March, the development cycle is fairly similar to that for fall shows with several minor exceptions.

The cycle runs about five to seven months behind the fall cycle. So for example, while new shows are beginning to go into production in July and August, network executives are busy taking pitches for mid-season shows.

Mid-season pitching will continue into the fall. And while the networks are busy deciding which fall shows to pick up during their spring, they'll continue meeting with producers and writers about their various mid-season scripts.

Purchasing for mid-season is about one-quarter to one-third the volume of fall purchases and there is no formal "pilot week." During the summer months the networks will review the mid-season prospects and select those shows that seem most likely to succeed or fill an expected weakness in the fall line-up.

Long Form Development Cycle

Long form development follows a much less restricted schedule and generally occurs on a year-round basis. Pitching and production go on simultaneously.

Before each season begins, the long form development departments have a rough idea of how many movies and of what types they'll need to fill the schedule. It could be thirty, fifty, seventy, or anywhere in-between.

Numbers vary considerably from network to network and from season to season. One major influence on this is the number of specials and sporting events the network may choose to program in a given year.

302

It is also affected by the replacement philosophy at play at any given time. When a series show turns up with bad numbers, some executives opt to pull it immediately and throw in a back-up replacement. Others might juggle the schedule and plug gaps for a few weeks with additional movies.

Networks generally have a ratio of three scripts developed for every MOW or miniseries produced and aired. Knowing this they pace their buying of pitches accordingly. Whenever they have enough scripts in development or projects in production they are "closed" for pitching purposes.

Selling the Pitch

The big day has finally come. You're going into the network accompanied by your producer and the studio executive.

After a few minutes of chit-chat, you'll once again make your presentation. It'll be short, sweet, and to the point. By now you know it as well as your own name. Everyone contributes their particular expertise. And for at least the third time you'll either meet with a pass or a definite maybe.

A few days or weeks later, the answer comes back. No. It just doesn't mesh with their needs. And it's off to the next place. This time you stroll into another network and make your pitch again. Another "maybe" and you wait.

Finally, the studio calls back. It's a yes!

Closing the Deal

If you haven't been able to get an agent before, you will now. There's a real deal with hard cash to close. You may call a few agents, but chances are agents will be calling you. Remember, everyone's always on the lookout for the next big hot talent, and that just might be you.

The studio will make their deal with the network and your if-come deal memo will be translated into a full contract for services in accord with all WGA regulations, or if you're a producer, whatever else you may have worked out.

The deal will specify time schedules for delivery as well as payments due for each stage. Now it's possible that the deal may not be guaranteed, meaning the network, if not satisfied, can cut you off at any point. Although the provision is frequently added, it's rarely invoked.

And if you're the writer, and they're paying you for the project, you have no ownership rights to the materials you create. You can be bumped and replaced by another writer on your own project without recourse, provided the network and studio follow all the terms of the contract.

Being rewritten has happened to the best writers in Hollywood, and should that event come to pass, there's really very little you can do except take the money and run to your next project.

But let's look at the bright side. You've got a deal to write or produce a TV-movie script. You've made it to the major leagues and you're playing with the big boys. Whether you stay there is now up to you and the fates.

Selling the Pilot/MOW Script

If your project is accepted, behind the scenes your producer and your studio executive will be lobbying the network to choose your piece. If you've got heavyweight talent involved, they'll get into the action as well.

And don't forget your agent. Going into production guarantees a far bigger payoff for you and commission for them. It also gives them the chance to package a director and stars.

Suffice it to say that it can get real political. Everybody is pushing for their side. May the best script and the most powerful team win. Hopefully that script is yours. The odds are three to one for an MOW, twice that or more for a pilot.

Further complicating the odds process is the fact that certain heavyweights in town will be totally immune to the numbers and waiting game. Whereas a network might order thirty to forty MOWs a year, a fair percentage of these will come from preexisting deals with guaranteed production commitments. The same holds true for pilots.

Companies such as Steven Bochco's or Aaron Spelling's might have a guaranteed commitment from the network. This means in effect that from the moment they pitch or present a new idea for a show, the outcome is certain. That show is going to get made.

Networks make commitment deals like this with the very best talent around town in order to ensure that they gain access to the services of these talented people.

Big name stars are also frequently the beneficiaries of these types of deals. The lead of a series that a network wants to keep happy often gets a commitment for his or her next series or for a TV movie.

Types of commitments vary considerably. A writer/producer team with a great track record might get a guaranteed script commitment. This means that if they pitch a fairly reasonable idea, they'll definitely get the go-ahead to write (and get paid for) a script.

A pilot commitment means that the creative team is guaranteed that they will definitely go all the way through the script process and have the ability to see their project filmed as a pilot.

A guaranteed series commitment is a promise that the network will pay for the script, the pilot, and a specified number of episodes for a new show. Deals of this sort are clearly the most expensive and risky, and consequently, are rarely given out — but they are given out. When Jeff Auerbach was president of Blake Edward's television company, they obtained just such a deal for a series for Blake's wife, film star Julie Andrews.

For the struggling freelancer there is a downside and an upside to these types of commitments. Heavy guarantees by a network to existing heavyweight talent make it more difficult for newcomers and second-tier players to break through.

If a network shoots fifteen pilots out of seventy-five pilot scripts, the odds are one in five. But if half of those fifteen pilots are shot because of preexisting commitments, the odds of anyone else winning this lottery jump to one in ten.

How can this help you? At first glance it seems like it can't, but if you dig deeper and find out who has existing commitments with the networks, you can try to pitch your projects to them first. A success there will then streamline your development process because you'll be the beneficiary of the prior commitments.

Pilot/MOW Production Order

The creative team that does the best job in creating and marketing its script with the network is going to end up getting the production order.

For TV series pilots this is a key step in a still difficult and challenging race. There are more obstacles still ahead.

But for MOWs a production order is pretty much as close as you can get to knowing that your script is going to be filmed and aired.

If a network is feeling particularly optimistic about a pilot script before it's shot, it may even authorize several back-up scripts for the actual series. This is so that the show can be raced into production if necessary. Orders of this type are more common for mid-season shows, which by their nature are designed to fill in the gaps created by failed shows.

Another common type of order, again primarily used for mid-season, is called the "short order." Right from the start the network views this show as a serious contender for the schedule. Instead of focusing on a single pilot, they concentrate on creating six episodes.

Shows of this sort typically air around February. If it's a success, as was the case with *Kate and Allie* and *Moonlighting*, the network will be able to factor this information into its fall season planning meetings held in April and May.

Moonlighting was actually a two-hour pilot followed by a six-episode short order. Its ratings that first spring were not strong, but it was enough of a critical success that ABC opted to renew it the following year. Their hunch proved correct and it was a smash hit for the next three seasons.

Pilot/MOW Production

Once the order is awarded to the studio, pre-production begins. First on board is usually a director, followed closely by the casting of the stars. A production team, including a line producer, is brought on to handle the actual physical production of the show.

If you're the writer, you may be brought in to make additional adjustments to the script during the shooting, but by and large the writer is generally considered a nuisance around the set by most directors.

From this point on they consider the project their own and don't particularly care for the opinion of the writer. The guild ensures writers' rights to be on the set, but generally your time is better spent writing or selling your next project. Unless of course you're specifically asked to be around for rewrites.

Hollywood is, remember, the product of collaboration and it's time to let others do their job of bringing your idea to the screen.

Of course you may feel like you've been abused when your script becomes unrecognizable to what you originally envisioned. This happens. The first few times around there's not much you can do.

It's for this reason successful writers frequently become producers, directors, or both. They see this as a means to safeguard their artistic vision. It's also a means of developing clout that will help down the road.

The best way to accomplish this goal is not to interfere when you're just starting out, but to watch, look, and listen to what the other players are doing and how they're doing it. If you feel that you can do a better job, then by all means start doing it.

Meanwhile, if your project is an MOW, the next steps are simple. Go to the wrap party and the publicity screening, hobnob with the celebrities, and then invite your friends over to watch the MOW on the night it airs.

For the uninitiated, MOW publicity screenings are rarely the glamorous events one sees on *Entertainment Tonight* or CNN's *Hollywood Minute*. They're pretty much straight business affairs with the cast, crew, creative executives, and writers from the various trade magazines in attendance.

Wrap parties are also usually low-key affairs. It's a production company's way of saying thank you to the crew and cast. Still, a lot of bigwigs will show up and if you're into food, it's usually top-notch.

Series Selection

If what you've been involved with is a pilot, there usually won't be a public or publicity screening. After all, no one knows whether you've reached the end goal — being picked up for series production.

As we noted earlier in the section on development seasons, this is now the time for the senior studio executives to push metal to the floor in their lobbying efforts. Their goal is short and simple: Convince the network through whatever means possible that your show is the one they need to pick up for next year.

Lobbying for this takes all forms and includes every power play imaginable.

For network executives it's a particularly intense time. Each one has invested his or her ego and prestige on a particular favorite project. Their careers depend on success and they're wary of anything that stands in the way. There's much competition between the executives in each department and much competition between departments for favorable spots on the schedule.

For writers and producers at this point there's not too much to do but wait and plan the next steps in your career. If you've gotten this far, you're hot and consequently this is the best time to strike that next deal.

Series Order and Production

If your show is among the lucky chosen few, congratulations. The next phase will be for your studio and producer to assemble a full show staff of writers, directors, and the physical production team.

Chances are you'll land a job on the ongoing series. However, because you're still new to the game, a senior writer/producer will probably be brought in as show runner. Show runners are veterans who know what's required to get a show mounted each and every week.

Even if you have the title and status that puts you above the show runner, our advice is to shut up and listen, at least for the first few weeks or episodes.

Again, let the people who know what they're doing, do what they do best. When you've got the requisite skills, that'll be your time to take over.

Many talented writers have been fired off of their own first show because they failed to heed that simple bit of advice. Ego is no substitute for experience. And if you coordinate your creative ideas with the show runner rather than fight him or her, you'll have a much better chance of achieving your end goal of keeping your job and ensuring that your show stays on the air.

Production orders for a new show vary considerably. Heavyweight veterans with a star cast might get a full season pick up of twenty-two to twenty-four episodes, but that's rare. More typical are shorter commitments of six, nine, or thirteen episodes.

If your show goes in the ratings dumper, the networks want to be able to bail out as fast as possible at the lowest cost. But if you're good, maybe you'll be the one to go all the way.

Current Shows

Orders for new shows are generally given out after the New York scheduling meetings. Depending either on the faith the network has in a particular show or on the nature of the deal they originally made with the production entity behind it, a production order will be handed out for a given number of shows.

Once a show is given the go-ahead for regular season production, oversight of that show is transferred from the respective network's development department to the current programming department.

An executive from current programming is assigned to that show, and may have anywhere from seven to twelve shows to monitor. At some networks, show assignments are divided into comedy and drama groupings. At other networks, assignments may be done more randomly.

Current programming executives, usually at the director level, have minimal clout over a new show. Their primary function is to serve as a liaison between the show's producers and the network senior staff. They will monitor all the stories, scripts, and film dailies or sitcom tapings.

Should there be a minor problem or conflict, they will try to resolve it, but if the situation escalates, they will quickly report back to the vice-president of current programs who will then resolve the dispute. Essentially current executives want to make sure that a show stays on track, that the stories turned out are consistent with the underlying philosophy for the show that's been hammered out in development.

More often than not the current exec is interfacing with a veteran show runner who will usually have far more experience than the executive. Ellen Endo-Dizon, formerly a vice-president of current comedy at Embassy TV and the senior vice-president of production at Republic Pictures, once compared giving notes to having a gun. Smart network executives know that when they walk into a story or script meeting, it's as if they have a gun with only six shots. Their corrective notes had best be on target and limited in number. If they make too many comments, they'll be perceived as amateurs who should be totally ignored and if they make fewer comments than necessary, then the show may not work as well as it should. Responsibility for its failure may then rest on their shoulders.

Typical Purchase Orders

On average, the typical number of episodes of a full season of any given prime-time series is twenty-two. On rare occasions this escalates to twenty-four or even twenty-six, but these are the exceptions.

In the early days of television, orders were often as high as thirty-six episodes per year. The burden of production, however, was too much. With the networks currently having the rights to air each episode of a show it purchases from a studio twice, an order of twenty-two shows allows it pretty much to cover the fifty-two weeks of the year. Obviously, two times twenty-two is only forty-four, but keep in mind there are many weeks, especially during the holiday season, when normal programming is interrupted for specials, sporting events, or blockbuster miniseries.

Even so, to produce enough shows to fill the calendar for six months usually requires a full nine months or more of production work.

The various tasks of laying out stories, casting each episode, drafting scripts, handling pre-production chores and actually filming or taping are all labor and time intensive. It's exhausting work, especially on film shows that may depend on a single lead actor.

Bear in mind that TV production works at light-speed compared to theatrical features. The typical theatrical motion picture with a 120-page script may take three to four months to shoot. That works out to roughly a page a day.

By comparison, the average one-hour TV script is about forty-four pages long and it's usually shot in seven to ten working days. That works out to anywhere from four to seven pages a day. Add to that the time for rehearsals and you can see that it's difficult to move from shooting one episode to another in less than two weeks. Even so, to fit into the rigors of a tight production calendar, it's necessary for the director of one episode to be in production while the director of the next episode is in pre-production.

Tom Greene, a top-notch writer-producer for such shows as *Magnum, P.I.*, *Wildside*, and *Knight Rider*, has often told us how overlapping production schedules put an enormous burden on the writing staff. Changes in scripts are constant right through shooting. And since the show runner tends also to be the head writer and rewrite person, the time and pressure are intense.

Given these circumstances, it is more typical of networks to give out limited orders on new shows. Whereas a veteran show with a seasoned staff may get an early order for a full twenty-two episodes, networks hesitate to give a large order to a new show.

The most common limited order is for thirteen episodes. An order of this size is large enough for a studio to gear up a full-scale effort to get the show staff together and begin pre-production. If all goes well in the early stages and the ratings are acceptable, the show will get what's known as a "back nine," or an additional order of nine shows, bringing the total to twenty-two.

If the network is less confident in the chances of success but still feels the show is worth a shot, they will give out a short order of six episodes. Sometimes they'll tack on an order of an additional three scripts. If the show takes off, it'll help the staff to continue the flow of production by having the extra three scripts ready to roll out.

Less common formerly was an up-front order of nine shows. Now, however, as networks scramble to cut costs, more and more nines are appearing where one might have seen an order of thirteen before.

There are various exceptions to these general rules. Occasionally shows created directly for the syndication market, such as *Swamp Thing* or *Thunder in Paradise*, which Tom Greene also produced, might get multi-season orders of thirty-six, forty-four, or more episodes. These shows are shot on budgets much lower than normal network fare. The large orders enable them to cut costs through long-range planning. They can double up on sets, locations, and even film footage.

Following, for your reference, is a list of television producers of movies of the week.

Television Drama Producers

Alexander/Enright & Assocs.	Gross-Weston Prods.
Blue Andre Prods., Inc.	Grossbart/Barnett/Iezman Ent.
C.M. Two Prods.	Hill/Fields Entertainment
Carla Singer Prods.	Jones Entertainment Group
Cosgrove-Meurer Prods.	Karen Danaher-Dorr Prods.
Craig Anderson Prods.	The Kushner-Locke Co.
Dave Bell Associates	Larry Thompson Organization
Freyda Rothstein Prods.	Larry White Prods.
Gimbel-Adelson Productions	Lion's Leap Prods.
Green/Epstein Prods.	The Manheim Co.

Marian Rees Associates
Morgan Hill Films
O'Hara-Horowitz Prods.
Papazian-Hirsch Entertainment
Patchett Kaufman Entertainment
The Polson Co.
Preston Stephen Fischer Co.

Rosemont Prods. Ltd.
Stonehenge Prods.
Susan Baerwald Prods.
Symphony Pictures
Ten Four Prods.
Tomahawk Films
Von Zerneck-Sertner Films

Television Thriller Producers

CPC Entertainment
Diana Kerew Prods.

The Landsburg Co.

Chapter 20.

Financing Sources for Motion Pictures

T his chapter will give you an overall view of the different forms of financing used and/or available for moviemakers.

We prepared this chapter with the guidance of UCLA Extension Film School instructor Mr. Alan Gadney. He is an award-winning filmmaker, author, and publisher who has packaged, secured financing for, written, produced, and directed feature motion pictures. He has won forty-nine international awards for his work in twelve countries, and has written fifteen books and several screenplays. Alan has a master's degree from USC's School of Cinema-Television.

UNDERSTAND YOUR FINANCING OPTIONS

There are two major paths to financing. One is to seek financing within the film and television industry; the other is to locate funding independent of the entertainment industry. Each path offers benefits and drawbacks.

ENTERTAINMENT INDUSTRY FINANCING

There are traditional sources that finance motion pictures, television, and related projects. The financial players are highly sophisticated movie financing experts, and they may have stringent requirements that you cannot meet — such as a superior and highly commercial screenplay, star acting talent, big name director and producers, distribution deals and rights presales in place, and so forth. Traditional industry financing sources include:

Major Studios, Networks, Producers, Distributors

Looking toward the electronic future, the major studios have already begun to increase their individual distribution slates from only a dozen annual releases a few years ago, to forty or more per year. ⚓ **About half of those releases are acquisitions of films either made completely independently of the major studios,** or indirectly financed by the studios through some sort of production financing or distribution guarantee (sometimes called a prearranged Negative Pickup). The remainder of their releases are either financed completely in-house (within the studio) or co-financed and co-produced with others.

Entertainment Lenders (Banks)

Entertainment lenders make loans for interest and they require collateral. ⚓ Collateral for movie loans comes in the form of (1) a bankable distribution deal with a creditworthy distributor — a major studio for example, (2) the preselling of rights to the domestic ancillary and foreign markets in the form of a bankable contract — such as a letter of credit, and/or (3) individual guarantees of credit — e.g., your rich uncle. It may take some or all of the above to secure a movie loan, and then it may be for only a portion of the needed budget. You may still have to bring in equity investors to make up the deficit.

International Sources

There are numerous sources of international funding securable by international entertainment financing experts, including ⚓ **overseas tax shelters, foreign equity investors, international co-productions and below-the-line** (mechanical charges, crew labor, extras, art and set costs, camera, electrical, wardrobe, transportation, raw-film stock, and post-production) **facilities deals.** Some countries have **blocked**

funds available, and **limited grant and subsidy programs**. But remember, each form of funding has its own requirements and restrictions. With international funding, you will usually have to shoot in the foreign country, bring in a certain amount of U.S. dollars, possibly for above-the-line salaries (writer, executive producer(s), producer(s), director, and principal members of the cast), and you will most probably need an international financing expert to set up and guide you through the deal. Also, the countries that you will be forced to shoot in may have adverse working or political conditions, or other drawbacks.

INDEPENDENT FINANCING SOURCES

If you do not wish to deal with traditional movie financing sources, or cannot meet their requirements, you can take the other route and go independent.

Passive Investors

✿ Potential independent investors **include everyone from highly sophisticated multi-millionaires to people with only a small nest egg.** You can sell them an investment in your project either through a broad-based Public Securities Offering, or individually through a Private Solicitation. But you must be aware of the many restrictions . . .

Because these investors will not be <u>actively</u> involved in the management of your production, you will be selling them a <u>passive</u> security (probably a share in a limited partnership or stock in a corporation or some other form of security) and thus what you sell, how you sell it, and to whom, will be regulated by the securities laws of both the United States federal government and the individual states that you are selling in. ✿ **The best advice is to get a good securities attorney to guide you through the intricate disclosure and selling process.**

To make an offering, you must have the proper securities documents in place. Please do not try to put together a securities disclosure document by yourself. ✿ **The penalties for even unwittingly violating federal and state securities laws can be horrendous.**

316

Active Financial Partners

The benefit here is that securing active business partners is not the sale of a passive security — because Financial Business Partners will be <u>actively</u> involved in your business in important management and decision-making positions. ☙ **They are part of your business and will help run your production operation.** And they can be openly solicited. You are seeking partners to be actively and financially involved in your production business. (And remember, they <u>must</u> be actively involved, because if they are not, then they may be considered to be passive investors, and you may be in violation of state/federal securities laws.) ☙ The drawback of course is that they <u>are</u> actively involved in your business. **They may not know anything about the movie business** (they sell used cars), **may have their own personal agendas** (they want their girlfriend to star in the film), **and may cause you massive problems that will not be worth the hassle.**

Grants and Gifts

This is the granting or gifting of financing, many times with strings attached (such as, the grant source owns your production). There are usually a limited number of sizable grants available and the competition is usually intense. Generally, the grant amounts may be too small for larger productions; however, the feature *Stand and Deliver* was financed primarily through grant monies, as many outstanding documentaries, shorts, and experimental projects have been.

Self-Financing

Under this scheme you do not look for outside financing but instead ☙ **look to yourself, your family, close friends, and acquaintances.** You raise a little money (possibly a personal loan from your wealthy Aunt Martha), borrow some from your family, sell your stamp collection, and put the rest on your credit cards. Then, to reduce your budget to rock bottom, you do all sorts of creative deals for those services and facilities that you cannot afford. (This is why the "thank you" credits on no-budget films can run for ten minutes.)

🔑 **You use extensive deferments for the cast and crew, borrow as much as you can, pay for everything else on extended credit, and slip into hard-to-get locations unannounced to "grab" some shots.** Some even pretend to be student filmmakers to get around permit restrictions. A number of inexpensive first films have been made this way by recognized directors Robert Townsend, Spike Lee, Paul Bartel, John Sayles — and the list goes on and on. Robert Rodriguez's *El Mariachi* is a recent $7,000 example.

Create a Strong Package and Presentation

🔑 **The traditional motion picture industry package usually consists of a finished screenplay, stars, a name director, and possibly a name producer or executive producer.** The sophisticated producing-financing entity will take care of, and possibly dictate, the rest of the movie packaging process — creation of the budget, production plan and schedule, marketing plan, selection of cast and crew, and so forth.

🔑 If, on the other hand, you are seeking **independent financing, your package and presentation will need to be far more complex.** Independent financing sources normally only provide the funding. You provide the production expertise and business plan, and you control the production. Therefore, your independent package will **consist of not only the script, acting and key creative talent, director, and producer, but also a detailed budget, complete production and marketing plans, financial plan and deal structure, possibly an income projection, and any special servicing or facilities arrangements you may have in place.**

And whether you are approaching independent or studio financial sources, you should always present your package in a professional manner — bound in a good-looking quality cover, complete with typeset text, title logo artwork, and photos or illustrations if appropriate, preferably in color. Too many independent producers invest in a

318

professional budget and production board, but then skimp on a dull, low-grade presentation that looks more like a high school term paper than an exciting production-financing plan designed to get investors to part with their money.

Seek Independent Financing

If you do not have a "knock 'em dead" screenplay, if you cannot put together a "Studio Package" or other industry financing requirements, or if you are a smaller budget producer making a highly personal artistic feature and need total control, then traditional movie industry financing such as studio deals, rights presales, international bank loans, and expensive stock offerings will probably not work.

But not to worry. 🖋 Simply go to the many independent financing sources instead — **regional investors, financial partners, family-friend financiers, grants, and contributors.** These sources exist throughout the country (and the world), and with **a good commercial project, solid production-marketing plan, and an artistic presentation supported by clever cost cutting, creative deal-making, tenacity, talent, and timing, you can raise your necessary funding.** Others have, why not you?

🖋 Use Creative Financing Techniques

These include such methods as step-financing, deal sweeteners at both recovery and profits, and partial cash financing.

PARTIAL CASH FINANCING

First, you budget your project. 🖋 **Then you raise only the cash required to actually make the picture** (such as 50 to 75 percent of the budget), and you as the producer make creative deals for the rest of your budget requirements such as cast/crew deferments, equipment discounts, extended credit on facilities and services, loans, contributions, and product placement trade-outs. The benefit to your financiers is they get full profit participation (100%) on the investor side for only

319

putting up a percentage (say 66%) of the capital needed. You as the producer have supplied the rest through deals. Richard Linklater shot *Slacker* in Texas on a $151,000 budget — only $26,000 (17% of the budget) was cash, the remaining $125,000 was deferred.

Make the Deal Investor Oriented

Structure in "Deal Sweeteners" that favor the financiers so that they can recover their investment and make some profit before other participants. 🦒 **Deal sweeteners serve to make your package "investor oriented" and more attractive to funders.**

ACCELERATED RECOVERY

When profits are returned to your production company from the distribution and sales sources, traditionally the financial investors/partners recover their original capital contributions first, before profits are divided and paid to other participants. 🦒 You can "sweeten" the financiers' recoupment position **by giving them as close to 100% of income as is feasible until they have completely recovered their original investment.** Mitigating factors might include contractual payments of star profits from gross income, payment of outstanding expenses, loans, and talent deferments, and small deductions for production company operating expenses.

FINANCIAL BONUS

To further sweeten the financiers' recovery position, you could also add a bonus to the recovery amount. Thus, your financiers first recoup all (100%) of their original capital contributions. Next they receive a bonus percentage of their original contributions, such as 10% or 20% to make up for lost interest (so that they are actually recovering their original investment at 110% or 120%). After this, further income becomes profits.

ACCELERATED PROFITS

Profits are usually divided between the financiers, production company, and possibly third parties, such as important acting or creative talent. **☙ Again, to sweeten the deal for your financiers, you can accelerate their profits on a sliding scale so that your financiers initially receive higher profits than the production company until profits are returned to them up to certain levels.** An example might be a 70/30 split (between financiers/producers) until an amount equal to the financiers' original investment has been earned in profits. Then the formula slides to 60/40, then levels out at 50/50 (and possibly the split can then reverse to favor the producers first at 40/60 and then increasing to 30/70). Thus, if the picture pays off, the financiers first earn the most, and if the picture goes through the roof, the producers earn the most in the long term.

Cut Budget Costs

Scale down your budget to the essentials and put your investors' money on the screen where it should be. **☙ Investors do not like to see a lot of expensive middlemen and extravagant living — no chauffeured limousines, expensive gifts, personal servants and gourmet catering — this reeks of all the wasteful policies that they have heard over and over about Hollywood-type productions.** But your production is not "Hollywood." It is probably independent, financially conservative, and possibly a smaller budget. With creative planning and clever scripting you may be able to avoid the high-cost sets and effects, expensive aerial and underwater sequences, and chaotic crowd scenes with babies. Tighter budgets mean breaking even faster, which means faster profits for you and your financiers.

☙ If you are interested in learning more about financing, read John W. Cones' new book: *43 Ways to Finance Your Film(s).*

Here are the 43 ways to finance your picture:

STUDIO/INDUSTRY FINANCING

1. The Studio/In-House Production Deal
2. The Studio Production-Financing/Distribution Agreement
3. Studio-Based Independent Production Company Financing
4. Independent Distributor Financing
5. Domestic Studio Facilities Deals
6. Lab Deals
7. Talent Agency Financing
8. End User Financing
9. Completion Funds

LENDER FINANCING

10. Lender Financing Without Distributor Contracts
11. Negative Pick-ups
12. Artificial Pick-ups
13. Pre-Sale Financing of Feature Films

INVESTOR FINANCING

Active Investor (Non-Securities Vehicles)

14. The Self-Funded Sole Proprietorship
15. Business Plans
16. Investor Financing Agreement
17. Joint Venture Financing
18. The Initial Incorporation

Passive Investor (Securities) Vehicles

19. The Investment Contract
20. Limited Partnerships (generally)
21. Limited Liability Companies
22. Corporate Financing (generally)
23. The Out of State "Foreign" Corporation
24. "S" Corporations
25. Small Corporate Offering Registration (SCOR)
26. Regulation "A" Corporate Stock or Limited Partnership Offerings
27. Regulation S-B Public Offerings
28. S-1 Public (Registered) Offerings
29. Over-the-Counter Companies
30. A NASDAQ Company
31. Stock Exchange Companies
32. Convertible or Participatory Debt Instruments
33. Regulation "D", Rule 504 (Private Placement) Offerings
34. Regulation "D", Rule 505 (Private Placement) Offerings
35. Regulation "D", Rule 506 (Private Placement) Offerings

FOREIGN FINANCE OPTIONS

36. Blocked Currency or Blocked Funds Deals
37. Foreign Currency Deals
38. Foreign Below-the-Line or Facilities Deals
39. International Co-Productions (involving formal treaties)
40. Foreign Tax Shelter/Incentives
41. Foreign Government Grants of Subsidies
42. Foreign Debt Capitalization Programs
43. Foreign Equity Financing

Chapter 21.

Financing Sources for Television

U ntil 1993, federal laws allowed for studios to produce and sell series to the network, but the network only had the right to air each episode or movie twice.

This purchase or payment is called a **"license fee."** Essentially it is the amount of money the network gives to the studios to produce each episode of a show.

Amounts vary considerably, but current license fees might run around $600,000 to $700,000 per half-hour. For a one-hour drama, double that, and for a two-hour movie, quadruple it.

In the past decade, inflation has caused the cost of production to exceed the license fee for each episode. A production company may have to eat or **deficit finance** each episode to the tune of several hundred thousand dollars.

Multiply this times twenty-two episodes a year, and you suddenly realize that the studios LOSE millions of dollars every year for the privilege of airing shows on the networks.

Only players with deep pockets can afford these kinds of losses. Why do they do it then? Because a hit show can make hundreds of millions of dollars back in the secondary or syndication markets.

After the second airing, all rights to the show revert back to the studio or producer. In effect, the networks "rent" the shows they air.

The studios then resell the shows that have aired on the network into syndication around the country and the world.

That's why you'll see shows like *Who's the Boss?* or *Cheers,* or even *I Love Lucy,* forever. The studios have sold them into syndication in specific markets, such as New York or New Orleans or Los Angeles, for a specific number of runs.

Much of the profit in television these days comes from syndication sales. It was the sale of *The Cosby Show* into syndication that turned its producers, Bill Cosby and the Carsey-Werner Company, into mega-millionaires.

To effectively syndicate a show, however, a studio usually has to keep a show on the air for upwards of three to five years, and preferably, seven.

Why? To air a show, such as *The Cosby Show* or *Facts of Life* or *Silver Spoons*, in syndication five days a week for six straight months requires a minimum of 130 episodes. That's nearly six years' worth of work. And not many shows last six years.

So obviously, when studios buy or create product, they're looking for those with staying power, because if they don't stay, they not only lose money deficit financing initial production, they will also get minimal returns on their efforts to balance the books through syndication. It is the few hits they create that allow them to experiment with all of their failures.

And in a world where the stakes are so high, the players are cautious and looking to hedge their bets.

Chapter 22.

Distribution

T his chapter will deal with the do's and don'ts of cutting a distribution deal. As you know, we can have access to finances to produce our film by having a distribution company advance some money or give us a letter of intent. Mark Litwak, an entertainment attorney, journalist, screenwriter, television producer, university professor, and the author of *Reel Power* and *Dealmaking in the Film & Television Industry: From Negotiations to Final Contracts*, will take you through the distribution maze. Again, don't worry about it. You probably will sell your project to a seasoned producer, so you don't have to worry about the details of distribution, but at least you will understand how it works.

There are several ways to develop or produce a film. Beginning with an idea or the movie rights to an existing literary property, a studio can hire a writer to create a script. The studio's development staff works with the writer to craft the story. Most scripts developed by studios never get produced.

Other movies begin with a script developed outside the studio. Here a writer, working on his or her own, or hired by an independent producer, writes a screenplay. After it is finished, it may be packaged (joined) with other elements (e.g., a star or director) and presented to the studio for financing and distribution. The big three talent agencies (CAA, ICM, and William

Morris) are responsible for most packaging.

Sometimes films are both developed and produced away from the studio or company that ultimately distributes them. These independently produced projects are often dependent on investors or presale distribution deals (selling off various foreign distribution rights) to finance production. The producer then enters into an acquisition agreement with the distributor for release of the picture. This is called a negative pick-up deal.

Although the terms of negative pick-up deals vary, the studio/distributor typically pays for all distribution, advertising, and marketing costs. The studio/distributor and producer share profits. Because the producer has taken the risk of financing production, he or she probably can obtain a better definition of net profits than if he/she made the film with studio financing. Profits may be split 50/50 between the distributor and producer without a deduction for a distribution fee. Of course, the independent producer takes the risk that if the film turns out poorly, no distributor will want it. Then the producer can incur a substantial loss.

In a negative pick-up deal, the distributor will often agree to give the producer an advance of his/her share of the profits. The producer can use this money to repay investors. Producers will want to obtain as large an advance as possible because they know they may never see anything on the back end of the deal (i.e., no profits).

The distributor wants to pay as small an advance as possible and usually resists giving an amount that is more than the cost of production. Its executives will propose, "We'll be partners. We will put up all the money for advertising and promotion. If the picture is successful, we will share in its success." Sound good?

Unfortunately, distributors have been known to engage in creative accounting, and profit participants rarely see any return on their share of "net profits" because of the way that term is defined. Consequently, the shrewd producer tries to get as large an advance as possible. He/she also tries to retain foreign rights and keep them from being cross-collateralized. (This means the monies earned from several markets are pooled. For example, let's say your picture made $1 million in England and lost $1 million in France. If those territories were cross-collateralized, and you were entitled to a percentage of the net revenue, you would get nothing. On the other hand, if the territories were not cross-collateralized, you would get your percentage of the English revenues and the distributor would absorb the loss incurred in France.)

Negotiating the Distribution Deal

The most important advice I can offer filmmakers seeking distribution is, ☜ *Don't brag about how little money you spent to make the picture before you conclude your distribution deal.* You may feel proud of making a great-looking picture for a mere $400,000. But if the distributor knows that is all you have spent, you will find it difficult to get an advance beyond that. It would be wiser not to reveal your investment, recognizing that production costs are not readily discernible from viewing a film. Remember, the distributor has no right to examine your books (assuming the distributor has not provided financing). What you have spent is between you, your investors, and the I.R.S.

Negative pick-up deals can be negotiated before, during, or after production. Often distributors become interested in a film after viewing it at a film festival and observing audience reaction. All the studios and independent distributors have one or more staffers in charge of acquisitions. It is the job of these acquisitions executives to find good films to acquire.

It is not difficult to get acquisition executives to view your film. Once production has been announced, don't be surprised if they begin calling you. They will track the progress of your film so they can see it as soon as it is finished — before their competitors get a shot at it.

From the filmmaker's point-of-view, you will get the best distribution deal if you have more than one distributor interested in acquiring your movie. That way you can play them off against each other to get the best terms. But what if one distributor makes a pre-emptive bid for the film, offering you a $500,000 advance, and you have only 24 hours to accept the offer? If you pass, you may not be able to get a better deal later. It is possible you may fail to obtain any distribution deal at all. On the other hand, if you accept the offer, you may be foreclosing the possibility of a more lucrative deal that could be offered to you later. Consequently, it is important to orchestrate the release of your film to potential distributors to maximize your leverage.

Orchestrating the Release

❧ **Keep the film under wraps.** Don't show your film until it is finished. Executives may ask to see a rough cut. They will say, "Don't worry. We're professionals. We can extrapolate and envision what the film will look like with sound and titles." Don't believe them. Most people can't extrapolate. They will view your unfinished film and think it amateurish. First impressions last.

The only reason to show your film before completion is if you are desperate to raise funds to finish it. The terms you can obtain under these circumstances will usually be less than those given on completion. If you must show a work in progress, exhibit it on a Moviola or flatbed editing table. People have lower expectations viewing a film on an editing console than when it is projected in a theater.

❧ **Arrange a screening.** Invite executives to a screening; don't send them a video cassette. If you send a tape to a busy executive, he will pop it into his VCR. Ten minutes later the phone will ring, and he hits the pause button. Then he watches another 10 minutes until his secretary interrupts him. After being distracted 10 times, he passes on your film because it is "too choppy." Well, of course it's choppy with all those interruptions. You want to get the executive in a dark room, away from distractions to view your film with a live audience — hopefully one that will respond positively. So rent a screening room, invite all the acquisition executives you can, and pack the rest of the theater with your friends and relatives, especially Uncle Herb with his infectious laugh.

✎ **Make the buyers compete against each other.** Screen the film for all distributors simultaneously. Some executives will attempt to get an early look — that is their job. Your job is to keep them intrigued until it is complete. You can promise to let them see it "as soon as it is finished." They may be annoyed to arrive at the screening and see their competitors. But this will get their competitive juices flowing. They will know that they better make a decent offer quickly if they hope to get the film.

✎ **Obtain an experienced advisor.** Retain an experienced producer's rep or entertainment attorney to negotiate your deal. Filmmakers know about film, distributors know about distribution. Don't kid yourself and believe you can play in their arena and win. There are many pitfalls to avoid. Get yourself an experienced guide to protect your interests. Any decent negotiator can improve a distributor's offer enough to outweigh the cost of his or her services.

✎ **Investigate the distributor.** Always check the track record and experience of each distributor. As an entertainment attorney who represents many independent filmmakers, I often find myself in the position of trying to get unscrupulous distributors to live up to their contracts. I am amazed at how many distributors refuse to abide by the terms of their own distribution agreements. The savvy filmmaker will carefully investigate potential distributors by calling filmmakers who have contracted with them. I recently read a Standard & Poor's report on a distributor and was shocked to learn that the company was $2.3 million in arrears on royalty payments. One can also check the Superior Court Dockets in Los Angeles to see if a company has been sued.

♈ Selecting a Distributor: A Checklist

1. Amount of advance.

2. Extent of rights conveyed. Domestic and/or foreign? Ancillary rights? Are any markets cross-collateralized? Does the distributor deal in every market or use subdistributors?

3. Is there a guaranteed marketing commitment?

4. Does the producer have any input or veto power over artwork and theater selection in the top markets?

5. Track record, financial health, and reputation of distributor.

6. Are monthly or quarterly accounting statements required? Does the filmmaker have the right to audit the books?

7. To what extent does the distributor plan to involve the filmmaker in promotion and publicity?

8. Marketing strategy: demographics of intended market, grassroots promotion efforts, film festivals, release pattern, etc.

9. Split of revenues and accounting of profits: Is there a distribution fee? Overhead fees? If a subdistributor is used, are double distribution fees deducted? Is the distributor using a subsidiary company as subdistributor? Does the subdistributor also earn a profit? How are the profits divided?

10. Distributor leverage with exhibitors. Can the distributor collect monies owed? What terms does the distributor typically give exhibitors?

11. Any competing films handled by distributor? Conflicts of interest? Will the distributor favor their in-house films over those acquired from outside?

12. Does the producer have the right to regain distribution rights if the distributor pulls the plug on distribution?

13. Personal affinity and rapport between producer and distributor executives.

Note: If you need Mark Litwak's services, see Chapter 24.

NEGATIVE PICK-UP CHART

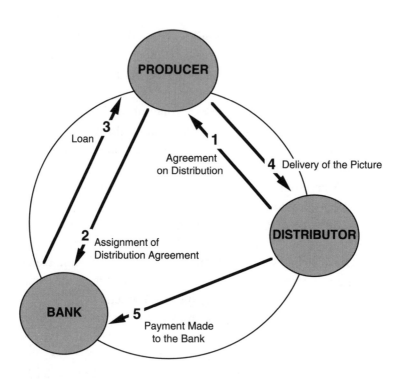

© De Abreu and Associates

PART II

DIRECT ACCESS TO HOLLYWOOD

Chapter 23.

Direct Access to Hollywood

CONGRATULATIONS! YOU MADE IT.

Now it's the time for you to put into action all that you've learned.

As David Permut said, "The power in the business is the material." As Paul Mazursky stated, "If you want to get into this business, get the rights to a story, a book, or a screenplay." As Gale Anne Hurd shared with you, "If you don't make the commitment to your job your top priority, someone else will, and you won't succeed." As Robert Wise advised, "Have passion and be patient and persistent." As Alex Ho said, "Be up-front and honest about things." As Mark Rydell emphasized, "Be a creative producer, a person of taste." As Arthur Hiller recommended, "....submit, submit, submit, submit, submit...."

And as Christopher Vogler quoted the great Marcus Aurelius, "If you work at that which is before you following right reason seriously, vigorously, calmly, without allowing anything else to distract you ... if you hold to this, expecting nothing, fearing nothing, but satisfied with your present activities according to nature and with your heroic truth in every word and sound which you utter, you will live happy. There is no one who is able to prevent it."

TRUE STORY SUBMISSION
FOR POTENTIAL SALE OF FILM RIGHTS

If you have the rights to a true story, you may want to submit it to:

BREAKING IN PRODUCTIONS
Attention: Ms. Pennington
433 N. Camden Drive, Suite 600
Beverly Hills, CA 90210

B.I. Productions is a production company that specializes in true stories.

To Submit True Stories, Please Send:

1. A one-page cover letter introducing or explaining your story.

2. A signed release form — use the release form that we have provided on the next page.

3. Copies of news articles, if any, about your true story.

4. A typewritten treatment of your story on $8\,^1/_2$ X 11-inch pages. No more than five to eight pages.

5. A $10.00 non-refundable processing fee. Make check payable to Breaking In Productions.

6. A self-addressed stamped envelope.

Note: Within four to six weeks, you will receive a written response.
MATERIALS SENT TO US WILL NOT BE RETURNED TO YOU
DO NOT SEND ANY MATERIALS WITHOUT RELEASE FORM

IMPORTANT

IF YOU SUBMIT YOUR TRUE STORY, BREAKING IN PRODUCTIONS HAS NO OBLIGATIONS TO YOU, EXCEPT FOR THOSE STATED IN THE RELEASE FORM PROVIDED BY BREAKING IN PRODUCTIONS. YOU ARE NOT OBLIGATED IN ANY WAY UNTIL A FORMAL WRITTEN AGREEMENT, IF ANY, IS ACCEPTED AND SIGNED BY YOU.

336

BREAKING IN PRODUCTIONS RELEASE FORM
TRUE STORIES

To Whom It May Concern:

I am concurrently submitting to you with this release form a true story in the format of a _____ [introductory letter, synopsis, treatment or script/manuscript] titled: _____, (hereafter the "Material"), whose principal characters are _____

_____

WGA Registration No.: _____Number of Pages:_____
        (if any)

I agree and understand that:

(1) Because of your position in the entertainment industry: a) you receive many ideas, formats, stories, suggestions, and other materials which you do not solicit or otherwise request; b) you generally do not accept, consider, or review unsolicited material unless the person submitting the material has signed this Agreement; c) you would not accept, consider, or review the Material if I did not sign this Agreement; and d) no confidential relationship is established by submitting the Material to you.

(2) I may submit the Material or similar material to persons other than you. I have kept at least one copy (or duplicate) of all the Material submitted to you.

(3) You need not return the Material to me. If you choose, you may make and keep a copy (or a duplicate) of the Material, but are not obligated to do so. You may present this Material to third parties.

(4) You will review the Material within a reasonable period of time after you receive a copy of this Agreement which I have signed. If you decide that you wish to use the Material or any elements or aspects of the Material for any purpose, then you and I may negotiate in good faith to reach a written agreement covering your use of the Material and any compensation or payment.

(5) I am not waiving, and this Agreement will not limit, my copyright of the Material. I understand that you may use in any fashion:

337

a) any matter which is made available to you and which contains elements or aspects which are similar to protectable literary property contained in the Material, and/or b) any elements or aspects of or matter contained in the Material which is not original with me, new, unique, concrete, and novel and/or which is in the public domain. I will not sue you or bring any action or proceeding against you if you use any such matter, and I shall not be entitled to an injunction or other equitable remedy if such a suit, action, or proceeding is brought.

(6) You have no obligations to me (including any obligation to compensate or make payments to me, unless you expressly agree to do so), except for those expressly stated in this Agreement.

(7) I hereby state that: a) the Material was created and is owned free and clear of all other interests only by me; and b) I have full right to submit the Material to you and to comply with this Agreement. I will fully reimburse you if you incur any losses, damages, or expenses (including lawyers' fees) because any of the statements made by me in this release form are not true.

(8) If either you or I transfer, assign, or license any rights under this Agreement, the person making the transfer, assignment, or license will still be responsible for performing his/her/its obligation under this Agreement.

(9) If more than one party signs this Agreement as the submitting party, then references to "I" or "me" throughout this Agreement shall apply to each such party, jointly and severally.

(10) I have read and have received a signed copy of, and understand this Agreement. You have made no representation, oral or written, of any kind to me. This Agreement states our entire agreement.

(11) This Agreement is governed by and construed under the laws of the State of California, applicable to agreements entered into and to be fully performed therein.

DATE: SIGNATURE(S):

NAME (PRINTED):
ADDRESS:
CITY:

338

SCREENPLAY SUBMISSION

If you have a completed screenplay, you may want to submit it to:

CHRISTOPHER COLUMBUS
SCREENPLAY DISCOVERY AWARDS™
Attention: Mr. Abreu
433 N. Camden Drive, Suite 600
Beverly Hills, CA 90210

The Christopher Columbus Society for the Creative Arts(R.) S.M. created the Screenplay Discovery Awards to discover and develop new spec screenplays. The Society provides selected screenwriters with what they need most: professional feedback and direct access to Hollywood. Of those selected, if any, first, second, and third place winners will be offered film rights options of up to $10,000.00.

To Submit Screenplays, Please Send:

1. A request for guidelines and regulations.

2. A self-addressed stamped envelope.

Note: Within two weeks from receipt of your request, the Society will send you an application and release form.

DO NOT SEND ANY SCREENPLAY(S) WITHOUT APPLICATION/RELEASE FORM.

MANUSCRIPT AND BOOK SUBMISSION
FOR POTENTIAL PUBLICATION AND/OR FILM RIGHTS

If you have a completed manuscript or book, you may want to submit it to:

CUSTOS MORUM PUBLISHERS
OPUS MAGNUM DISCOVERY AWARDS™
Attention: Mr. Abreu
2049 Century Park East, Suite 1100
Los Angeles, CA 90067

Custos Morum Publishers created The Opus Magnum Discovery Awards to discover new manuscripts. Of those selected, if any, first, second, and third place winners will be offered film rights options of up to $10,000.00.

To Submit Manuscripts/Books, Please Send:

1. A request for guidelines and regulations.

2. A self-addressed stamped envelope.

Note: Within two weeks from receipt of your request, the publishers will send you an application and release form.

DO NOT SEND ANY MANUSCRIPT(S) WITHOUT APPLICATION/RELEASE FORM.

340

PRODUCERS' PACKAGING DIRECTORIES

STUDIOS AND PRODUCERS
Hollywood Creative Directory
3000 Olympic Blvd., Ste. 2413
Santa Monica, CA 90404
(310) 315-4815
(800) 815-0503 outside California

AGENTS AND MANAGERS
Hollywood Agents and Managers Directory
3000 Olympic Blvd., Ste. 2413
Santa Monica, CA 90404
(310) 315-4815
(800) 815-0503 outside California

DIRECTORS
Directors Guild of America
Directories for (A) Agents or (B) Members
7920 Sunset Blvd.
Los Angeles, CA 90046
(213) 851-3671, (310) 289-2000

LITERARY AGENTS AND WRITERS
Writers Guild of America
Directories for (A) Literary Agents or (B) Members
8955 Beverly Blvd.
West Hollywood, CA 90048
(310) 550-1000

ACTRESSES AND ACTORS
Academy Players Directory
8949 Wilshire Blvd.
Beverly Hills, CA 90211
(310) 247-3000

Chapter 24.

Professional Sources

DISCLAIMER

The following lists are comprised of reputable industry professionals whom the authors recommend. However, publisher and authors shall have neither liability nor responsibility to any person or entity with respect to any loss or damage caused or alleged to be caused directly or indirectly by either the professionals listed and/or their services to the reader(s).

AGENTS

We recommend that you order the literary agents list from the Writers Guild of America or the *Hollywood Agents/Managers Directory* (310) 315-4815. You will have access to dozens of agencies. For your perusal, we have included a few agencies that sometimes represent new writers who have been introduced through qualified referrals.

The Agency
1800 Avenue of the Stars, Ste. 400
Los Angeles, CA 90067
(310) 551-3000

The Gersh Agency
232 N. Canon Drive
Beverly Hills, CA 90210
(310) 274-6611

H.N. Swanson, Inc.
8523 Sunset Boulevard
Los Angeles, CA 90069
(310) 652-5385

United Talent Agency
9560 Wilshire Boulevard, Ste. 500
Beverly Hills, CA 90212
(310) 273-6700

**DO NOT SEND ANY MATERIAL TO THESE AGENCIES.
THEY WILL NOT TAKE UNSOLICITED MATERIAL.**

ATTORNEYS

John W. Cones, Esq.
1324 Marinette Road
Pacific Palisades, CA 90272
(310) 477-6842

John W. Cones is a securities/entertainment attorney, lecturer, and author of *Film Industry Contracts* (computer disk is available), *Film Finance and Distribution,* and *43 Ways to Finance Your Film(s)*, among others. We highly recommend his books.

Mark Litwak, Esq.
P.O. Box 3226
Santa Monica, CA 90408
(310) 450-4500

Mark Litwak is an entertainment attorney, a journalist, and the author of *Reel Power, Dealmaking in the Film & Television Industry,* and *Contracts for the Film & Television Industry* (computer disk available). We highly recommend his books.

Gregory Victoroff, Esq.
ROHDE & VICTOROFF
1880 Century Park East, Ste. 411
Los Angeles, CA 90067
(310) 277-1482

Greg Victoroff is an author (*Photography & Law, Visual Artists Business & Legal Guide*) and copyright attorney who provides legal representation for writers, producers, celebrities, public figures, authors, and publishers and is a specialist in publishing contracts, copyrights, life story options, motion picture and television rights, and libel and privacy review.

344

CONSULTANTS

CAREER CONSULTANT

Ms. Donie A. Nelson
Career Strategies for Writers
5035 Overland Avenue
Culver City, CA 90230
(310) 204-6808

Donie Nelson is a career and marketing consultant. Drawing from her years of experience in the film and television industry as a development executive who has worked extensively with screen-writers, studios, independent producers, agents, etc., she counsels writers on the best way to market a specific script, or on the best ways for a writer to get representation and attention for their work in general.

RESEARCH CONSULTANT

Ms. Lynn Rosenberg
8306 Wilshire Boulevard, Ste. 249
Beverly Hills, CA 90211
(310) 285-0100

"In-depth research can often make the difference
between an authentic script and one that isn't."

Ms. Rosenberg provides research services for writers, directors, and producers. She also specializes in guiding newcomers with their own research.

345

SCHOLARSHIPS AND CONTESTS

SCHOLARSHIPS AND GRANTS

For information regarding contests, fellowships, and grants we highly recommend that you acquire the reference book *Dramatists Sourcebook*, published by Theater Communications Group, Inc., 355 Lexington Avenue, New York, NY 10017, (212) 697-5230.

SCREENWRITING CONTESTS

The Christopher Columbus Screenplay Discovery Awards
Christopher Columbus Society for the Creative Arts
433 N. Camden Drive, Ste. 600
Beverly Hills, CA 90210

The Diane Thomas Contest
UCLA Extension
10995 Le Conte Avenue
Los Angeles, CA 90024

The Nicholl Fellowships
The Academy of Motion Picture Arts and Sciences
8949 Wilshire Boulevard
Beverly Hills, CA 90212

Writer's Aide
1685 S. Colorado Boulevard, Ste. 237
Denver, CO 80222
(303) 430-4839

The Writer's Aide is the most comprehensive source for information regarding screenplay contests. You should order their package.

PROFESSIONAL SERVICES

SCREENPLAY ANALYSIS & CONSULTATIONS

HOLLYWOOD INK
7537 Kimdale Lane
Hollywood, CA 90046

Hollywood Ink is a professional script consultation service for serious writers who desire assistance in revising, rewriting, or replotting existing works. Depending on the length and type of script, fees range from $500 to $750 per analysis and consulting session. Critiques focus on means to improve strength of story line, plot consistency, conflict and its resolution, dramatic content, character development, and dialogue.

To Submit Screenplays, Please Send:

1. A request for guidelines and fee structure.

2. A self-addressed stamped envelope.

DO NOT SEND SCREENPLAY BEFORE RECEIVING GUIDELINES/RELEASE FORM.

PROFESSIONAL SERVICES

SCREENPLAY ANALYSIS & CONSULTATIONS

STORYTECH
Christopher Vogler
President
941 Amoroso Place
Venice, CA 90291
(310) 822-1587 • Fax (310) 305-8645

Storytech is a literary consulting service dedicated to helping writers, producers, directors, and studio executives shape their stories. Its founder, Christopher Vogler, is the author of the award-winning book, *The Writer's Journey: Mythic Structure for Storytellers and Screenwriters*, and has lectured internationally on story structure. He is a story consultant for Walt Disney Feature Animation, and has consulted on movies at Touchstone, Warner Bros., Twentieth Century Fox, and other major studios. Storytech provides expert professional evaluation and development notes on screenplays and manuscripts.

To submit your project(s), please contact
Storytech before sending any materials.

348

PROFESSIONAL SERVICES

SCREENPLAY ANALYSIS & CONSULTATIONS

Ms. Madeline DiMaggio
P.O. Box 1172
Pebble Beach, CA 93953
(408) 373-7776

Ms. DiMaggio, author of *How to Write for Television*, has worked as a story editor and creative consultant to Paramount and NBC, and has written over thirty hours of produced film in prime-time television, television pilots, soaps, animation, and motion pictures. Ms. DiMaggio's services include script critiquing, script rewriting, and story development for writers interested in presenting treatments to Hollywood.

Mr. Michael Hauge
HILLTOP PRODUCTIONS
P.O. Box 55728
Sherman Oaks, CA 91013
(818) 995-8118

Michael Hauge, author of the award-winning book *Writing Screenplays That Sell*, offers a critique and consultation service for scripts, treatments, and story lines.

Dr. Linda Seger
2038 Louella Avenue
Venice, CA 90291
(310) 390-1951 • Fax (310) 398-7541

Dr. Linda Seger is an international script consultant, lecturer, founder of the Seger Method, and author of *Making a Good Script Great, Creating Unforgettable Characters: The Art of Adaptation,* and *Turning Fact and Fiction into Film.* Dr. Seger has provided her services to major studios, directors, and writers.

PROFESSIONAL SERVICES

SCRIPT AND TREATMENT WRITERS

Ms. Sandy Steinberg
17968 Boris Drive
Encino, CA 91316
(818) 342-9794

Ms. Steinberg offers writing and/or polish services for your scripts and/or treatments. She presently works with directors, producers, studios, and writers — beginners and experienced.

Ms. Dara Marks
(310) 390-1628

Ms. Marks is an experienced writer who offers writing and consultation services for your scripts and/or treatments. She works with both beginners and experienced screenwriters.

Note:
For access to writers for hire, please refer to the Writers Guild of America list of agents or *The Hollywood Agents & Managers Directory*. Other sources for access to writers for hire are career consultants, story consultants, seminars, and writers' groups.

PROFESSIONAL SERVICES

SEMINARS - WORKSHOPS

Ms. Madeline DiMaggio
P.O. Box 1172
Pebble Beach, CA 93953
(408) 373-7776

Ms. DiMaggio offers a six-month workshop in which writers meet once a month to develop and write or rewrite feature films and television scripts. The goal of the workshop is for the writer to have a completed first draft screenplay or a polished screenplay, ready for market, by the end of the six-month period. She is an established working writer (both television and feature) presently under contract at Walt Disney Studios.

Mr. Michael Hauge
HILLTOP PRODUCTIONS
P.O. Box 55728
Sherman Oaks, CA 91013
(818) 995-8118

Michael Hauge, author of the award-winning book *Writing Screenplays That Sell*, offers his weekend screenwriting seminar throughout the U.S., Canada, and England.

Mr. Robert McKee
TWO ARTS, INC.
12021 Wilshire Boulevard, Ste. 868
Los Angeles, CA 90025
(310) 312-1002 or (212) 463-7889

Mr. McKee is a highly regarded screenwriting teacher and known Broadway actor. His seminars are attended both by newcomers and well-established industry professionals, from stars to directors.

PROFESSIONAL SERVICES

SEMINARS - WORKSHOPS

Dr. Linda Seger
2038 Louella Avenue
Venice, CA 90291
(310) 390-1951 • Fax (310) 398-7541

Dr. Linda Seger is an international script consultant, lecturer, founder of the Seger Method, and author (*Making a Good Script Great, Turning Fact and Fiction into Film, From Script to Screen*) who offers screenwriting seminars in the U.S. and throughout Europe.

Mr. David Trottier
The Screenwriting Center
2034 E. Lincoln, #300
Anaheim, CA 92806
(714) 251-1073

The Screenwriting Center provides writing seminars, correspondence courses, and script analysis. Also available are an audio cassette program, an industry formatting guide, and books, including the *Screenwriter's Bible*. For information, please call the Center.

Mr. John Truby
Truby's Writers Studio
1737 Midvale Avenue
Los Angeles, CA 90024
(310) 575-3050 ext. 8

Mr. Truby provides ongoing workshops, from story structure to advanced screenwriting both for television and features. His studio offers multiple services to new and experienced screenwriters, from audio tapes to writers' computer software.

PROFESSIONAL SERVICES

SEMINARS - WORKSHOPS

Mr. Christopher Vogler
STORYTECH
941 Amoroso Place
Venice, CA 90291
(310) 822-1587

Christopher Vogler, author of the award-winning book *The Writer's Journey*, offers screenwriting seminars throughout the U.S. and Europe. For information and schedules, please contact Storytech.

Prof. Richard Walter
L.K. SEMINARS
15303 Ventura Boulevard, Ste. 900
Sherman Oaks, CA 91403
(800) 755-2785

Professor Walter has been the screenwriting chairman of UCLA for the past seventeen years. He is a well-known author (*The Art, Craft, and Business of Screenplay Writing*), lecturer, and fiction writer. He consults with new and experienced screenwriters on their works in progress. His seminars, which are produced by Leslie Kallen Seminars, take him throughout North America. Video and audio tapes are available.

Writer's Connection
P.O. Box 24770
San Jose, CA 95154-4770
(408) 445-3600 • Fax (408) 445-3609

Writer's Connection serves writers working in all genres of writing. Their services include a monthly newsletter, reference books, and conferences, including "Selling to Hollywood."

PROFESSIONAL SERVICES

PRODUCTION WORKSHOP

Hollywood Film Institute • Two-Day Workshop
Mr. Dov S-S Simens • (800) 366-3456
5225 Wilshire Blvd., Ste. 410
Los Angeles, CA 90036

HFI, founded by Dov S-S Simens, who has taught at USC, UCLA & NYU film schools, has condensed long film school courses into intensive crash courses that last only one weekend each. Courses include: **Financing, Directing, Screenwriting, and Independent Filmmaking.** HFI has the second largest mail order bookstore pertaining to the film-theater arts. All students receive graduation diplomas.

SCREENWRITING PUBLICATIONS

FORUM-Screenwrite NOW! • (410) 592-3466
P.O. Box 7-CSS, Long Green Pike
Baldwin, MD 21013-0007

Member benefits include discounted script analysis, products, and contests as well as *Screenwrite NOW!* magazine. This magazine is the world's largest periodical dedicated to the screenwriter. To join, send $48.00 ($68.00 Foreign) for full year membership. We highly recommend that you join this organization.

The Hollywood Scriptwriter • (805) 495-5447
1626 N. Wilcox Avenue, Ste. 385
Hollywood, CA 90028

This newsletter is published monthly by Kerry Cox. *The Hollywood Scriptwriter* was founded in 1980 and its goal has always been to provide practical answers, advice, and guidance from working professionals. We highly recommend that you subscribe to this invaluable, critical source of information.

GUILDS, UNIONS, AND OTHER
INDUSTRY ORGANIZATIONS

Academy of Motion Picture
Arts and Sciences (AMPAS)
8949 Wilshire Blvd.
Beverly Hills, CA 90211
(310) 247-3000

Actors Equity Association
6430 Sunset Blvd., Ste. 700
Los Angeles, CA 90028
(213) 462-2334

Actors Equity Association
165 W. 46th St.
New York, NY 10036
(212) 869-8530

American Federation of
Television and Radio
Artists (AFTRA)
6922 Hollywood Blvd., 8th Fl.
Hollywood, CA 90028
(213) 461-8111

American Federation of
Television and Radio
Artists (AFTRA)
260 Madison Ave., 7th Fl.
New York, NY 10016
(212) 532-0800

American Film Market Assn.
12424 Wilshire Blvd., Ste. 600
Los Angeles, CA 90025
(310) 447-1555
(Distributors & Production Cos.)

Directors Guild of America
7920 Sunset Blvd.
Los Angeles, CA 90046
(310) 289-2000

Directors Guild of America
110 W. 57th St.
New York, NY 10019
(212) 581-0370

Independent Feature Project (IFP)
104 W. 29th St., 12th Fl.
New York, NY 10001
(212) 465-8200

Independent Feature
Project/West (IFP/West)
1625 Olympic Blvd.
Santa Monica, CA 90404
(310) 392-8832

355

Producers Guild of
America (PGA)
400 S. Beverly Dr., Ste. 211
Beverly Hills, CA 90212
(310) 557-0807

Sundance Institute
4000 Warner Blvd.
Burbank, CA 91522
(818) 771-9191

Screen Actors Guild (SAG)
5757 Wilshire Blvd.
Los Angeles, CA 90036
(213) 954-1600

Writers Guild of America West
8955 Beverly Blvd.
West Hollywood, CA 90048
(310) 550-1000

Screen Actors Guild (SAG)
1515 Broadway, 44th Fl.
New York, NY 10036
(212) 944-1030

Writers Guild of America East
555 W. 57th St.
New York, NY 10019
(212) 767-7800

LIBRARIES AND BOOKSTORES

American Film Institute
Library
2021 N. Western Ave.
Los Angeles, CA 90027

Margaret Herrick Library
(AMPAS)
333 S. La Cienega Blvd.
Beverly Hills, CA 90211

Doheny Memorial Library
Univ. of Southern California
University Park
Los Angeles, CA 90089

New York Public Library
Telephone Reference and
General Information
(212) 340-0849

Larry Edmunds' Cinema
and Theatre Bookshop
6644 Hollywood Blvd.
Hollywood, CA 90028

New York Public Library
for the Performing Arts
40 Lincoln Center Plaza
New York, NY 10023

Samuel French Theatre
and Film Bookshop
7623 Sunset Blvd.
Hollywood, CA 90046
(213) 876-0570

Samuel French Theatre
and Film Bookshop
11963 Ventura Blvd.
Studio City, CA 91604
(818) 762-0535

PUBLICATIONS

Advertising Age
740 N. Rush St.
Chicago, IL 60611
(advertising industry)

Poets & Writers
72 Spring St.
New York, NY 10011
(for literary writers/poets)

American Journalism Review
8701 Adelphi Rd.
Adelphi, MD 20783
(journalism/communications)

Publishers Weekly
249 W. 17th St.
New York, NY 10011
(book publishing industry)

Editor & Publisher
11 W. 19th St.
New York, NY 10011
(newspaper publishing)

Science Fiction Chronicle
P.O. Box 2730
Brooklyn, NY 11202
(for sci-fi/horror writers)

Folio
P.O. Box 4949
Stamford, CT 06907
(magazine publishing)

The Writer
120 Boylston St.
Boston, MA 02116
(for writers)

Horn Book Magazine
14 Beacon St.
Boston, MA 02108
(children's literature)

Writer's Digest
1507 Dana Ave.
Cincinnati, OH 45207
(for writers)

Kirkus Reviews
200 Park Avenue South
New York, NY 10003
(book publishing)

TRADE PUBLICATIONS

Daily Variety
5700 Wilshire Blvd.
Los Angeles, CA 90036

Weekly Variety
5700 Wilshire Blvd., Ste. 120
Los Angeles, CA 90036

The Hollywood Reporter
5055 Wilshire Blvd.
Los Angeles, CA 90036

Weekly Variety
249 W. 17th St., 4th Fl.
New York, NY 10011

WRITERS' GROUPS

American Book Producers
Association
160 Fifth Ave., Ste. 604
New York, NY 10010

Association of Authors
Representatives
10 Astor Pl., 3rd Fl.
New York, NY 10003

American Medical Writers
Association
9650 Rockville Pike
Bethesda, MD 20814

Association of Desk-Top
Publishers
4507 30th St., Ste. 800
San Diego, CA 92116

American Society of
Journalists & Authors
1501 Broadway, Ste. 302
New York, NY 10036

The Authors Resource
Center
P.O. Box 64785
Tucson, AZ 85718

American Translators Assn.
1735 Jefferson Davis Hwy.
Arlington, VA 22202

The Authors Guild
330 W. 42nd St., 29th Fl.
New York, NY 10036

Associated Writing Programs
Tallwood House, Mail Stop 1E3
George Mason University
Fairfax, VA 22030

The Authors League of
America
330 W. 42nd St., 29th Fl.
New York, NY 10036

Copyrighters Council
of America
7 Putter Ln.
Linnick Bldg. 102
Middle Island, NY 11953

Council of Authors &
Journalists c/o Uncle Remus
Regional Library System
1131 East Ave.
Madison, GA 30650

Council of Literary
Magazines & Presses
154 Christopher St., Ste. 3C
New York, NY 10014

The Dramatists Guild
234 W. 44th St.
New York, NY 10036

Editorial Freelancers
Association
71 W. 23rd St., Ste. 1504
New York, NY 10010

Education Writers Association
1001 Connecticut Ave., NW
Ste. 310
Washington, DC 20036

Freelance Editorial Assn.
P.O. Box 380835
Cambridge, MA 02238

International Association of
Business Communicators
1 Hallidie Plaza
San Francisco, CA 94102

International Assn. of
Crime Writers
North American Branch
JAF Box 1500
New York, NY 10116

International Television Assn.
6311 N. O'Connor Rd.
Ste. 230
Irving, TX 75039

Int'l Women's Writing Guild
Box 810, Gracie Station
New York, NY 10028

Mystery Writers of
America
17 E. 47th St., 6th Fl.
New York, NY 10017

National Association of
Science Writers
Box 294
Greenlawn, NY 11740

National Writers Club
1450 S. Havana, Ste. 424
Aurora, CO 80012

National Writers Union
873 Broadway
Ste. 203
New York, NY 10003

PEN American
Center
568 Broadway
New York, NY 10012

Poetry Society of
America
15 Gramercy Park
New York, NY 10003

Poets & Writers
72 Spring St.
New York, NY 10012

Publication Services Guild
P.O. Box 19663
Atlanta, GA 30325

Romance Writers of America
13700 Veterans Memorial Dr.
Ste. 315
Houston, TX 77014

Science-Fiction Fantasy
Writers of America
5 Winding Brook Dr., Ste. 1B
Guilderland, NY 12084

Society of American
Business Editors & Writers
Univ. of Missouri/76 Gannett Hall
Columbia, MO 65211

Society of Amer. Travel Writers
1155 Connecticut Ave., NW, #500
Washington, DC 20036

FILM SCHOOLS

The AFI Center for Advanced
Film and Television Studies
2021 N. Western Ave.
Los Angeles, CA 90027

Columbia University
Film Division
School of the Arts
513 Dodge
New York, NY 10027

New York University
Tisch School of the Arts
721 Broadway
New York, NY 10003

University of California,
Los Angeles
Dept. of Film and Television
405 Hilgard Ave.
Los Angeles, CA 90024

UCLA Extension
10995 Le Conte Ave.
Los Angeles, CA 90024

University of Southern California
School of Cinema-Television
University Park
Los Angeles, CA 90089

BOOKS

If you cannot find these books at your local bookstore, please contact:
Samuel French Theatre & Film Bookshop
7623 Sunset Blvd., Los Angeles, CA 90046, (213) 876-0570

Adventures in the Screen Trade
by William Goldman

The Art, Craft, and Business
of Screenplay Writing
by Richard Walter

The Art of Dramatic Writing
by Lajos Egri

Contracts for the Film &
Television Industry
by Mark Litwak

Dealmaking in the Film &
Television Industry
by Mark Litwak

From Script to Screen
by Dr. Linda Seger

Film Finance & Distribution
by John W. Cones

Film Industry Contracts
by John W. Cones

Creating Unforgettable
Characters
by Dr. Linda Seger

43 Ways to Finance Your Film(s)
by John W. Cones

Film Directors:
A Complete Guide
by Lone Eagle Publishing

The Complete Guide to
American Film Schools
by Ernest Pintoff

How to Sell Your Screenplay
by Carl Sautter

How to Write for Television
by Madeline DiMaggio

How to Write a Movie in
21 Days
by Viki King

The Complete Guide to Standard
Script Formats
by Cole/Haag

The New Screenwriter Looks
at the New Screenwriter
by William Froug

Turning Fact and Fiction
into Film
by Dr. Linda Seger

Reel Power
by Mark Litwak

Making a Good Script Great
by Dr. Linda Seger

Successful Scriptwriting
by Kerry Cox
and Jurgen Wolfe

Screenwriting Tricks of the
Trade
by William Froug

Screenplay
by Syd Field

Dramatists Sourcebook
by Theater Communications Grp.

The Writer's Journey
by Christopher Vogler

Screenwriter's Bible
by David Trottier

Writer's Market
by Writer's Digest Books

Writing Screenplays That Sell
by Michael Hauge

COMPUTER PROGRAMS

If you are unable to find the programs listed below, contact:
The Writers Computer Store, (310) 479-7774
11317 Santa Monica Blvd., Los Angeles, CA 90025

Formatting programs:
Scriptor (Mac & IBM), Warren Script Applications (with Microsoft
Word), SuperScript Pro, Script Perfection (with Word Perfect)

Script writing programs:
ScriptWare, Movie Master (IBM), Final Draft (Mac)

Story development programs:
Collaborator, IdeaFisher, Plots Unlimited, Storyline (Mac & IBM)

Chapter 25.

Sample Query Letters and Contracts

WARNING — DISCLAIMER

T his book is designed to provide information in regard to the subject matter covered. It is sold with the understanding that the publisher and authors and advisors are not rendering legal or other professional services.

It is not the purpose of this book to reprint all the information that is otherwise available to authors, but to complement, amplify and supplement other texts.

DO NOT USE ANY OF THESE SAMPLE CONTRACTS

Please use the services of a qualified entertainment attorney.

Every effort has been made to make this book as complete and as accurate as possible. However, there may be mistakes both typographical and in content. Therefore, this text should be used only as a general guide and not as the ultimate source of contracting information. Furthermore, this collection of contracts contains information only up to the printing date.

Since the authors, advisors, and publisher cannot foresee changes in the law, the jurisdictions where these contracts might be used, or project all the circumstances where they might be used, the authors, advisors, and publisher shall have neither liability nor responsibility to any person or entity with respect to any loss or damage caused or alleged to be caused directly or indirectly by the information contained in this book.

AGREEMENT AND CONTRACT TERMINOLOGY

Finder's Fee Agreement: An agreement between two or more parties that establishes the fee to be paid to one party for finding a property and/or a financier for another party.

Non-Disclosure Agreement: An agreement between two parties for one party not to reveal information provided to such party by another.

Letter Agreement: A short, written agreement in the form of a letter. Normally, it doesn't include all of the terms and provisions that one would find in the more complete agreement. The letter agreement is used to shorten the negotiation process, until a complete or longer agreement is prepared.

Deal Memo: A shortened version of a contract. A memorandum of the minimum negotiated terms for the main points agreed to by all parties involved, written in a letter agreement format.

Option/Purchase Agreement: A negotiated written agreement which provides to the option buyer, who pays an option fee, the exclusive right to develop or sell the property during a specified period of time, and, if specified contingencies are met, the right to purchase the property.

We highly recommend that you acquire *Film Finance & Distribution — A Dictionary of Terms* by John W. Cones.

364

Note

Minimum payments to actors, directors, and writers are set by collective bargaining agreements by the Screen Actors Guild, AFTRA, Directors Guild of America, and Writers Guild of America. These minimums only apply to guild members and signatory companies.

LIST OF SAMPLE CONTRACTS AND LETTERS

Samples of these contracts and letters are provided on the following pages:

IMPORTANT

Due to space constraints, our sample agreements were shortened. Therefore, substantial portions of these agreements have been omitted. Normally, agreements of this nature can have up to fifty pages and if they include net profit definitions, can even exceed one hundred pages.

A — QUERY LETTERS

A query letter is a short but detailed letter written to interest someone in your project. It is an important selling tool since it introduces you and your project. Its purpose is to tease the reader so much that he or she wants to see more or to meet with you. There is no single formula for a query letter, in format or substance, but here are a few pointers that should help:

Queries are single-spaced, professional business letters. They need to be neat, clean, well presented, and well thought out.

The person you are writing to should be addressed by name and title in the address, and addressed formally (i.e., "Dear Mr. Doe" not "Dear John") in the salutation.

If possible, limit the query letter to one page.

The opening of your letter should be strong enough to grab the reader's attention. Often, the log line of a project or script you are promoting helps in composing a strong opening and focuses immediately on the purpose of the letter.

Provide brief, relevant details about the project, and include any special expertise you have that is important to the project.

Mention briefly any appropriate materials you have enclosed with the letter.

Make clear in your closing paragraph any follow-up action on your part.

B — LETTER TO ACQUIRE RIGHTS

August 7, 1996

Mr. John Doe
12345 Main Street
Genericville, WA 00000

Dear Mr. Doe:

I am writing to inquire if the theatrical and film rights to your story are still available.

I was fortunate to be able to speak with Joanne Jones, the reporter with *XYZ Newspaper*, and she was kind enough to give me your name and address.

Your powerful story touched me greatly. I deeply feel that such a story should be shared with others.

I would appreciate it if we could arrange to speak at your earliest convenience. Please call me collect at (310) 000-0000.

Yours cordially,

John Brown

C — QUERY LETTER AFTER ACQUISITION OF RIGHTS

July 25, 1993

Mr. John Doe, Producer
Such-and-Such Studio
54321 Main Street
Los Angeles, CA 00000

Dear Mr. Doe:

As we discussed on the phone last week, I have recently acquired the rights to the true life saga of Jane Jones, the first American woman to serve as a combat pilot in the Air Force. In recent hostile actions over the Persian Gulf, Ms. Jones was credited with shooting down an enemy fighter aircraft.

Enclosed is a treatment (or script) based on Ms. Jones's experiences, which I believe would make an excellent movie along the lines of a *Top Gun* or *Thelma and Louise*.

I appreciate your consideration of my project and look forward to your reactions and comments. I'll call you soon so we can discuss the treatment further.

Sincerely,

John Brown

D — SUBMISSION RELEASE FORM

To Whom It May Concern:

I am concurrently submitting to you with this release form a [script, treatment, manuscript] titled:_____, (hereafter the "Material"), whose principal characters are_____

WGA Registration No.: _____Number of Pages:_____
     (if any)

I agree and understand that:

(1) Because of your position in the entertainment industry: a) you receive many ideas, formats, stories, suggestions, and other materials which you do not solicit or otherwise request; b) you generally do not accept, consider, or review unsolicited material unless the person submitting the material has signed this Agreement; c) you would not accept, consider, or review the Material if I did not sign this Agreement; and d) no confidential relationship is established by submitting the Material to you.

(2) I may submit the Material or similar material to persons other than you. I have kept at least one copy (or duplicate) of all the Material submitted to you.

(3) You need not return the Material to me. If you choose, you may make and keep a copy (or a duplicate) of the Material, but are not obligated to do so. You may present this Material to third parties.

(4) You will review the Material within a reasonable period of time after you receive a copy of this Agreement which I have signed. If you decide that you wish to use the Material or any elements or aspects of the Material for any purpose, then you and I may negotiate in good faith to reach a written agreement covering your use of the Material and any compensation or payment.

(5) I am not waiving, and this Agreement will not limit, my copyright of the Material. I understand that you may use in any fashion: a) any matter which is made available to you and which contains

elements or aspects which are similar to protectable literary property contained in the Material, and/or b) any elements or aspects of or matter contained in the Material which is not original with me, new, unique, concrete, and novel and/or which is in the public domain. I will not sue you or bring any action or proceeding against you if you use any such matter, and I shall not be entitled to an injunction or other equitable remedy if such a suit, action, or proceeding is brought.

(6) You have no obligations to me (including any obligation to compensate or make payments to me, unless you expressly agree to do so), except for those expressly stated in this Agreement.

(7) I hereby state that: a) the Material was created and is owned free and clear of all other interests only by me; and b) I have full right to submit the Material to you and to comply with this Agreement. I will fully reimburse you if you incur any losses, damages, or expenses (including lawyers' fees) because any of the statements made by me in this release form are not true.

(8) If either you or I transfer, assign, or license any rights under this Agreement, the person making the transfer, assignment, or license will still be responsible for performing his/her/its obligation under this Agreement.

(9) If more than one party signs this Agreement as the submitting party, then references to "I" or "me" throughout this Agreement shall apply to each such party, jointly and severally.

(10) I have read and have received a signed copy of, and understand, this Agreement. You have made no representation, oral or written, of any kind to me. This Agreement states our entire agreement.

(11) This Agreement is governed by and construed under the laws of the State of California, applicable to agreements entered into and to be fully performed therein.

DATE: SIGNATURE(S):

NAME (PRINTED):
ADDRESS:
CITY:

E — SHORT FORM RELEASE AND CONSENT AGREEMENT
[your name]
[your address]

AGREEMENT made by and between _____ [insert name of person(s) you are interviewing], his/her heirs, executors, successors and assigns (hereafter "Subject"), and _____ [insert your name] (hereinafter referred to as "Producer").

WITNESSETH:

In consideration of the mutual covenants herein contained, the parties agree as follows:

In return for the opportunity to be involved with this project and other good and valuable consideration, the receipt and sufficiency of which is hereby acknowledged, Subject hereby gives Producer its principals and associates, employers, employees, and agents, and any other person(s) or entity with whom they may contract for the use of Subject's information disclosed in meeting(s), interview(s) and/or other communications that Subject had with Producer, the absolute right and permission to copyright, publish and/or to use and reuse in any medium and for any purpose whatsoever, including but not limited to promotional and advertising uses and other trade purposes, any information disclosed by Subject, as well as using Subject's name in conjunction therewith.

[insert name of city],[insert date]   Producer

[Note: your title will be Producer]

_____   _____

Name:[name of person(s)   Name:[your name]
you interviewed]

_____   _____

(Signed):   (Signed):[your name]
Date: Date:

F — FINDER'S FEE AGREEMENT

1.0   As an inducement to _____ [insert name of person finding project or financier] for presenting to _____ [your name or company name, if any] a _____ [story, manuscript, book or screenplay] written by_____ [name of author, if any] currently titled_____ [name of project], _____ [your name or company] agrees that if the material is optioned by_____ [your name or company] in any form, and a development deal is negotiated and _____ [your name or company] or any of its officers become a producer or co-producer on this venture _____ [your name or company] will pay _____ [name of person] the sum total of _____ percent (_____%) of any and all gross monies or other consideration earned or received by _____ [your name or company] at any time in connection with the _____ [story, book, screenplay, manuscript]. This fee to be paid in less than fourteen (14) days after the receipt date of monies paid to _____ [your name or company]. Access to and copies of any agreement concerning the payment of such funds to be made available to _____ [name of person] upon request.

1.1_____ [your name or company] and _____ [name of person] acknowledge and agree that if any legal action takes place because of a violation of the terms of this agreement, the prevailing party shall be entitled to recover all attorney's fees and expenses incurred for this same litigation.

2.0 This Agreement is governed by and construed under the laws of the State of_____ [name of your state].

_____ [your name or company]
_____ [your addresss]
SIGNATURE: _____
Dated: _____ 19 _____
_____ [name of person finding project or financier]
SIGNATURE: _____

G — NON-DISCLOSURE AGREEMENT

This agreement (hereinafter referred to as the "Agreement") is made by and between _____ [insert your name] whose address is _____ [insert your address] (hereinafter referred to as "Producer") and _____ [insert name of Prospective Buyer/Big Producer/Financier] whose address is _____ [insert address] (hereinafter referred to as the "Prospective Buyer") on this the _____ day of _____, 19 ____ [insert date, month, year].

The Producer has certain proprietary concepts and literary characters currently embodied in graphic artwork and in textual material (the "Documents"). The proprietary concepts, literary characters, and documents are called _____ [insert name of project] (the "Project").

The Prospective Buyer would like to review the Project for possible use in a feature length motion picture. The Producer is interested in selling and/or licensing some or all of the Project to the Prospective Buyer.

Therefore, the parties to this Agreement agree as follows:

1. AUTHORIZED USE — The Prospective Buyer may review the Documents and the Project to determine the desirability of entering into an agreement with the Producer regarding the Prospective Buyer's use of the Project. Before the Prospective Buyer, an employee or any representative of the Prospective Buyer may view the Documents, the Prospective Buyer shall require such individual who will view the Documents to read this Agreement and sign an agreement substantially identical to this Agreement.

2. DAMAGES — Since the concepts, characters and documents relating to the Project are valuable trade secrets belonging to the Producer, if the Prospective Buyer or anyone to whom the Prospective Buyer discloses breaches this Agreement, the Prospective Buyer shall pay liquidated damages of the greater of either (a) twenty-five percent

373

(25%) of gross sales of goods or services related to the Project, or (b) $100,000. In addition, the parties to this Agreement recognize that the above stated liquidated damages are an inadequate remedy for a breach of this Agreement, thus the Producer shall also be entitled to injunctive relief in the event that the Prospective Buyer or someone to whom the Prospective Buyer discloses the Project, breaches this Agreement.

3. EVALUATION TIME LIMITS — If the Prospective Buyer decides not to enter into an agreement with the Producer to use the Project, the Prospective Buyer shall return the Documents to the Producer by Federal Express on the next business day following such decision, to the address set out below:

[insert your name and address]

In any event, unless the Producer gives him/her express consent to extend the evaluation time, the Prospective Buyer shall return the Documents by Federal Express to the Producer at the above address within two (2) weeks from the date of signing this Agreement. The Producer may be reached at the following phone number(s) if the Prospective Buyer wishes to obtain an extension of time for the Project evaluation:

[insert your phone number(s)]

4. TERMINATION AND APPLICABLE LAW — This Agreement terminates when the Project becomes public information, unless, in breach of this Agreement, the Prospective Buyer or those to whom the Prospective Buyer discloses the Project, are partly responsible for information relating to the Project becoming public. The law of the state of_____ [insert name of state] shall apply to the Agreement. The State District Courts in_____ [insert names of county and state], have jurisdiction and venue over any dispute involving this Agreement.

PROSPECTIVE BUYER/BIG PRODUCER/FINANCIER

_____ [insert Prospective Buyer's name]
SIGNATURE: _____

H — LETTER EXTENDING OPTION AGREEMENT

[Insert name and address of person or company you are sending the letter to.]

Re:_____ [name or title of project].

In return for the payment of $_____ , and other good and valuable consideration, the receipt and sufficiency of which are hereby acknowledged, I,_____ [writer or owner of rights' full name], owner of all rights in and to the [treatment, manuscript, or screenplay], presently entitled _____ [insert name of treatment, manuscript, or screenplay] grant _____ [your name or company] an extension of our existing exclusive option agreement dated _____ (copy attached hereto) for twelve (12) consecutive months starting on _____ (Expiration date of initial Option) [this time limit is up to you and the other party] .

Dated:_____, 1995

_____   _____
[your name typed]   [writer or owner of rights' name]
[title, if any]
[your address]

Enclosed:
1. Copy of original Option Rights/Purchase Agreement dated _____ signed and agreed by both parties:_____ [name of writer], and_____ [your name] for_____ [your company's name].

I — SHORT FORM OPTION AGREEMENT
[MANUSCRIPT — NON-FICTION]

For the valuable consideration of $_____, receipt and sufficiency of which is hereby acknowledged, the undersigned _____ [writer's full name in caps] hereby grants to_____ [your name or company name, if any] and its heirs, representatives, successors and assigns, the exclusive option to acquire all motion picture, television, video cassette, subsidiary, ancillary, allied and incidental rights, title and interest throughout the world in perpetuity in and to the original non-fiction manuscript currently titled_____ [manuscript's title] (hereafter the "Property"). _____ [writer's last name in caps] reserves all book publishing rights, live stage rights, publishing and stage rights to author-written sequels to _____ [manuscript's title] and all subsidiary rights to such sequels, including without limitation, books-on-tape and other such recorded rights (hereafter "Reserved Rights")._____'s [your name or company name, if any] rights shall include the exclusive right to create a screen adaptation of_____ [manuscript's title] as well as all future screen adaptations, including all television, motion picture, and other dramatic rights (other than author's Reserved Rights), including without limitation dramatic rights in and to any sequel and remake versions thereof, the title and characters of the Property (except as they conflict with the Reserved Rights) and the copyright, renewals, and extensions of such copyright.

This option shall be effective immediately upon signature by both parties and through_____, 19___. _____ [your name or company name, if any] may renew the option for an additional three months for an additional sum of $_____, payable prior to the expiration of the initial option period. All option payments made to _____ [writer's name in caps] shall be applied to the otherwise non-reducible purchase price of $_____.

It is understood that_____ [your name or company name, if any] shall use its best efforts to cause_____ [writer's name] to write the first draft and set of revisions at terms to be negotiated in good faith; however, this option agreement is not contingent on his/her so doing.

WARRANTIES AND INDEMNIFICATION

Author hereby states that the Property was created and is owned free and clear of all other interests only by Author. In addition, Author has the full right to comply with this agreement. Author will fully reimburse _____ [your name or company] if any losses, damages, or expenses (including lawyers' fees) are incurred because any or all of the statements made in this agreement are not true.

ACCEPTED AND AGREED TO:

_____ [your company name, if any]

by: _____   by:_____

_____ [your name]_____ [title]
[writer's full name in caps]

_____   _____

Date   Date

J — SHORT FORM ASSIGNMENT AGREEMENT
[PUBLISHED WORK — NON-FICTION]

For the sum of $ _____, and other good and valuable consideration, receipt and sufficiency of which is hereby acknowledged, the undersigned _____ [insert writer's full name] hereby grants to _____ [your name or company name, if any] (hereinafter referred to as "Purchaser") and its heirs, representatives, successors and assigns, the exclusive option to acquire all motion picture, television, video cassette, subsidiary, ancillary, allied and incidental rights, title and interest, throughout the world in perpetuity, in and to that certain original non-fiction work described as follows:

Title:_____

Written By: _____

Publisher:_____

Date and Place of Initial Publication: _____

Copyright Registration No.: _____

and including all contents thereof, all present and future adaptations, sequels and versions thereof, the title and characters thereof, and copyright therein and all renewals and extensions of such copyright.

WARRANTIES AND INDEMNIFICATION: Author hereby states that the Property was created and is owned free and clear of all other interests only by Author. In addition, Author has the full right to comply with this agreement. Author will fully reimburse Purchaser if any losses, damages, or expenses (including lawyers' fees) are incurred because any or all of the statements made in this agreement are not true.

The undersigned and Purchaser will enter into a full option agreement relating to the transfer of the foregoing rights in and to said non-fiction work within 30 days. This assignment is expressly made subject to all of the terms, conditions, and provisions contained in said literary option agreement.

The undersigned has executed this assignment as of this _____ day of _____, 19___.

_____ [writer's name]

378

K — SHORT OPTION AGREEMENT
[DEPICTION OF LIFE STORY]

This shall constitute an agreement between _____ [insert your name or company name, if any] and _____ [writer's name] (_____ [writer's last name in caps]) to option and purchase the exclusive motion picture, television and allied rights in regard to the life story of _____ [insert name of person] as depicted in articles written by _____ [writer's last name in caps], as follows:

1. OPTION: _____ [your name or company name, if any] shall have the exclusive, irrevocable ONE (1) year option, to exploit and develop the above-mentioned life story and literary property in the aforementioned media. In consideration, _____ [your name or company name, if any] shall pay _____ [writer's last name in caps] $ _____, which is non-applicable towards the purchase price. _____ [your name or company name, if any] shall have the right to automatically extend the option period for an additional one (1) year period in return for an additional payment of $ _____.

2. PURCHASE PRICE: $ _____

3. CONSULTING SERVICES: [insert writer's name in caps] shall receive a fee of $ _____ as a consultant's fee.

4. BILLING: Producer shall use its best efforts to see to it that _____ [insert writer's last name in caps] receives screen credit such as "Based on an article by [insert writer's name]," size, style, and placement to be at producer's discretion.

5. NET PROFITS: 5% of 100% of the net profits as defined in producer's standard definition of net profits attached hereto.

WARRANTIES AND INDEMNIFICATION: Writer hereby states that the life story rights are owned free and clear of all other interests only by Writer. In addition, Writer has the full right to comply with this agreement. Writer will fully reimburse _____ [your name or company] if any losses, damages, or expenses (including lawyers' fees) are incurred because any or all of the statements made in this agreement are not true.

Agreed to: Agreed to:

_____   _____

[writer's name]   [your name/company
(Date)   name, if any] (Date)

L — OPTION AGREEMENT
[LIFE STORY — FOR TELEVISION]

This shall constitute an agreement between_____ [insert your name or company name, if any] (_____) [your last name or company abbreviated, if any, in caps] and _____ [insert writer's or holder of rights' name] (_____)[last name of person in caps] to option and purchase the exclusive motion picture, television and allied rights in regard to his/her personal and professional life story, as follows:

1. OPTION: (___) [your last name in caps] shall have the exclusive, irrevocable six (6) month option for the sum of $_____, which is non-applicable toward the purchase price. (_____) [your last name in caps] shall have the right to automatically extend the option period for an additional one (1) year period for the sum of $_____, which payment is applicable toward the purchase price.

380

2. PURCHASE PRICE: $_____ if the pilot program is one (1) hour or $_____ if the pilot program is two (2) hours.

3. SERIES SALES BONUS: If twelve (12) or more episodes based on the pilot are initially ordered,_____ [insert writer's name or holder of rights' name in caps] shall receive a one-time-only bonus of $_____. For an order of less than twelve, the series sales bonus shall be reduced pro rata by the number of episodes initially ordered less than twelve.

4. SERIES ROYALTY: For the concept,_____ [writer's last name in caps or holder of rights' last name in caps] shall receive a royalty of $_____ per episodes sold.

5. SERIES SERVICES:_____ [writer's last name or holder of rights' last name in caps] shall render non-exclusive services to producer as consultant for the fee of $_____ per original episode for the life of the series.

6. BILLING:_____ [writer's last name in caps or holder of rights' last name in caps] shall receive screen credit as consultant on a separate card; size, style, and placement to be at producer's discretion.

7. NET PROFITS: In addition to any other compensation paid to _____ [writer's last name or holder of rights' last name in caps] hereunder, _____ [writer's last name or holder of rights' last name in caps] shall also receive 7% of 100% of producer's net profits which shall be pursuant to producer's standard definition of net profits, attached hereto.

Agreed to: Agreed to:

_____   _____
[writer or holder   [your name or company
of rights' name]   name, if any]
(Date)   (Date)

M — SHORT FORM OPTION AGREEMENT
[OPTION OF NOVEL]

For the sum of $ _____, and other good and valuable consideration, the receipt and sufficiency of which are hereby acknowledged, the undersigned _____ (hereinafter referred to as "Owner/ Author") hereby grants to_____ (hereinafter referred to as "Purchaser"), the exclusive and irrevocable right and option to purchase the motion picture and other rights (hereinafter referred to as "Rights") in and to all literary, dramatic and/or musical writings and material contained in that certain published novel titled_____ (hereinafter referred to as "Property"), written by Author, and all revisions, adaptations, dramatizations and translations thereof and additions thereto and the title thereof, all as set forth in that certain Long-Form Option Agreement (hereinafter referred to as the "Long-Form Agreement") between Owner and Purchaser. Purchaser's option to purchase said rights shall be for a period of _____ ( ) months, commencing on _____, 19___, and Purchaser may extend such option for _____ additional _____ month periods, for the additional sum of $ _____, pursuant to the terms and conditions to be set forth in the Long-Form Agreement.

PURCHASE PRICE: $ _____.

WARRANTIES AND INDEMNIFICATION: Author hereby states that the Property was created and is owned free and clear of all other interests only by Author. In addition, Author has the full right to comply with this agreement. Author will fully reimburse Purchaser if any losses, damages, or expenses (including lawyers' fees) are incurred because any or all of the statements made in this agreement are not true.

The parties acknowledge that this Short-Form Option Agreement should be read in conjunction with the Long-Form Agreement, and in the event of any conflict between the provisions of this instrument and the Long-Form Agreement, the provisions of the Long-Form Agreement shall control.

IN WITNESS THEREOF, the undersigned have executed this instrument as of _____, 19_____.

Agreed to: Agreed to:

_____   _____
Owner/Author   Production Company

N — PRODUCER/WRITER AGREEMENT

The following sets forth the principal terms of the agreement between_____ ("Producer"), on the one hand, and_____ ("Writer"), on the other, in connection with the project currently entitled _____ [insert name of screenplay].

1. Producer hereby engages Writer to write a first draft and a first set of revisions (the "Work") of the project currently entitled_____ _____[insert name of screenplay] intended as a theatrical motion picture (the "Picture"). The Work shall be based upon the story and ideas as agreed between Producer and Writer.

2. The first draft shall be delivered not later than _____, 19___. Producer shall thereafter have a four-week reading period. The first set of revisions shall be delivered not later than _____, 19____.

3. In consideration for the services to be rendered by Writer hereunder, Producer shall pay Writer the guaranteed sum of $_____ payable as follows:

(a) The sum of $_____ upon the later of execution of this letter agreement or commencement of services.

(b) The sum of $_____ upon delivery of the first draft.

(c) The sum of $_____ upon commencement of writing services for the first set of revisions and;

(d) The sum of $_____ upon delivery of the first set of revisions.

4. Producer shall have the exclusive right to "set up" the project at a studio and/or with one or more third party financiers. The terms of the third party's option and acquisition of the Work shall be negotiated between Writer's representatives and such third party in good faith and Writer shall be entitled to retain all of the terms of Writer's employment by Producer which shall be negotiated in good faith upon Producer's or Writer's request. Such terms and conditions shall be within customary industry parameters for writers in the motion picture industry in Los Angeles. The terms to be negotiated in good faith shall include, without limitation, an optional rewrite and polish, sole and shared credit bonus, passive payments for sequels, remakes and television productions and a first opportunity to write subsequent productions, representations and warranties, credit, anti-injunctive relief, notice, suspension, default, and termination.

5. Writer agrees to execute the attached Certificate of Authorship as well as all other documents reasonably necessary to effectuate the purposes of this agreement.

6. Writer shall accord Producer a first negotiation right in connection with the project currently entitled_____ [insert name of script]. If and when Writer is prepared to exploit such project, Writer shall first offer Producer the right to produce the picture on terms then to be negotiated in good faith. In the event Writer and Producer cannot agree upon terms, after fifteen (15) business days, Writer shall have no

further obligation to Producer with respect to_____
_____[insert name of script].

7. If Producer has not "set up" the Picture on or before the date twenty-four (24) months after Writer delivers to Producer the first set of revisions of the Work, then Writer shall have the non-exclusive right to "set up" the Picture without Producer, provided Producer shall continue to have the right to set up the Picture pursuant to the terms hereof for an additional year; provided, further, if Producer has not "set up" the Picture within three (3) years then the Picture will revert to Writer. If Writer sets up the Picture at any time pursuant to the foregoing sentence (i.e., either after twenty-four (24) months or after the Picture reverts), upon entering into an agreement with a third party to develop, produce, finance or exploit the Picture in any fashion, Writer shall pay to Producer an amount equal to all sums expended by Producer in connection with the Picture plus interest and an amount equal to 5% of 100% of the net profits of the first motion picture (and all sequels) which net profits shall be defined, computed, accounted and paid to Producer in the same manner as they are to Writer.

8. This agreement shall be governed by and construed pursuant to the laws of the State of _____ [insert name of your state]. This agreement represents the entire understanding between the parties and may not be amended except in writing and signed by all parties hereto.

Dated: _____, 19 ___.

Agreed to: Agreed to:

_____   _____

[name of "Producer"]   [name of "Writer"]

O — CERTIFICATE OF AUTHORSHIP

I,_____ [insert name of writer], hereby certify that pursuant to and subject to an employment agreement ("Employment Agreement") between_____ [name of producer] ("Producer") and me dated as of _____, 19___, in connection with the motion picture project presently entitled _____ [insert name of script] (the "Picture"), all literary material of whatever kind or nature, written or to be written, furnished or to be furnished, by me (all such literary material being referred to herein as the "Material") was and/or will be solely created by me as a "work-made-for-hire" specially ordered or commissioned by Producer for use as part of the Picture with Producer being deemed the sole author of the Material and the owner of all rights of every kind or nature, whether now known or hereafter devised (including, but not limited to, all copyrights and all extensions and renewals of copyrights) in and to the Material, with the right to make all uses of the Material throughout the universe (subject to the Employment Agreement) and all changes in the Material as Producer deems necessary or desirable.

To the extent permitted by applicable law, I hereby waive the "moral rights of authors" as said term is commonly understood. It is agreed that my consideration for the Material is included in the compensation to be paid pursuant to the Employment Agreement.

Subject to Article 28 of the Writers Guild of America Basic Agreement, I jointly and severally warrant and represent that I have the right to execute this document and, except to the extent used as the basis therefor, that the Material is or shall be original with me and to the best of my knowledge, does not and shall not defame or disparage any person or entity or infringe upon or violate the rights of privacy, publicity or any other rights of any kind or nature whatsoever of any person or entity and is not the subject of any litigation or of any claim that might give rise to litigation. I shall defend (with counsel acceptable to the Producer), indemnify and hold harmless Producer, the corporations comprising Producer, its and their employees, officers, agents, assigns and licensees from and against any and all liability,

386

claims, costs, damages and expenses (including reasonable attorneys' fees and court costs) arising out of or in connection with a breach of the foregoing covenants, warranties and representations.

I agree to execute any documents and do any other acts as may be reasonably required by Producer or its assignees or licensees to further evidence or effectuate Producer's rights as set forth in this Certificate of Authorship or the Employment Agreement. Upon my failure promptly to do so, I hereby appoint Producer as my attorney-in-fact for such purposes (it being acknowledged that such appointment is irrevocable and coupled with an interest) with full power of substitution and delegation.

I further acknowledge that (i) in the event of any breach hereunder by Producer, I will be limited to my remedy at law for damages, if any, and will not have the right to terminate or rescind this Certificate or the Employment Agreement or to enjoin the distribution, advertising or exploitation of the Picture, (ii) nothing herein shall obligate Producer to use my services or the results or proceeds thereof in the Picture or to produce, advertise or distribute the picture, and (iii) this Certificate shall be governed by the laws of the State of_____ [insert name of state] applicable to agreements executed and to be performed entirely therein.

Subject to the Employment Agreement, Producer's rights with respect to the Material and/or my services may be freely assigned and licensed and its rights shall be binding upon me and inure to the benefit of any such assignee or licensee.

Employer and I have caused this document to be executed this _____ day of _____, 19___.

_____

[name of writer]

P — LETTER AGREEMENT
[TELEVISION]

This is a sample of an executed deal memo letter of agreement between a writer and purchaser. The names, dates, and screenplay titles used in this sample agreement are fictitious, and the sample is furnished for informational purposes only. It is not intended to offer legal advice in any manner. To protect your own interests, we highly recommend that you obtain the services of a qualified entertainment attorney, who can advise you on the needs of your agreements and/or contracts.

June 15, 1995

Mr. John Doe
Such-and-Such Productions
13 Main Street
Any City, Middle America 00000

Dear John,

As per our conversation today, I am sending you the basic points that I am looking for if we cut a telefilm deal.

1. Option Monies:

   (a) $1,000 for the first six months;

   (b) $2,500 for an additional six months;

   (c) $6,500 for an additional six months.

2. Script Adviser: $2,500 payable upon commencement of the rewriting process.

3. Purchase Price: $75,000 payable upon commencement of principal photography.

4. Net Profits: 5% of 100% of net profits defined on (production house) standard of net profits subject to good faith negotiation.

5. Advances: $7,500 upon first sale in foreign syndication; $5,000 upon first sale in domestic syndication.

6. Concept fees: Fee to be discussed with you if it goes to series.

CO-PRODUCER PACKAGE:

I would like to be able to attach myself to this project as co-producer.

7. Co-Producer Fee: $30,000 payable over the period of principal photography.

Yours sincerely,

John Brown

Q — LETTER OF AGREEMENT — DEAL MEMO
[TELEVISION]

This is a sample of an executed letter of agreement between a writer and producer related to sale of the work to television. The names, dates, and screenplay titles used in this sample agreement are fictitious, and the sample is furnished for informational purposes only. It is not intended to offer legal advice in any manner. To protect your own interests, we highly recommend that you obtain the services of a qualified entertainment attorney, who can advise you on the needs of your agreements and/or contracts.

April 30, 1995

Mr. John Doe
Such-And-Such Entertainment Company
4321 Elm Street
Sometown, CA 90000

Re: "A Mysterious Tale" by John Brown

Dear Mr. Doe:

This letter shall confirm the agreement between yourself and me, John Brown ("writer"), with regards to my writing services on the above-mentioned project.

This agreement is on an if-come basis, meaning that if we are able to have the network order a script on the above-referenced property, then the following deal will be activated:

1) Should the writer be employed to write a script based on the above-referenced property, compensation for one run shall be $50,000. This shall entitle you to story, first draft, revision and polish.

2) In the event that a picture is produced based on the script, the writer will receive a $10,000 bonus for sole credit or a $5,000 bonus for shared credit.

3) If the writer receives sole writing credit, he will receive 5% of 100% of net proceeds and 2 1/2% of 100% of net proceeds if he shares credit.

4) In the event that the picture is released theatrically, the standard 100-50/50 formula shall be applied.

5) In the event that a sequel is produced, writer is entitled to 50% of his passive participation, or 33 1/3% in the event of remake.

If the above meets with your approval, please sign below in the designated space, and return the original letter to me.

Sincerely,

John Brown

Agreed to and accepted by:

_____

Authorized Signatory
Such-and-Such Entertainment Company

R — DEAL MEMO
[MOTION PICTURE]

This is a sample of an executed deal memo letter of agreement between a writer and purchaser. The names, dates, and screenplay titles used in this sample agreement are fictitious, and the sample is furnished for informational purposes only. It is not intended to offer legal advice in any manner. To protect your own interests, we highly recommend that you obtain the services of a qualified entertainment attorney, who can advise you on the needs of your agreements and/or contracts.

May 13, 1995

Mr. John Doe
Such-and-Such Entertainment Company
4321 Elm Street
Any City, California 00000

Re: "A Mysterious Tale" by John Brown

Dear Mr. Doe:

This letter shall confirm the agreement between Such-And-Such Entertainment Company ("Purchaser"), and John Brown ("Author"), for Purchaser to acquire certain motion picture, television and allied rights in and to the screenplay entitled "A Mysterious Tale" ("Property") for the purpose of producing a theatrical motion picture, television motion picture or miniseries ("Picture").

I understand the terms of the agreement to be as follows:

1. OPTION:

A. Commencing on May 13, 1995, Purchaser shall have an exclusive and irrevocable six-month option in which to acquire certain motion picture, television and allied rights in and to the Property. As consideration for such option, Purchaser will pay Author $1,000, which sum shall be payable immediately. The foregoing option shall be applied against and in reduction of the purchase price.

B. Purchaser shall have the right to extend the option for an additional six-month option period by giving written notice and by payment to Author of an additional $1,000 on or before the initial six-month option period expires. The foregoing option payment shall not be applied against and in reduction of the purchase price.

2. CASH PURCHASE PRICE:

If Purchaser exercises the option to exploit the Property as a television movie or miniseries, the purchase price shall be $75,000 (less option monies paid to Author pursuant to Paragraph 1A). If Purchaser exercises the option to exploit the Property as a theatrical motion picture, the purchase price shall be $150,000 if the budget (including contingency and bond) is less than $20 million. The purchase price shall be $250,000 if the budget is greater than or equal to $20 million. The applicable purchase price shall be payable to Author in full upon the earlier of: (a) exercise of the option (which notice shall be in writing on or before the end of the applicable option period); or (b) commencement of principal photography of the first production based upon the Property.

3. CONTINGENT COMPENSATION:

If the WGA accords Author sole screenplay or teleplay credit Author shall receive 5% of 100% of the net profits from the Picture and all elements thereof, from all sources and in all media. If Author receives no credit or shared credit, Author shall receive 2 1/2% of 100% of the net profits. Net profits shall be calculated and defined per Purchaser's standard definition of net profits, subject to good faith negotiation within customary industry parameters.

4. TELEVISION SERIES:

Purchaser shall not have the right to exploit Property as a television series without Purchaser and Author negotiating the terms thereof (including, but not limited to, per episode royalty, spin-off royalty, reruns and profits) in good faith.

5. CREDIT:

Author shall receive credit on all Pictures produced hereunder on a separate card, in the main titles and in paid ads under Purchaser's control, including in any otherwise excluded ads if the director receives credit.

> A. Subject to the WGA, such credit shall read "Screenplay by John Brown".

> B. Author shall receive credit on all other versions and formats (e.g., video cassette, remakes, sequels, etc.).

6. THEATRICAL RELEASE:

If the Purchaser exploits the Property as a television movie and if there is a domestic theatrical release of the Picture or any portion thereof prior to the initial U.S. television broadcast, Author will receive 100% of the compensation paid pursuant to Paragraphs 2 and 3. If there is a domestic theatrical release of the Picture subsequent to the initial U.S. television broadcast, Author will receive 50% of the compensation paid pursuant to Paragraphs 2 and 3. If there is a foreign theatrical release of the Picture prior or subsequent to the initial U.S. television broadcast, Author will receive 50% of the compensation paid pursuant to Paragraphs 2 and 3. The applicable fixed compensation shall be payable upon release.

7. SEQUELS AND REMAKES:

Author shall receive 50% of the compensation payable pursuant to Paragraphs 2 and 3 for each sequel and 33 1/3% of the same for each remake of the Picture. This fixed compensation will be paid to Author upon commencement of principal photography of the applicable production.

8. RESERVED RIGHTS:

All rights not granted to Purchaser hereunder are reserved to Author. Author reserves the following rights, without limitation: live stage, Author-written sequels and prequels, audio cassette (books on tape, books on cassette), live television, live dramatic tape, radio and all publication rights. Notwithstanding the above, for the purpose of advertising and promotion, Purchaser shall be entitled to publish summaries and synopses of Property not attributable to Author, not exceeding 7,500 words and not for sale or resale. Purchaser shall not be entitled to publish a novelization or photonovelization of the teleplay or Property without Purchaser and Author negotiating the terms thereof in good faith.

9. MISCELLANEOUS:

A. The parties shall negotiate in good faith the compensation for Author for any other exploitation of the Property. Author shall also receive a free video cassette in a format of Author's choice of each Program based on the Property. Author agrees to sign a customary letter prohibiting Author from duplicating or exploiting the cassette commercially.

B. Purchaser shall name Author as an additional insured on Purchaser's errors and omissions policy for the Picture.

C. There shall be no relief of Purchaser's obligations hereunder if Purchaser assigns its rights and interest in and to Property to any third party other than a so-called "major" or "mini-major" production, financing, or distribution entity.

D. Purchaser shall pay directly or reimburse Author for any pre-approved expenses in connection with Author's services.

E. Author represents that he has the sole right and authority to make and enter into this agreement and to convey the rights herein granted without restriction or limitation.

F. All checks and notices from Purchaser to Author shall be made in the name of John Brown, 1234 Main St., City, State.

10. <u>OTHER TERMS</u>:

Other terms and conditions incorporated by reference herein are all those that are customary in agreements of this type in the United States television and motion picture industries, subject to good faith negotiation within customary industry parameters. The parties intend to enter into a long-form agreement incorporating the terms herein and other such terms and conditions.

Please contact me immediately if the above is in any way inconsistent with your understanding of the agreement. Otherwise this letter shall constitute a firm and binding agreement until such time, if any, as a more formal document is executed by all parties. If all is in order, please sign this original and three copies and return them to me.

Sincerely,

John Brown
Dated: _____, 19 ___.
AGREED TO AND ACCEPTED

_____

Such-And-Such Entertainment Company
By:_____

About the Authors

CARLOS DE ABREU

Carlos de Abreu is a best-selling author, screenwriter, producer, development professional, and marketing expert.

He studied economics at the University of Witwatersrand, South Africa, and film at the University of California, Los Angeles.

He has executive produced various projects, including *Breaking In Hollywood* and *Justice on Trial*, and he has multiple feature projects in active development and co-production.

Mr. de Abreu co-founded The Christopher Columbus Society For The Creative Arts(R.)S.M. and established The Christopher Columbus Screenplay Discovery Awards™.

He co-authored the national best-seller *Husband, Lover, Spy: A True Story* and presently is writing *The Bastard* and *Blowback*. His prior works include *Mozambique the Last Good-Bye*, *Sworn to Silence*, and *The WDG Manual: The Art of Writing the Perfect Screenplay*.

HOWARD JAY SMITH

Howard Jay Smith is Vice-President of Production for Kamin & Howell Entertainment and an instructor at UCLA Extension Writers' Program. His film and writing classes have been among the university's top-rated and highest attended. His numerous guests have included actress-writer Carrie Fisher; *Die Hard* creator Steven De Souza; *Roseanne* executive producer Bob Myer; and top Hollywood authors, including Linda Seger and Syd Field.

An award-winning writer published in the *Washington Post* and *Horizon* magazine, he has worked as a freelance producer-writer on more than fifty film, TV, commercial and video projects which were developed at Columbia, TriStar, NBC, ABC-TV, Republic Pictures, and numerous independent production companies.

For Columbia-Embassy Television, Mr. Smith oversaw the production of five MOWs and more than seventy-five episodes for sitcoms, including *Who's the Boss?*, *Diff'rent Strokes*, and *The Facts of Life*.

Prior to that he was a development executive at ABC-TV where he worked as manager of drama series development. Among the top hits launched during his tenure there were *Moonlighting*, *Spenser: For Hire*, and *MacGyver*, among others.

A Phi Beta Kappa, Magna Cum Laude graduate of the American Film Institute, Nanyang University of Singapore, and the University of Buffalo, Mr. Smith is a three-time winner of the Washington, D.C., Arts and Humanities Commission Writer's Fellowship.

Bibliography

Avallone, Susan, and Lechner, Jack, comps. and eds. *Film Producers, Studios, Agents and Casting Directors*. 2nd Edition. Beverly Hills, Lone Eagle, 1990.

Bates, James. "Strike Tears Hollywood Hyphenates Down Middle." *Los Angeles Times*, July 19, 1988.

Brookfield Communications, Inc. industry research reports.

"Box Office Reports." *The Hollywood Reporter,* January 4, 1994.

Brown, Les. *Les Brown's Encylopedia of Television*. New York, Zoetrope, 1982.

Brown, Rich. "From Marconi to HDTV." *Broadcasting*, December 9, 1991.

Byrge, Duane. "Box Office Inferno Ignited by $16 Million 'Doubtfire.'" *The Hollywood Reporter*, January 4, 1994.

Capital Cities/ABC, Inc. Annual Report & Form 10-K, 1992; Report to Shareholders, Third Quarter 1993; "Highlights & Milestones," 1953-1992

Carolco Pictures Inc. Form 10-Q, September 30, 1993; Form 8-K, October 20, 1993.

Cones, John W. *Film Finance & Distribution*. Los Angeles, Silman-James Press, 1992.

Du Brow, Rick. "NBC Has Grand Plans for Carsey-Werner's 'Grand.'" *Los Angeles Times,* December 9, 1989.

Eller, Claudia. "Sale of Eszterhas Script Scores a Screenwriters' Breakthrough." *Los Angeles Times*, May 19, 1994.

Fox, David J. "3rd Highest Grossing Year Despite Fewer Tickets Sold." *Los Angeles Times*. Washington Edition, January 4, 1994.

General Electric Company. Annual Report, 1992; Form 10-K, December 31, 1992.

Gerstein, Marc H. "Capital Cities/ABC." *The Value Line Investment Survey,* September 24, 1993.

————. "CBS Inc." *The Value Line Investment Survey*, September 24, 1993.

————. "Paramount Comm." *The Value Line Investment Survey*, December 3, 1993.

————. "Turner Broadcasting." *The Value Line Investment Survey*, September 24, 1993.

————. "Viacom, Inc." *The Value Line Investment Survey*, September 24, 1993.

Grover, Ronald. "Crying All the Way to the Oscars." *Business Week*, March 15, 1993.

Grover, Ronald, and Landler, Mark. "Waiting for a Megadeal." *Business Week*, January 10, 1994.

Harris, Kathryn, and Lippman, John. "Viacom, Cable Giant TCI Discuss Joint Venture." *Los Angeles Times*, March 30, 1994.

Hollywood Creative Directory. Volume No. 21, Winter/Spring 1994. Santa Monica, Hollywood Creative Directory, 1994.

Hollywood Creative Directory. Volume No. 22, Summer 1994. Santa Monica, Hollywood Creative Directory, 1994.

Hollywood Reporter, The, January 4, 1993.

Hollywood Reporter, The, January 8, 1992.

Honeycutt, Kirk and Parker, Donna. "NL Pays $4 Mil for Black's 'Kiss.' " *The Hollywood Reporter*, July 22-24, 1994.

Hoover, Gary, Campbell, Alta, and Spain, Patrick J., eds. *Hoover's Handbook of American Business, 1994*. Austin, The Reference Press, 1993.

————. *Hoover's Handbook of American Business, 1992*. Austin, The Reference Press, 1991.

————. *Hoover's Handbook of World Business, 1993*. Austin, The Reference Press, 1992.

Kaye, Jeff. "In the Center of the Action." *Los Angeles Times*, December 9, 1989.

King, Thomas R. "Three Hollywood Studios Wage Close Fight for Box-Office Crown." *Wall Street Journal,* January 4, 1993.

Krantz, Michael. "What Do Women Watch?" *GQ*, August 1993.

Landler, Mark. "NBC Could Use a Good Script Doctor." *Business Week,* March 15, 1993.

Landler, Mark, DeGeorge, Gail, and Grover, Ronald. "Paramount: Not So Fast Barry." *Business Week,* January 10, 1994.

LIVE Entertainment Inc. Annual Report, 1992; Form 10-K, December 31, 1992; LIVE home video catalogue.

Lubove, Seth, and Weinberg, Neil. "Creating a Seamless Company." *Forbes,* December 20, 1993.

Marich, Robert. "MGM Finishes Restructuring." *The Hollywood Reporter*, January 4, 1994.

Marshall, Rick. *The History of Television.* New York, Gallery Books, 1986.

Martin, James A. "Are You Breaking the Law?" *Macworld,* May 1994.

McClellan, Steve and Eggerton, John. "Getting the Picture: TV Takes the Stage." *Broadcasting,* December 9, 1991.

McNeil, Alex. *Total Television: A Comprehensive Guide to Programming from 1948 to the Present.* 3rd Edition. New York, Penguin Books, 1991.

Metro-Goldwyn-Mayer, Inc. Form 10-K, December 31, 1992.

Orion Pictures Corporation. Form 10-Q, November 30, 1993; Annual Report 1993; "Orion Pictures Corporation." January 1994.

Miller, Annetta and Nayyar, Seema. "Networks, Networks, Everywhere." *Newsweek,* November 15, 1993.

Monush, Barry, ed. *International Motion Picture Almanac*, 64th Edition. New York, Quigley Publishing Company, 1993.

Moshavi, Sharon. "Entertainment & Information." *Forbes*, January 3, 1994.

Murphy, A.D. "Industry Sheds Those B.O. Blues." *The Hollywood Reporter,* January 4, 1994.

———. "Record Box Office at $5.24 Billion." *The Hollywood Reporter,* January 3, 1994.

———. "Warners' 19% Makes It a Threepeat." *The Hollywood Reporter*, January 3, 1994.

———. "World Rentals for U.S. Distribs Break $4 Billion." *The Hollywood Reporter,* May 3, 1994.

Paramount Communications Inc. Form 10-K, October 31, 1992; Annual Report, 1992.

Public Broadcasting Service. 25th Anniversary, 1969-1994 press kit.

Sharav, Ben. "Time Warner." *The Value Line Investment Survey,* December 3, 1993.

Sony Corporation (Sony Kabushiki Kaisha). Annual Report, 1993; "Consolidated Results for the Second Quarter and the Six-Month Period Ended September 30, 1993"; Form 20-F, March 31, 1993.

Spain, Patrick J., Campbell, Alta, and Chai, Alan, eds. *Hoover's Handbook of Emerging Companies, 1993-1994.* Austin, The Reference Press, 1993.

Spelling Entertainment Group Inc. Form 10-Q, September 30, 1993; Form 10-K, December 31, 1992; Annual Report, 1992; "Spelling: The Glitz Is Back." *TV Program Investor,* November 30, 1992; "Research Report." L. H. Friend, Weinress & Frankson, Inc.; "Tom Carson, MGM CFO, Set to Take Same Post for Spelling Entertainment." News Release, September 7, 1993; "Spelling Entertainment and Republic Pictures Announce Agreement in Principle to Merge." News Release, September 13, 1993.

Standard & Poor's *Industry Surveys.* March 17, 1994, March 11, 1993, March 12, 1992, March 14, 1991, July 5, 1990, March 16, 1989.

Swort, Edmund H.. "Disney (Walt)." *The Value Line Investment Survey,* December 3, 1993.

———. "New Line Cinema." *The Value Line Investment Survey,* December 3, 1993.

Time Warner Inc. Annual Report, 1992; Form 10-K, December 31, 1992.

Turner Broadcasting System, Inc. Third Quarter Report, September 30, 1993, Form 10-K, December 31, 1992; Annual Report, 1992.

"Viacom Sells Its Stake in Lifetime for $317.6 Mil." *Investor's Business Daily,* March 30, 1994.

Viacom Inc. Form 10-K/A, Amendment No. 2, December 31, 1992.

Walker, John, ed. *Halliwell's Filmgoer's and Video Viewer's Companion.* 10th Edition. New York, HarperPerennial, 1993.

Walt Disney Company, The. Annual Report, 1992.

Ward's Business Directory of U.S. Private and Public Companies, 1994. Volume 5. Detroit, Gale Research Inc., 1993.

Ward's Business Directory of U.S. Private and Public Companies, 1992. Volume 5. Detroit, Gale Research Inc., 1993.

Wells, Jeffrey. "The Bigger the Bucks, the Longer They Need to Age." *Los Angeles Times,* October 4, 1992.

Wiseman, Paul, and Cox, James. "Lawsuit Casts Another Cloud Over Viacom Bid." *USA Today,* December 16, 1993.

Index

A

417

Warner, Jack 235
Warner, Sam 235
Warner/Amex 257
Washington, Denzel 70, 288
Washington Post 59
Waterdance, The 37
Waterland 240
Way Down East 222
Wayne, John 76
Wayne's World 224, 242
Wayne's World 2 225
WB Network 236, 247
Weaver, Sigourney 288
Weekend at Bernie's II 228
Weekly Variety 245
Weinstein, Harvey and Bob 238
Weitz, Richard 263
We're Back! 232
Werner, Tom 256
West Side Story 38, 222, 293
Westinghouse 249
What Price Glory? 229
What's Eating Gilbert Grape 225
What's Love Got to Do With It? 234
When a Man Loves a Woman 140
White Christmas 224
Whitmore, James 42
Who's Afraid of Virginia Woolf? 236
Who's the Boss? 131, 325
Who's the Man? 240
Wide Sargasso Sea 240
Wide World of Sports 247
Wilder Napalm 228
Wildside 311
William Morris Agency 147, 261, 326
Williams, Robin 287
Willie & Phil 53
Willis, Bruce 288

Wilmot, Mollie 46
Wilshire Court Productions 224
Winds of War, The 212
Winger, Debra 290
Wings 224
Winkler Films 284
Wise, Robert 38, 39, 335; the three P's 293
Wiseguy 255
Witches of Eastwick, The 203
Witness 15
Witt-Thomas-Harris 198
Wizan Film Properties, Inc. 284
Wizard of Oz, The 222
Women's Wear Daily 248
Woods, James 290
Works made for hire 78
Wrestling Ernest Hemingway 237
Writers: scripts and treatments 350
Writer's Aide 346
Writers Computer Store 362
Writer's Connection 353
Writer's Digest 30, 66
Writers' fees 215; network television 217, 218
Writers Guild of America 29, 106, 123, 207, 278, 285, 300, 304, 341, 343, 350, 365; minimums 215, 292; registration 79, 81
Writers Guild of America East 80
Writers Guild of America West 80
Writer's Journey, The 33, 155, 348, 353
Writer's Market 67
Writing: idea/concept/story 96; log line 95; step-by-step guide 95; story structure 96
Writing groups 29, 68; addresses 359, 360
Writing Screenplays That Sell 156, 349, 351

427

Order Form

Custos Morum Publishers

2049 Century Park East, Suite 1100
Los Angeles, CA 90067 • Fax: (310) 288-0257

Please send the following:

Quantity		*Special Price*	*Sub-Total*

___**HUSBAND, LOVER, SPY** ($21.95@) = **$18.00**   _____
By Janice Pennington with Carlos de Abreu— **Best-seller**

OPENING THE DOORS TO HOLLYWOOD
___**HOW TO SELL YOUR IDEA** ($22.95 @) = **$18.00**   _____
STORY, BOOK, SCREENPLAY
By Carlos de Abreu and Howard Jay Smith

SUBTOTAL   _____
SHIPPING/HANDLING (See Below)   +   _____
Calif. RESIDENTS add 8.25% SALES TAX   +   _____

TOTAL ENCLOSED $ _____

Make check or money order payable to:
CUSTOS MORUM PUBLISHERS

Name:

Address:

City: State: Zip:

Telephone: (   )

SHIPPING & HANDLING
1 book – $3.50   2 books – $5.50   3 books – $6.00
Each book thereafter an additional $1.00

All prices subject to change without notice